ALL OUR CHILDREN LEARNING

A Primer for Parents, Teachers, and Other Educators

Benjamin S. Bloom

Distinguished Service
Professor of Education
The University of Chicago

McGraw-Hill Book Company

NEW YORK   ST. LOUIS   SAN FRANCISCO   AUCKLAND
BOGOTÁ   GUATEMALA   HAMBURG   JOHANNESBURG   LISBON
LONDON   MADRID   MEXICO   MONTREAL   NEW DELHI   PANAMA
PARIS   SAN JUAN   SÃO PAULO   SINGAPORE   SYDNEY
TOKYO   TORONTO

To Sophie

First paperback edition, 1982

1234567890DODO898765432

ISBN 0-07-006121-1

Library of Congress Cataloging in Publication Data
Bloom, Benjamin Samuel, date
   All our children learning.

   Includes index.
   1. Curriculum planning.   2. Home and school.
3. Educational research.   I. Title.
LB1570.B59   375'.001   80-14349
ISBN 0-07-006118-1
    0-07-006121-1 (pbk)

CONTENTS

PREFACE

When invited by Thomas Quinn, my editor at McGraw-Hill, to have a series of my papers published as a special collection, I gave serious thought to what value—other than personal vanity—such a book might have. It seemed to me that many of my books were scholarly efforts which went into a particular problem, method, or theory into greater detail than many teachers, parents, and other educators might care to venture. These books were intended for a limited audience of scholars, researchers, testers, and advanced students in schools of education. Even though many of these books were circulated throughout the world in various translations and have had a considerable influence on the school systems of many countries, they were read by a relatively small number of educational specialists in each country. This especially was true where the books emphasized complex statistical methods and highly specialized testing and psychometric methods.

In contrast to my books were a number of my papers which were originally given as presentations to large and varied audiences for some special occasion. Later, these were published as journal articles or as chapters in a book. The fact that they were originally given as speeches to general audiences made it likely that the language of the papers was straightforward with a minimum of technical details. As I reread these, I became convinced that the publication of a selected set of the papers might communicate some of my ideas and research to a wider audience than most of my books could possibly reach.

I then asked a group of my students and friends to check my papers to determine which ones they regarded as the more significant ones for persons interested in education as parents, teachers, students of education, administrators, or educational specialists. They selected thirteen of these papers as the ones which best communicated some of my major ideas about education and the schools. These papers are grouped under four headings and within each group are arranged from the more recent to the earlier papers.

Overviews of Education

The first set consists of papers which provide a summary of

what we have learned about education during the past two decades. In contrast, "Innocence in Education" deals with what we have learned about education and the educative process in the United States. This paper focuses on the topics where educational research has made the greatest impact on our views about the schools, classrooms, teachers, students, and learning. "Implications of the IEA Studies for Curriculum and Instruction" summarizes what we have learned by studying the schools, teachers, and students of twenty-eight countries. It represents a view of contemporary education from a worldwide perspective. Those of us who were involved in these International Educational Achievement (IEA) studies were surprised by the vast differences in school learning when the different nations are compared. Finally, "Twenty-five Years of Educational Research" describes the effects of earlier research on our present understanding of the educational process.

This initial set of papers should be of interest to almost all readers of this book. They put into brief form a modern reconception of education in and out of the schools.

Home and School

The second set of papers deals with the relations between the home and the school. Learning goes on in both the home and the school, and it is the relation between these two institutions that explains much of the learning success of some students and the difficulties of other students. In some ways, the interaction between the home and the school is the central problem in modern education throughout the world. If this is handled well, most children find school to be an interesting and rewarding place. If this is handled poorly, children are likely to dislike school because they are rarely rewarded for their learning by either the school or the home.

These three papers, "Early Learning in the Home," "The Effect of the Home Environment on Children's School Achievement" and "Stability and Change in Human Characteristics: Implications for School Reorganization," could be read with profit by most parents who are concerned about the educational progress of their children. Elementary-school teachers, principals, and curriculum specialists should also be aware of the ideas developed in these papers.

Instruction and Curriculum Development

The third set of papers, on instruction and curriculum development, is introduced by Professor Lorin Anderson, who points out the basic ways in which these papers are interrelated and their consequences for our thinking about education and the classrooms. The first two papers, "New Views of the Learner" and "Learning for Mastery," bring into view a new understanding of the great learning potential of virtually all students in the school. These new views are not matters of faith or hope; they are based on research findings in many classrooms in the U.S. and abroad. Schools can be vastly improved in the instruction they provide for all students, and these changes have important effects on students' learning, their attitudes and interests, and their mental health. While these two papers should be of special interest to parents and teachers, they are relevant to all persons interested in the improvement of education and the schools.

The other two papers, "Peak Learning Experiences" and "The Role of the Educational Sciences in Curriculum Development," are likely to be of special interest to curriculum makers, teachers, and persons directly concerned with the changing process of education in the schools and the ways in which these changes can be most effective.

Evaluation

The final set of papers, on evaluation, are introduced by Professor George Madaus, who points out the ways in which they help us understand the role of evaluation in determining the learning progress of individual students. Madaus points out that evaluation also provides procedures for improving student learning, instruction, and the curriculum. In some ways educational evaluation has been one of the clearest and most powerful sets of methods developed over the past quarter of a century. These methods may be either destructive or very positive forces in education, depending on how they are used.

The paper, "Changes in Evaluation Methods," briefly describes a modern conception of the role of evaluation in improving school learning. It can be read with some profit by all readers of these papers and especially by teachers, administrators, and students of education. The two remaining papers, "Some Theoretical Issues Relating to Educational Evaluation" and

"Changing Conceptions of Examining at the University of Chicago," may be of special interest to educational researchers, evaluators, students of education, and some teachers and administrators.

ACKNOWLEDGMENTS

T he author gratefully acknowledges that permission to include these papers in this book was freely given by the editors and publishers of the journals or books in which they originally appeared.

"Innocence in Education," *SCHOOL REVIEW* 80 (1972): 332–352. By permission of the University of Chicago Press.

"Implications of the IEA Studies for Curriculum and Instruction," *SCHOOL REVIEW* 82 (1974): 413–435. By permission of the University of Chicago Press.

"Twenty-Five Years of Educational Research," *AMERICAN EDUCATIONAL RESEARCH JOURNAL*, 3 (1966): 211–221. By permission of the American Educational Research Association.

"Early Learning in the Home," Paley Lecture, University of California at Los Angeles, 1965. By permission of the Dean of the School of Education, UCLA.

"Stability and Change in Human Characteristics: Implications for School Reorganization," *Educational Administration Quarterly*, 2 (1966): 35–49. By permission of the editor.

"New Views of the Learner: Implications for Instruction and Curriculum," *Educational Leadership*, 35 (1978): 563–576. By permission of the editor.

"Learning for Mastery," *The Evaluation Comment*, May, 1968, Vol. 1, No. 2. By permission of the Center for the Study of Evaluation, University of California, Los Angeles.

"The Role of the Educational Sciences in Curriculum Development," *International Journal of the Educational Sciences*, 1 (1965): 5–15. By permission of the Pergamon Press.

"Peak Learning Experiences," in Provus, M. (Ed.) *Innovations for Time to Teach*, Washington, D.C.: National Education Association, 1966. By permission of the National Education Association.

"Changes in Evaluation Methods," in Glaser, R. (Ed.) *Research and Development and School Change*. Hillsdale, New Jersey. Lawrence Erlbaum Associates, Publishers. 1978. By permission of the Editor and the Publisher.

"Some Theoretical Issues Relating to Educational Evaluation," In Tyler, R. (Ed.), *Educational Evaluation*, 68th Yearbook of the National Society for the Study of Education, Part 2, University of Chicago Press, 1969. By permission of the Editor of the National Society for the Study of Education.

"Changing Conceptions of Examining at the University of Chicago," in Dressel, P. (Ed.), *Evaluation in General Education.* Brown Publishing Co., Autumn, 1954. By permission of the Editor.

Introduction

**New Directions in Educational Research and
Educational Practice**

These papers can be read from the perspective of what amounts to a worldwide revolution in educational research and in our understanding of some of the factors that directly influence learning. As a result of the new ideas gained from this research, student learning can be improved greatly, and it is possible to describe the favorable learning conditions which can enable virtually all students to learn to a high standard.

These new ideas have been successfully applied in many classrooms throughout the world. How quickly these ideas will be tried in the local schools will depend upon the leadership in these schools, the public demand for improvement in school learning, and the role to be played by schools of education in the training of teachers. In some countries the leadership in applying the new research to the schools has been assumed by the curriculum centers, which weave these new ideas into the instructional material and into the training of teachers for the instructional processes to be used in the new curriculum.

There are several features which account for the striking qualities of these new research developments. The simplest is the movement from a study of the characteristics of teachers and students to direct observation of the learning taking place in the interactions between teachers and students in the classroom. To put it in the most direct terms, there has been a movement away from the study of the actors (teachers and students) to the study of teaching and learning as they take place in the classroom. Increasingly, educational researchers are doing studies under classroom conditions in which they study particular teaching-learning processes and the changes they produce in both learners and teachers. Central in these studies is the concern about the causal links between the underlying processes and the qualitative and quantitative changes in the learning of students.

Perhaps the most important change, however, is the movement from what I have termed *fixed or static* variables to variables which are *alterable* either before the teaching-learning processes or as a part of these processes. It is this shift in the variables used which, to me, is central in the new view of education. This shift enables researchers and educators to move from an emphasis on prediction and the classification of students to a concern for causality and the relations between means and ends in teaching and learning. This concern has resulted in new ways of understanding, explaining, and altering human learning.

1

The search for alterable variables and the causal processes by which they can be altered is a relatively recent step in educational research, but I am confident that it will be an important part of educational research and practice for the next decade.

If parents, teachers, and other educators are really convinced that a good education is absolutely essential for all who live in modern society, then we must all search for the alterable variables and processes which can make a difference in the learning of children and youth in or out of the school. Such alterable variables will do much to explain the learning process, and they can do even more to directly improve the teaching and learning processes in the schools. The basic task of research is to further our understanding of how such processes can be altered and what their consequent effect will be on students, teachers, and learning.

The small number of alterable variables which are described here and in the papers in this book are only a few of the variables that have already been studied by researchers and used by teachers. Studying these has already made a great difference in our understanding of school learning. But, most importantly, they have brought about major changes in our view of learners and their amazing potential for learning. It is my hope that this small list will be rapidly expanded in the next decade and that these variables will become equally central for teachers, parents, and researchers. When they are thoroughly understood and well used, they will bring about the most profound changes in the schools and in the society.

In the following pages I will describe some of these new alterable variables and contrast them with the fixed or nonalterable variables they replace. In the discussion of each of these variables, I will indicate what both education and students stand to gain from the use of these newer ideas in the schools. In each case, the reader is referred to the selected papers in this book where the ideas are more fully developed.

Time Available for Learning versus Time the Student Is Engaged in Learning

We have always recognized time as a central factor in all learning. Schools allocate so many years for different subjects such as reading, literature, arithmetic, science, social studies, and so on. In addition, the schools determine the number of school days in each school year and the number of hours per week that will be assigned to each part of the curriculum. Time in the sense of years, days, and hours *available* for school learning becomes a relatively fixed or stable variable. To make significant alterations in these time allocations requires major legal, economic, and other policy changes at the state or community level. Only rarely can a group of teachers or local school administrators make drastic changes in these time allocations. Because these time allocations are much the same for most of the students, they account for only small differences in the learning of individual students within a classroom or school.

Quite in contrast to the concept of fixed *time available* for learning is the alterable variable of *time-on-task* (e.g., active learning time, time that students are engaged in learning). If two students are in the same classroom and one is actively engaged in learning for 90 percent of the classroom period while the other student is actively engaged for only 30 percent of the classroom period, there will be quantitative as well as qualitative differences in the learning during that time period for the two students.

One method of appraising the level of time-on-task is by observing at various intervals whether or not a particular student is *overtly* engaged in the learning—paying attention, doing work assigned, or in some way responding in a relevant way to the instruction and the instructional material. A second method is to determine the extent to which the student is *covertly* (in thought) engaged in the learning. There are various methods (stimulated recall, interviews, or questionnaires) of determining whether the student is *thinking* in relevant ways about what is going on in the classroom or whether his thoughts are unrelated to the classroom teaching-learning processes. Most studies report an index of time-on-task as the proportion of the classroom period the individual student was actively participating in the learning.

The studies on this variable show that the percentage of time-on-task (for individual students or groups of students) is highly related to subsequent measures of achievement and to subsequent indices of interests or attitudes toward the learning. In turn, time-on-task is largely determined by the quality of instruction and the extent to which the students have the cognitive prerequisites for each new learning task. Put in another way, students cannot actively engage in the learning if the instruction is poor and/or they are unable to comprehend what is being taught and what they are to do.

What is most important is the strong evidence that the amount of active engaged time in the classroom *can be altered* during a sequence of learning tasks. Thus, consider two groups of students who are comparable at the beginning of a new course in terms of their aptitude or previous achievement. One group learns the subject under conventional conditions, while the second group learns the subject under a very high quality of instruction (mastery learning or some other procedure which maximizes learning). During the first learning task both groups are likely to be very similar in percentage of time-on-task. On the second learning task the percentage of time-on-task will tend to be greater for the high-quality-of-instruction group and lower for the poorer-quality-of-instruction group. If both groups are followed over a series of learning tasks, it will be found that the high-quality-of-instruction group *increases* greatly in percentage of time-on-task while the low-quality-of-instruction group *decreases* greatly in percentage of time-on-task. On the final learning task the two groups (who were very similar on the first learning task) will be very different. And, in turn, these differences will be reflected in their achievement differentials, their motivation for further learning of the subject, and their self-confidence in their learning ability.

Time-on-task is then one of the variables that accounts for learning differences among students, among classes, and even among nations. Time-on-task can be altered positively (or negatively) by the instructional process, and this has direct consequences for student learning and student interest in learning.

These ideas about time and learning are central in the chapters "New Views of the Learner" and "Learning for Mastery." They are also developed further in chapter 1, "Implications of the IEA Studies for Curriculum and Instruction."

Intelligence versus Cognitive Entry

During much of the present century, educators have made use of intelligence and aptitude tests to predict later school achievement. In general, the statistical relations between these tests and later achievement have been found to be correlations of about $+.50$ to $+.70$. Most researchers and educators have interpreted these relations as indicating that these characteristics (intelligence and aptitude) *determine* the individual's potential for learning. They use them as a basis for making long-term decisions about selection, streaming, and even about the types of school programs to be assigned individuals. All too frequently, intelligence and aptitude scores determine the individual's opportunities for further education, support, and encouragement in the school and even the qualities of the interaction between the teacher and the student.

There is some evidence that intelligence test scores are alterable in the early years (ages 3 to 7), but there is little evidence of significant alteration in levels of intelligence as a result of school experiences in the later years. Less is known about the alterability of performance on specific aptitude tests. At least on the basis of present evidence, we may regard both intelligence and aptitude as highly stable characteristics during most of the school years.

Quite in contrast to intelligence and aptitude indices are *cognitive entry characteristics*. These are the specific knowledge, abilities, or skills which are the essential prerequisites for the learning of a particular school subject or a particular learning task. Such prerequisites typically correlate $+.70$ or higher with measures of achievement in a subject. Furthermore, when they are identified and measured, they *replace* intelligence and aptitude tests in the prediction of later achievement. That is, intelligence or aptitude tests add little or nothing to cognitive entry measures for the prediction of learning in a particular subject. All this is to say that cognitive entry characteristics are highly related to achievement and they have an obvious causal effect on later achievement. Especially is this true when sequential learning tasks are involved, where it may be impossible to learn learning task B unless a prior learning task A has been learned to an adequate level.

Cognitive entry characteristics are highly alterable because they represent particular content and skills which may be learned if they are absent, which may be reviewed if they have been forgotten, and which may be learned to a mastery level if they have been learned to a lesser level. In the next section of this introduction we will refer to feedback-corrective procedures as one major method for ensuring that cognitive entry characteristics are developed adequately for almost all students. In much of the mastery learning research in the schools, it is evident that the large gains in final achievement for the mastery students occurred because they were brought to high levels of achievement on the *prerequisites* for each new learning task. This is typically not done for students under conventional instruction.

Much of the variation in school learning is directly determined by the variation in students' cognitive entry characteristics. When means are found for ensuring that students reach adequate levels of competence on the essential cognitive entry behaviors, most students can be assured of high levels of school learning with very little variation in their achievement. The alterability of cognitive entry characteristics has the most profound implications for instruction, curriculum, and our views about the learning potential of almost all students in the schools.

These ideas about the role of intelligence and the importance of ensuring adequate cognitive entry levels are central in chapters 7 and 8, "New Views of the Learner" and "Learning for Mastery."

Summative versus Formative Testing

In most classrooms, achievement tests are used for summary or summative purposes. The summative test evidence is primarily used to classify or judge the student on the extent to which he has learned the content and objectives set for the course. The student's scores on each test are converted into school marks or other indices which compare each student with a set of norms or standards set by the teacher or the test makers. Typically, once the student has taken a test, he or she is marked; rarely is there opportunity for correcting one's errors or for being retested. In general, the basic notion is that the students have had equal opportunity to learn the subject over a defined period of time and they are then to be judged over what they have learned. This is repeated again and again during the school year.

It is frequently assumed that test results and school marks are the primary motivators for learning in the school. Marks based on tests are also assumed to be sound estimates of the *quality of the learning* as well as a proper index of the *quality of the learners*. Such marks are eventually the basis for major long-term decisions about the learners, including entry into different school programs, scholarships, and admission into higher education.

The use of summative testing-grading procedures results in highly predictable measures of school achievement. Typically, the correlations between achievement tests in the same subject at two points in time are usually above $+.70$ (depending upon the reliability of the separate tests). If carefully made standardized tests are used over a number of subjects, the correlations over a five-year period or longer tends to be $+.80$ or higher. For example, the relative rank-in-class of a student in grade 3 will effectively predict his rank-in-class in grade 8 or grade 11. Many researchers and educators infer from this constancy that differentials in achievement are nonalterable and that they are fixed by intelligence, heredity, home influences, or some other conditions outside of the school. It is assumed that the student and his background explain this remarkable stability of achievement and that the causes or remedies are not to be found within the schools. This assumption leads to the view that it is the student who has failed (or succeeded) and that the teachers, the instruction, the curriculum, and the school are not to be held responsible.

In contrast to summative tests used for grading and judging students is the use of tests and other evidence as an integral part of the formation of the learning. *Formative tests* are used primarily for feedback purposes in order to inform the student and the teacher about what has been learned well and what still needs to be learned. When the feedback is provided in relation to corrective procedures to help the student correct the learning errors, with additional time and help most students can reach the standard of achievement set by the teacher. Typically, a parallel formative test is used to determine when the student has completed the corrective process to the set standard. In various studies it is found that if only a small fraction of the students reach the mastery standard on the formative test given at the end of a particular two-week learning task, with an hour or two of corrective effort most of the students do reach the mastery standard when they are retested on a parallel formative test.

When formative tests and corrective procedures are used in this way over a series of learning tasks, the proportion of students reaching the mastery standard (before correctives) increases on each subsequent task until as many as 80 percent or 90 percent of the students are able to reach the mastery standard on the final learning tasks in the series. The amount of corrective help needed becomes smaller on successive learning tasks until only a few students need such corrective procedures. The students appear to be "learning to learn."

The use of formative tests in this way ensures that most of the students have the necessary cognitive prerequisites for each new learning task, that students have increased interest in the learning and greater confidence in their own ability to learn, and that they use more of the classroom time to engage actively in the learning process.

Such formative tests are also useful in helping the teacher determine which aspects of the learning task were learned well by the majority of the students and which were learned poorly by most of the students. This gives the teacher feedback in order to determine which ideas and skills need to be reviewed or retaught in a different way if the majority of students are to learn them to a high standard. The major change is that teachers do less in the way of judging and grading students on what they had learned by a particular date and they do more to see to it that each student learns what he or she needs as preparation for the next learning task(s).

Formative testing in relation to the corrective process may be considered as one example of cybernetic feedback-corrective procedures necessary for communication, body processes, and almost all human activities. In tutoring situations, the one-to-one relation provides so much interactive information that the feedback-corrective process is a natural part of the exchange between the tutor and tutee. However, since group learning is central in the schools, it is very difficult to provide adequate feedback-correctives for the teacher and the thirty or so learners in each classroom. As a result, much teaching may take place with inadequate learning on the part of many of the students. *Periodic* formative testing and corrective procedures, if used effectively, can improve the learning of most of the students. However, in the long run, the basic problem of group learning is to find ways of providing *continual* feedback-corrective processes as an integral part of the classroom teaching-learning interactions.

These ideas about testing and feedback-corrective processes are developed further in chapters 11 and 12, "Changes in Evaluation Methods" and "Theoretical Issues in Educational Evaluation." They are central in chapter 8, "Learning for Mastery," and chapter 7, "New Views of the Learner."

Teacher Characteristics versus Qualities of Teaching

Over the past half century there has been a great deal of research on *teacher characteristics* and their relationship to student learning. This research has been concerned with such characteristics as the age of the teachers, the training they have had, teaching experience, membership in teacher organizations, their personality and attitudes, and even their performance on achievement tests related to their field of teaching. In general, the relationship between such teacher characteristics and student learning has been very low. It may well be that researchers in the past have not selected the right teacher characteristics for study. However, based on the research done so far, it may be concluded that the characteristics of teachers have little to do with the learning of their students. And, even if they did show higher relations, most of the characteristics of teachers studied so far are static variables which are not directly alterable by in-service or other teacher-training programs.

Different from these many studies of teacher characteristics is the more recent research on the *qualities of teaching* that have a direct causal relation with student learning in the classroom. The research on these qualities of teaching is largely based on observational and experimental studies of teachers interacting with their students. Although there are many ways of doing this research, the theoretical approach of Dollard and Miller has been found to be very useful. Dollard and Miller have emphasized three major interactive characteristics of all teaching and learning—*cues, reinforcement,* and *participation. Cues* include the instruction as to what is to be learned as well as the directions as to what the learner is to do in the learning process. Much of the research relates student learning to the clarity, variety, meaningfulness, and strength of the explanations and directions provided by the teacher and/or the instructional material. *Reinforcement* includes the extent to which the student is rewarded or reinforced in his learning. Much of the research relates student learning to the variety of reinforcements provided, the frequency with which reinforcement is used, and the amount and kind of reinforcement given to different students in the class. *Participation* includes the extent to which the student is actively engaged in the learning. The research relates student learning to the extent to which he actively participates in using the cues, makes appropriate responses, and practices the responses until they have become a part of his repertoire. The research also includes the extent to which the instructor and/or the instructional method involves the different students in the class in overt as well as covert participation and response to the learning.

Observations of teacher interaction with students in the classroom reveal that teachers frequently direct their teaching and explanations to some students and ignore others. They give much positive reinforcement and encouragement to some students but not to others, and they encourage active participation in the classroom interaction from some students and discourage it from others. The studies find that typically the students in the top third of the class are given the greatest attention by teachers, while the students in the bottom third of the class generally receive the least attention and support. These differences in the interaction between teachers and students provide some students with much greater opportunity and encouragement for learning than is provided other students in the same classroom.

These qualities of teaching have been altered as a result of in-service education which provides teachers with feedback on what they are doing (or not doing) and with help to enable them to change the situation. Studies have found that when these interactions of teachers with their students are altered, there are significant improvements in student learning.

Teachers are frequently unconscious of the fact that they are providing more favorable conditions of learning for some students in the class than for other students. Generally, they are under the impression that they are giving all students equal opportunities for learning. When teachers are helped to secure a more accurate picture of their own teaching methods and styles of interactions with their students, they are increasingly able to provide favorable learning conditions for most of their students—rather than just for the top fraction of the class.

As the *qualities of teaching* become more central than the *characteristics of the teachers,* we will become clearer about the kinds of teacher training that can improve both teaching and learning. We will also become clearer about the variety of alterable conditions that can serve in the teaching-learning process. Tutors, aides, parents, and even other students can be helpful in promoting learning. New materials and media, new organization of classrooms, and new relations between teachers and students will be seen as important in contributing to the learning of the students.

These distinctions between *teachers* and *teaching* are most central in the papers "New Views of the Learner" and "Learning for Mastery." They are also developed in chapter 10, "Peak Learning Experiences," and chapter 1, "Implications of the IEA Studies for Curriculum and Instruction."

Parent Status versus Home Environment Processes

Teachers have long known that children coming from some homes learn better in school than children coming from other homes in the same communities. In general, it has been found that learning in the schools is related to the education and occupations of the parents, to the social class and socioeconomic status of the parents, and to their membership in particular ethnic groups and races. Sociological studies of socioeconomic status (which include parent education, occupation, and income) reveal moderate correlations between such indices and measures of school achievement. While such studies do demonstrate significant effects of the home on school achievement, they are not very helpful to the schools or to the parents, because these characteristics are not alterable. That is, there is little the school or the parents can do to alter the level of education, occupation, income, or ethnic characteristics. While such studies may be of some value for predicting levels of learning of groups of children, they offer no specific clues as to what the schools or the parents can do to improve the learning of the children.

Quite in contrast to these earlier studies of the characteristics of the parents are the more recent studies which emphasize what the parents *do* in interacting with their children. This research makes use of interviews and observational techniques to study the environmental processes in the homes—*the interactions between parents and their children.* Some of the home environmental processes which appear to be most significant are: the contribution of the home to the child's development of the mother tongue, the encouragement of the children to learn well, the aspirations of the parents for their children, the provision of help in learning when the child most needs it, and the ways in which time and space are organized in the home. The presence or absence of these qualities in the home are important determiners of the student's school achievement. In general, the effects of these processes are greatest with school achievement involving reading, vocabulary, and problem solving and least with spelling and arithmetic computation. These results suggest that the home has greatest influence on the language development of the child, general ability to learn, and motivation to learn well in school. The home has least influence on specific skills primarily taught in the school.

It is clear that when the home and the school have congruent learning emphases, the child has little difficulty in his later school learning. But when the home and the school have divergent approaches to life and to learning, the child is likely to be penalized severely by the school—especially when school attendance is required for ten or more years.

During recent years there has been a large number of studies which attempt to alter some of these processes in the home. These studies have made use of home visitors, special courses for parents, parent involvement in the schools for brief periods of time, as well as the provision of audio-visual and written materials and games to be used at various points in the child's development. This research makes it clear that many of these process variables are alterable and that most parents can do much to improve the school learning of their children.

Even when these variables cannot be altered in the home, a knowledge of the home environmental processes furnishes a basis for the development of programs of early childhood and primary education which can enable most of the children to learn well in school. The major point to be made is that there is a curriculum and teaching style in each home and that it is the variations in the home curriculum and teaching which account for much of the difference in children's preparation for the learning tasks in the school.

These ideas about the home are central in chapters 4 and 5, "Early Learning in the Home" and "The Effect of the Home Environment on Children's School Achievement." They also underlie the ideas in chapter 6, "Stability and Change in Human Characteristics—Implications for School Reorganization."

OVERVIEWS
OF
EDUCATION

Innocence in Education

After at least 5,000 years of educating the young in the home, in schools, and in the work place, educators frequently complain that almost nothing is really known about the educative process. The complaint becomes a rationalization for the failures of education and an excuse for the quick adoption (and equally rapid rejection) of new educational panaceas. Many educators appear to boast that they are in a state of *innocence* about education.

In striking contrast with professional educators are the host of journalists, reformers, and faddists who are quite certain that they have the true remedy for our educational ills. Most of them get a hearing in the mass media. The more persistent reformers have little difficulty in securing a grant to demonstrate their panacea and in collecting a following of educators who move in their wake for a few years. The libraries and basements of our schools still store the forgotten relics of fads and nostrums which were purchased because they promised to solve our educational problems.

In education, we continue to be seduced by the equivalent of snake-oil remedies, fake cancer cures, perpetual-motion contraptions, and old wives' tales. Myth and reality are not clearly differentiated, and we frequently prefer the former to the latter. It is not difficult to understand why the layman purchases fake cancer cures—he still yearns for a cure even when hope has been denied by a physician. But it would be difficult to explain why a reputable physician would purchase or advocate a fake cure. A parent in despair about the education of his child will seek a remedy no matter how farfetched because he also wants to hope. It is we educators who must look to our own field to ask why we have so much difficulty in distinguishing between myth and reality, or between sound remedies and worthless panaceas.

We have been *innocents* in education because we have not put our own house in order. We need to be much clearer about what we do and do not know so that we don't continually confuse the two. If I could have one wish for education during the next decade, it would be the systematic ordering of our basic knowledge in such a way that what is known and true can be acted on, while what is superstitution, fad, and myth can be recognized as such and used only when there is nothing else to support us in our frustration and despair. In addition, we need to know what new ideas are worth considering and how these ideas can and should be tested.

What do I mean by innocence? A decade ago, most of us were innocents with regard to the smoking of cigarettes. It was a costly habit which some condemned as vile and dirty, while others admired it as manly or sophisticated. No one claimed great virtues for smoking, but it was regarded as little more than a matter of individual taste and habit. Today, the effects of cigarette smoking on the incidence of lung cancer are widely known. We are no longer innocent about smoking cigarettes. We may continue to smoke cigarettes, but we do so with some knowledge of the possible consequences.

A decade ago, a manufacturer of electrical equipment found it expedient to dump the mercury by-products in the nearest body of water. These wastes sank out of sight, and as far as anyone knew that was the end of the matter. Now that researchers have established the links between mercury in the water, mercury in small fish, mercury in larger fish, and mercury deposits in the tissues of people who eat these fish, our manufacturer is no longer an innocent. Ten years ago, he was innocent when he dumped the mercury in the water. Today, if he does it, he does it from malevolence and a disregard for human values.

One could cite many instances in which innocence has been lost during the past few decades. These have been most dramatic with regard to phenomena that are not detectable by the senses (X-rays, carbon monoxide, etc.), that develop over a long time (lead poisoning, water pollution), or that are complex results of many forces in the society (economic cycles, crime, changes in social mores). New knowledge, new methods of detecting and measuring phenomena, and improved communication have made us aware of ways in which we are being influenced by the many forces around us. In some instances we have experienced great frustration because the loss of innocence has not been accompanied by effective ways of preventing or dealing with the problems that have been identified. In other instances, we have quickly learned how to deal responsibly with the new problems.

While I do not think we have equally dramatic instances in education, I believe that we should be less innocent in some aspects of education than we were two decades ago. And, I believe the next decade will establish other areas in which new knowledge and basic principles will force us to alter our educational institutions and educative processes—not so much from taste and whim but because our new awareness requires these changes.

Our innocence in education may, in part, be attributed to our addiction to *correlation and association* in our research. In contrast are those research procedures which seek to establish a *causal chain* that links one set of events to a relatively remote set of results or consequences. As long as we only know the correlation between two variables, we are not likely to be much affected. Our innocence is threatened when evidence accumulates under a wide variety of conditions that the relationships have a causal rather than only an associational basis. And our innocence is really challenged when some of the links between the phenomena are established.

One of the striking things about the loss of innocence is that a single clear presentation of a causal chain is sufficient to change almost everyone who understands and accepts the evidence. Especially for the professionals in a field, innocence may be challenged by a single lecture or publication which presents the links in a causal chain. The professional may persist in his practices, but he can never again do so as an innocent.

What I would like to do in this paper is point up seven areas or processes of education where our innocence is being threatened or challenged. For some of these areas, some of the causal links have already been established. For others, much work is still needed before the causal chain will become clear. I hope some parts of this catalog will be recognized by the readers of this paper and that many will join in the endeavor to do the conceptual and empirical research necessary to establish more complete causal relationships. It is my hope that each reader will prepare his own list of possibilities for reducing our innocence about education.

Individual Differences in Learning

Less than a decade ago, most educators accepted the idea that human capacity for school learning differed greatly from one person to another. While we differed in our estimates of the proportion who could learn effectively what the schools had to teach, most of us were certain that only a small percentage (10–15 percent) of students could really learn to some mastery level. Throughout the world, the proportion of students expected to *fail* in school varied from 5 percent to as high as 75 percent. We differed also in the causes we invoked to explain school-learning differences—genetics, motivation, socioeconomic status, language facility, docility, etc. But, we assumed that most of the causes of success or failure in school learning lay outside the school's or the teacher's responsibility. In our innocence, we were content to talk about *equality of opportunity,* by which we thought of each student being given the same learning conditions—it was the students who differed in their use of this opportunity.

More recently, we have come to understand that under appropriate learning conditions, students differ in the *rate* at which they can learn —not in the level to which they can achieve or in their basic capacity to learn. Fundamental research on these ideas is still in process. Studies in which these ideas have been applied to actual school subjects reveal that as many as 90 percent of the students can learn these school subjects up to the same standard that only the top 10 percent of students have been learning under usual conditions. As this research proceeds, special conditions have been discovered under which both the *level* of learning and the *rate* of learning become much the same from student to student. That is, there is growing evidence that much of what we have termed *individual differences in school learning* is the effect of particular school conditions rather than of basic differences in the capabilities of our students.

As we learn more about how individual differences in school learning are maximized or minimized, our responsibility for the learning of our students will become greater and greater. As our understanding of the learning process becomes greater, our loss of innocence will be accompanied by responsibilities and technical complexities which many of us will be loath to take on. Surprisingly, some of the professional and graduate schools have been first to take on these new responsibilities. The teachers at the elementary school level have been slow to learn about these ideas and to accept the responsibilities associated with the loss of innocence.

School Achievement and Its Effect on Personality

We have long been aware of the consistency and predictability of measures of school achievement over a number of years. We took this as further evidence of differences in human learning capacity and as validation of our grading and measurement procedures.

While we recognized some of the effects of consistently high or low achievement marks on the student's motivation for further learning and attitude toward the school, we were not aware of or much concerned about the ways in which school achievement influences the student's view of himself or his personality. After all, it was the student who was able or deficient—not the school or the educational process.

During the last two decades (and in part spurred on by the Supreme Court decision on school segregation) many scholars have been trying to determine the relation between school conditions, school achievement, and personality characteristics. Some have been searching for a direct relation between the student's success or failure in school and his view of himself. There is considerable evidence that repeated success in school over a number of years increases the probability of the student's gaining a positive view of himself and high self-esteem. Similarly, there is evidence that repeated failure or low performance in school increases the probability of the student's developing a negative view of himself and a lowered self-esteem. While these relationships between school marks and self-concept are relatively clear, much additional research is needed to establish the causal and interactive links between school achievement and self-view over a number of years.

What is more striking, but less certain, is the evidence that repeated success in school over a number of years (especially at the primary school level) appears to increase the likelihood that an individual can withstand stress and anxiety more effectively than individuals who have a history of repeated failure or low marks in school. To put it bluntly, repeated success in coping with the academic demands of the school appears to confer upon a high proportion of such students a type of immunization against emotional illness. Similarly, repeated failure in coping with the demands of the school appears to be a source of emotional difficulties and mental illness. Thus, while this research is beginning to draw parallels between immunization against physical diseases (e.g., polio, smallpox, etc.) and immunization against emotional diseases, it is also helping us to understand how schools may actually infect children with emotional difficulties. One question that is troubling some workers in this field is why some students who succeed admirably do not develop this immunization, while others who fail repeatedly are able to avoid the emotional difficulties that "should" be their fate.

Associated with some of this research is the remarkable finding that most of the emotional consequences are associated with teacher's marks and judgments rather than with the results of standardized achievement tests. Thus, it is possible to find two schools that do not overlap in their achievement measures, so that the lowest students in the superior school are slightly higher on the standardized achievement measures than the highest students in the inferior school. Under such conditions, the highest students in the inferior school have a more positive view of themselves than the lowest students in the superior school, even though the two groups of students have almost the same level of tested achievement. Indeed, the highest students in the inferior school have almost as positive a view of themselves and their capabilities as the highest students in the superior school. Perhaps the explanation has to do with the fact that most of the evidence of success or failure is in terms of teachers' marks and judgments, which the students receive daily, rather than standardized tests, which are given only once or twice a year with little interpretation to the students or parents. It is the perception of how well one is doing relative to others in the same situation that appears to be a key link between school achievement and personality effects.

Research on the relations between school achievement and mental health is far from complete. I believe that when it is fully established, it will have powerful effects on how we run our schools, mark our students, and even teach them. Especially when we are able to determine how to develop school learning more effectively, will we change from our present innocence about the long-term effects of school achievement (positive or negative) to a more complex view of education and our responsibilities for both the learning of our students and the more basic personality consequences of this learning?

Teachers versus Teaching

The selection and training of teachers have been central problems in education for many centuries. During the past fifty years there has been much research on teacher characteristics and their relation to student learning. This research was intended to improve the selection of students for teacher training and the selection of teachers for particular teaching positions. One could summarize most of this research with the simple statement that the characteristics of teachers have little relation to the learning of their pupils. In spite of the accumulation of a great deal of evidence on this point, in our innocence we still devote much effort to the selection of teachers and the recruitment of teacher-training students on the basis of scholastic aptitude, scholastic achievement, personality characteristics, and interests and attitudes.

More recently, some researchers have taken the position that it is the *teaching,* not the *teacher,* that is the key to the learning of students. That is, it is not what teachers are *like* but what they *do* in interacting with their students in the classroom that determines what students learn and how they feel about the learning and about themselves. This point of view has led to some of the most fundamental research about the nature of teaching, the role of the teacher in the classroom, and the kinds of learning materials that are useful in promoting particular kinds of learning.

As the role of teaching becomes more central than the characteristics of the teacher, we are likely to become clearer as to the kinds of preservice and in-service teacher training that can improve teaching. Even more important, research on this problem has already broadened our view of teaching from that of a single teacher teaching thirty students to the notion that tutors, aides, and even other students can be helpful in promoting learning. Finally, this view is enlarging our notion of the variety of conditions that can serve in the teaching-learning process. These include new materials and media, new organizations of classrooms, and new relations among teachers and students.

As we shift our attention from the teacher as a person to the variety of ways in which teaching-learning can take place, the nature of schools—their organization, buildings, and routines—will undergo marked transformations. Innocence in this area has already been challenged, and many of the consequences have already been seen in the schools. While we may no longer be innocent in this area, much research and development must take place before we will understand the many links in the teaching-learning process and the long-term consequences of these new developments for education in the schools and in the larger community.

What Can Be Learned?

When we observe teachers in the process of teaching, we note that there is much emphasis on the learning of information. When we examine teachers' quizzes and final examinations, we also note that most of the questions have to do with the remembering of information presented in the textbook or in the classroom. Schools, teachers, and textbooks are apparently directed toward filling a presumably "empty head" with things to be remembered. Although teachers, curriculum makers, and testers profess more complex objectives for education, the actual emphasis in the classrooms is still largely on the learning of specific information.

During the past two decades the professed objectives of education have changed from knowledge alone to a great variety of cognitive objectives including creativity. The objectives of education increasingly stress interests, attitudes, and values in the affective domain. And human relations, social skills, and new views of man in relation to his society and to himself are frequently expressed in these newer objectives of education.

The links between the learner and the learning process for some of the major cognitive objectives of education, such as application of principles and interpretation of new data, are well known. The links for some of the simpler affective objectives, such as interests and attitudes, are also known. However, there are many complex educational objectives for which we know very little about the kinds of learning processes needed. It is here that the links between the learner and the learning process must still be established.

Thus, while the view of what ought to be learned in the schools has broadened enormously, the teaching-learning processes for many of these new objectives are not fully understood. New research and development are necessary if our understanding of process is to match our new conceptions of educational objectives.

Even more important, classroom teaching in the schools has not caught up with what we already know about the teaching-learning processes necessary for many of the educational objectives which transcend *knowledge* as the primary goal of education. There is a wide gulf between what we want in education and what we do in education. While we want education to accomplish much more than the inculcation of knowledge, we are still partially innocent about how to do it. Even when the experts and gifted teachers know how to do it, this is only rarely transmitted to the majority of the teachers. It is the teachers who are still innocent about the relations between educational objectives and the teaching-learning process.

As we become more fully aware of what it is *possible* for education to do, we are left with major value considerations of what education *ought* to do. Perhaps, it is in this area that educators need to come to terms with themselves and with the rapid changes in students, society, and subjects of the curriculum. Decisions must be made about what is desirable and how to determine it before we shift to the more technical considerations of how to accomplish the new objectives and how to train teachers to support the necessary teaching-learning process.

Manifest and Latent Curriculum

When we talk about educational objectives, we quickly slip into thoughts about the content of education—the subject matter to be learned—and the behaviors that students should develop with relation to this subject matter. Our schools are thought of in terms of science, mathematics, social studies, foreign languages, literature, and the language arts. We organize curriculum centers and curriculum projects to develop the latest and best views on what should be learned. This, to use the words of the sociologists, is the "manifest" curriculum.

Textbooks are written for the manifest curriculum, syllabi are developed, teachers are trained to teach it, and tests are made to determine how much of this curriculum has been learned. There is no doubt about the importance of this curriculum—it is this to which we devote most of the money, time, and energy available to the schools.

During the past decade, sociologists, anthropologists, and social psychologists have been observing the schools, the ways in which they are organized, and the relations among administrators, teachers, and students. Slowly they have been discovering what may be termed the "latent" curriculum.

Schools teach much about time, order, neatness, promptness, and docility in this latent curriculum. Students learn to value each other and themselves in terms of the answers they give and the products they produce in school. Students learn how to compete with their age mates in school and the consequences of an academic and a social pecking order. The latent curriculum is probably a very effective curriculum for a highly urbanized and technologically oriented society. It develops some of the skills, attitudes, and values relevant to getting and keeping a job, the maintenance of a social status system in the larger society, and many of the attributes necessary for the maintenance of political stability.

Indeed, the latent curriculum is in many respects likely to be more effective than the manifest curriculum. The lessons it teaches are long remembered because it is so pervasive and consistent over the many years in which our students attend school. Its lessons are experienced daily and learned firmly. It is probable that the lessons of the latent curriculum are learned so well because they are spelled out in the behavior of the students and adults in the school and are only rarely verbalized or justified.

Where the manifest and the latent curricula are consistent and support each other, learning is most powerful. It is here that attitudes and values are probably learned most effectively. Where the manifest and the latent curricula are in conflict, one would expect the latent curricula to become dominant. It is not what we talk about but what we do that becomes important.

Schools can and do have considerable effects on both the cognitive and affective aspects of the manifest curriculum. But to judge the effects of schools only in terms of this curriculum is to ignore a great range of other influences resulting from the ways in which we have organized our schools and the processes involved in schooling. We have paid a high price for our innocence in this area because we have ignored the effects of the latent curriculum and because we have permitted so many aspects of this curriculum to develop in response to efficiency and convenience in managing students rather than in response to their educational needs.

Our innocence has been in giving our attention solely to the manifest curriculum while we overlooked the latent one. As we develop skill in recognizing and analyzing the latent curriculum and the relations between the two curricula, the schools will look very different to us. Much research will be necessary before we have a clear picture of the latent curriculum and the ways in which it affects students, teachers, and others in the schools. Even more will be required before we will understand how to alter the latent curriculum to make it more consistent with the manifest curriculum, or to make both manifest and latent curricula consistent with objectives of education which relate individual needs and the needs of the society.

Role of Testing

Of all the technical fields related to education, testing has developed most fully. This field has been most responsive to each new development in statistics and psychometrics. It has made excellent use of computer technology and high-speed scoring and data-processing procedures, and has led the way in defining and evaluating many of the possible objectives of education.

Testing has had a profound influence on decision making in many aspects of education. Tests provide the major evidence on which we select students for scholarships and for places in colleges, graduate schools, and professional schools. We use tests to determine whether our new curricula in science, in preschool education, or in medicine are effective.

In our innocence we have permitted testing to dominate education and to serve as the primary and often the only basis for our most important decisions about students, about teachers, and more recently about curricula and programs. This has had the effect of narrowing our view about what is important and of placing a quantitative emphasis on so many aspects of education. There has been a focus on the concrete, on the measurable, and on the products of education.

Only recently have we begun to ask more searching questions about this rapidly developing technology in education. We have begun to ask how testing and evaluation may serve education rather than dominate it. Some of the more exciting possibilities have emphasized the use of evaluation in the development of learning, teaching, and curricula. Some of the newer emphases have been on the process rather than on the product and on the affective as well as the more complex cognitive objectives of education.

Some workers in the field have been searching for ways in which evaluation can be helpful to teachers in improving the process of teaching. Others have found ways in which evaluation can be used to promote the process of learning. Another group has been searching for ways in which evaluation can be used in the actual formation of a new curriculum to insure that it will be the best possible for the students and teachers who will use it. Others have been using evaluation to set goals that students can attain and have found ways in which evaluation can be used to encourage students and help them develop a sense of accomplishment and a positive self-view.

There is a danger that the loss of innocence about the effects of testing will lead some educators to want to eliminate all testing. Steps already taken in this direction have the effect of eliminating measures of symptoms because we find them disturbing to teachers, students, and parents. The consequences of rash actions of this sort will be to lose many of the benefits evaluation can bring to teaching and learning. Tests can serve education without dominating it. The process of education can be markedly improved as we begin to understand how it can be facilitated by the appropriate use of educational evaluation. Many of the new strategies of teaching-learning are based on the use of formative evaluation at each stage of the process. New efforts to individualize education are dependent on major new efforts in evaluation at the beginning of, during, and at terminal points in the process of learning. It is likely that testing, which hitherto has been largely responsive to mass education, may become our most effective tool in helping the schools to relate education and teaching to the individual.

Education as Part of a Larger Social System

Education in Western societies is frequently equated with schooling. We support schools to give our children and youth an education. We empower schools to give formal recognition to the amount and type of education an individual has completed by the use of credits, certificates, and academic degrees. Most of our writing and research on education deal only with schools and schooling.

Recently, this equation of education and schooling has been attacked by scholars of education as well as by more radical reformers who insist that much learning can and does take place outside the school. But equally important, research on education and research on various aspects of the society have questioned some of the relations between the school system and other subsystems in the society.

Research into the relation between the schools and the home environment has been one of the more fruitful areas of study stimulated by these questions. Home is a powerful educational environment, especially during the preschool and primary school years. Studies of home environments in the United States, as well as in several other countries, reveal the effect of the home on language development, ability to learn from adults, attitudes toward school learning, and aspirations for further education and the occupational careers and life styles associated with education. It is clear that when the home and the school have congruent learning emphases, the child has little difficulty in his later schooling. But when the home and the school have very divergent approaches to life and to learning, the child is likely to be penalized severely by the school—especially when school attendance is required for ten or more years.

During the past half-decade we have begun to recognize some of the problems raised by disparities between home and school. One approach has been to preempt some of the years preceding regular school by placing children in preschool programs. Other attempts have been made to alter some aspects of the primary school. Still other efforts have been made to alter the home environment. There is no doubt that these attempts to alter the relations between home and school have raised many problems. The resolution of these problems and the appropriate relations between home and school will concern us for many years to come. While our innocence has been threatened by research on the relations between home environments and school, our present knowledge does not provide clear answers to the educational and moral questions raised by our new awareness of these relations.

Schools and peer groups are increasingly in conflict, and the individual appears to learn very different things in these two subsystems of society. Especially during adolescence do we find these two subsystems diverging. The conflicts between the values emphasized by schools and colleges and the values emphasized by various peer groups raise serious questions about the ways in which these two subsystems can be more effectively related. The very obvious differences between these subsystems have already had a marked effect on our innocence in this area. What we desperately need are research and scholarship which will point the way to the resolution of some of the more disturb-ing conflicts between the schools and adolescent peer groups.

Recent research by economists attempts to understand the relation-ships between the economic system of a nation and its educational system. It is evident that the relations between education and econom-ics may be very different for societies at different stages of industrial-ization as well as for societies which have very different political sys-tems. The view that education can be conceived of as investment in human capital has stimulated educators as well as economists to study the economic effects of different approaches to education. The view of education as both a consumer or cultural good and an investment in human capital alters many of our traditional views about education and its effects. This area of research raises long-term problems about the consequences of this view for support of the schools and support of students in the schools.

There are other subsystems in a nation—religion, mass media, the political system, the status system—which have very complex rela-tions with education. Perhaps the main point is that education is not confined to the school system and that very complex educational and other relations are found between the schools as a subsystem and the other subsystems within a society. While we have tended to think of a system of schooling as relatively insulated from other parts of the society, it is likely that the schools will be under pressure to relate more clearly to the other parts of the social system. Undoubtedly, we will come to regard education during the school-attending period, as well as before and after this period, as most appropriately the concern of many aspects of the society. Increasingly we will try to determine what can best be learned in the schools, what can best be learned elsewhere, and what can be learned only through an effective interrela-tion of different parts of the social system.

While we know much more about these matters than we did a decade ago, we are still quite innocent in this area. It is in these interactions of the subsystems of a nation in relation to both education and the great social problems that new understanding will most probably develop. One is hard pressed at this time to predict the consequences of this new understanding. But there is little doubt that our innocence will be most severely challenged in this area during the years ahead.

This paper has stressed the need for research which can establish causal links between particular events and relatively remote sets of results and consequences in the field of education. While this way of stating the problem suggests simple linear chains of causal relations, it does not preclude more complex interactive relations among events where *cause* and *effect* are not so easily labeled or permanently fixed. There is no doubt that education involves multiple causes as well as multiple effects and that complex problems in education are likely to be resistant to research based on simple notions of causation and determinism.

Five years ago I undertook to summarize the results of twenty-five years of educational research and concluded with the hope that more *powerful* research strategies might enable us to produce as many crucial substantive pieces of research in the next five years as had been produced in the previous twenty-five years.[1] It is left to others to determine whether this in fact has been accomplished. There is no doubt that the amount of educational scholarship and research has increased greatly and that the quality has improved, especially during the past eight to ten years. Resources have been made available to support educational research as well as the training of able, young scholars in this very demanding field. The partial catalog of advances presented in this paper and cited in the bibliography indicates that these resources have been well used.

These advances in our understanding of education and related phenomena have not always been reflected in our educational practices. I am convinced that little will be done until the meaning and consequences of these new advances are understood by educational scholars, educational leaders, and teachers. I have suggested that these new insights and understandings may be conceived of as the loss of *innocence* about the relations among educational phenomena. This way of posing the problem suggests that the burden of responsibility for appropriate actions and practices rests with the professionals in the field once new ideas are adequately communicated. But long experience in education has left me with the impression that innocence is not easily relinquished and new responsibilities are avoided as long as possible.

This paper has been adapted from a speech for the inauguration of Dean James I. Doi, College of Education, University of Rochester.
1. Benjamin S. Bloom, "Twenty-five Years of Educational Research," *American Educational Research Journal 3, no. 3* (1966): 211–21.

SELECTED BIBLIOGRAPHY

Individual Differences in Learning

Block, James H., ed. *Mastery Learning: Theory and Practice.* New York: Holt, Rinehart & Winston, 1971.

Bloom, B. S. *Individual Differences in School Achievement: A Vanishing Point?* Bloomington, Ind.: Phi Delta Kappa, 1971.

Carroll, John. "A Model of School Learning." *Teachers College Record* 64 (1963): 723–33.

Cronbach, L. J., and Snow, R. C. *Individual Differences in Learning Ability as a Function of Instructional Variables.* Final report: contract no. OEC 4-6-061269-1217, Washington, D.C.: Office of Education, 1969.

Gagné, Robert M., ed. *Learning and Individual Differences.* Columbus, Ohio: Charles E. Merrill Books, 1967.

School Achievement and Its Effect on Personality

Block, *Mastery Learning: Theory and Practice.* New York: Holt, Rinehart & Winston, 1971.

Brookover, W. B.; Shailer, T.; and Paterson, A. "Self-Concept of Ability and School Achievement." *Sociology of Education* 37 (1964) 271–78.

Kirkland, Marjorie C. "The Effects of Tests on Students and Schools." *Review of Educational Research* 41, no. 4 (October 1971): 303–50.

Stringer, L. A., and Glidewell, J. C. *Early Detection of Emotional Illnesses in School Children.* Final report. Saint Louis: Saint Louis County Health Department, 1967.

Torshen, Kay. "The Relation of Classroom Evaluation to Students' Self-Concepts and Mental Health." Ph.D. dissertation, University of Chicago, 1969.

Teachers versus Teaching

Anthony, Bobbie, C. M. "The Identification and Measurement of Classroom Environmental Process Variables Related to Academic Achievement." Ph.D. dissertation, University of Chicago, 1967.

Brophy, Jere E., and Good, Thomas L. "Teachers' Communication of Differential Expectations for Children's Classroom Performance: Some Behavioral Data." *Journal of Educational Psychology* 61, no. 5 (October 1970): 365–74.

Flanders, N. A. *Analyzing Teacher Behavior.* Reading, Mass.: Addison-Wesley Co., 1970.

Lahaderne, H. M. "Adaptation to School Settings: A Study of Children's Attitudes and Classroom Behavior." Ph.D. dissertation, University of Chicago, 1967.

Rosenshine, B. *Teaching Behaviors and Student Achievement: A Review of Research.* Stockholm: International Association for the Evaluation of Educational Achievement, 1970.

Ryans, David G. *Characteristics of Teachers.* Washington, D.C.: American Council on Education, 1960.

What Can Be Learned:

Bloom, B. S., ed. *Taxonomy of Educational Objectives: Cognitive Domain.* New York: David McKay Co., 1956.

Gagné, Robert M. *The Conditions of Learning.* New York: Holt, Rinehart & Winston, 1965.

Glaser, Robert. "Concept Learning and Concept Teaching." In *Learning Research and School Subjects,* edited by R. M. Gagné. Itasca, Ill.: F. E. Peacock Publishers, 1968.

Kohlberg, L. "Moral Education in the Schools: A Developmental Viewpoint." *School Review* 74, no. 1 (Spring 1966): 1–30.

Krathwohl. D. R.: Bloom, B. S.; and Masia, B. B. *Taxonomy of Educational Objectives: Affective Domain.* New York: David McKay Co., 1964.

McClelland, David C. "Toward a Theory of Motive Acquisition." *American Psychologist* 20, no. 5 (May 1965): 321–33.

Torrance, E. Paul. *Encouraging Creativity in the Classroom.* Dubuque, Iowa: W. C. Brown Co., 1970.

Manifest and Latent Curriculum

Dreeben, Robert. *On What Is Learned in School.* Reading, Mass.: Addison-Wesley Publishing Co., 1968.

Henry, Jules. *Culture against Man.* New York: Random House, 1965.

Jackson, Philip W. *Life in Classrooms.* New York: Holt, Rinehart & Winston, 1968.

Overly, Norman V., ed. *The Unstudied Curriculum.* Washington, D.C.: Association for Supervision and Curriculum Development, National Education Association, 1970.

Wilkinson, Rupert H. *Gentlemanly Power.* London: Oxford University Press, 1964.

Role of Testing

Bloom, B. S.; Hastings, J. T.; and Madaus, G. *Handbook on Formative and Summative Evaluation of Student Learning.* New York: McGraw-Hill Book Co., 1971.

Glaser, R., and Nitko, A. J. "Measurement in Learning and Instruction." In *Educational Measurement,* edited by R. L. Thorndike. Washington, D.C.: American Council on Education, 1971.

Lindvall, C. M., and Cox, R. C. *IPI Evaluation Program.* AERA Monograph Series on Curriculum Evaluation. Chicago: Rand McNally & Co., 1970.

Scriven, M. "The Methodology of Evaluation." In *Perspectives of Curriculum Evaluation.* AERA Monograph Series on Curriculum Evaluation. Chicago: Rand McNally & Co., 1967.

Tyler, Ralph W., ed. *Education Evaluation: New Roles, New Means.* National Society for the Study of Education, 68th Yearbook, pt. 2. Chicago: University of Chicago Press, 1969.

Education as Part of a Larger Social System

Home Environment

Coleman, James S., et al. *Equality of Educational Opportunity.* Washington, D.C.: Government Printing Office, 1966.

Dave, R. H. "The Identification and Measurement of Environmental Process Variables

That Are Related to Educational Achievement." Ph.D. dissertation, University of Chicago, 1963.

Hess, R. L., and Shipman, V. "Early Experience and the Socialization of Cognitive Modes in Children." *Child Development* 36 (1965): 869–86.

Stodolsky, S. "Maternal Behavior and Language and Concept Formation in Negro Pre-School Children." Ph.D. dissertation, University of Chicago, 1965.

Wolf, Richard. "The Measurement of Environments." In *Testing Problems in Perspective*, edited by A. Anastasi. Washington, D.C.: American Council on Education, 1966.

Economics

Blaug, Mark. *Economics of Education: A Selected Annotated Bibliography.* Oxford: Pergamon Press, 1970.

Bowman, M. J., et al. *Readings in the Economics of Education.* Paris: UNESCO, 1971.

Schultz, T. W. *The Economic Value of Education.* New York: Columbia University Press, 1963.

Other

Coleman, J. S. *The Adolescent Society.* Glencoe, Ill.: Free Press, 1961.

Coleman, James S., ed. *Education and Political Development.* Princeton, N.J.: Princeton University Press, 1965.

Coombs, Philip H. *World Educational Crisis.* New York: Oxford University Press, 1968.

Foster, Philip. *Education and Social Change in Ghana.* Chicago: University of Chicago Press, 1965.

Havighurst, R. J. *Human Development and Education.* New York: David McKay & Co., 1953.

Huberman, Michael. *Reflections on Democratization of Secondary and Higher Education.* International Education Year, UNESCO, no. 4. Paris: UNESCO, 1970.

Husén, T., ed. *International Study of Educational Achievement in Mathematics: A Comparison of Twelve Countries,* 2 vols. New York: John Wiley & Sons, 1967.

Husén, T., and Boalt, G. *Educational Research and Educational Change: The Case of Sweden.* New York: John Wiley & Sons, 1967.

Implications of the IEA Studies for Curriculum and Instruction

2

T he International Association for the Evaluation of Education Achievement (IEA) is an organization of twenty-two national research centers which are engaged in the study of education.[1] Organized in 1959, this group published a pilot study in 1962[2] and a study of mathematics achievement in 1967.[3] It has just published studies of achievement in science,[4] reading comprehension,[5] and literature,[6] and will in the near future publish studies of achievement in French as a foreign language,[7] English as a foreign language,[8] and in civic education.[9]

The IEA represents a cooperative approach to international research on educational problems. In each country there is a national research center which is involved as a cooperative partner in the cross-national research. This group of research centers has been concerned with the use of international tests, questionnaires, and other methods to relate student achievement and attitudes to instructional, social, and economic factors in each nation. The overall aim of this research is to establish generalizations which will be of value in education, not only in the participating countries, but throughout the world.

In addition to the international reports, each of the national centers is preparing a report in which its nation's results are discussed against the background of the international data and findings. In these national reports each center will highlight the results of its own country's research, explain these results, and suggest their curricular, instructional, and other implications.[10]

In this paper I will attempt to draw some of the overall implications for curriculum and instruction from the major results of the IEA surveys. But the important work on this subject will be the attempt by each of the national research centers to draw implications and suggest hypotheses that will make the greatest sense in terms of its own country's special conditions and problems.

International Instruments and Data Collection

A major feature of IEA is that its evaluation instruments and data-collection procedures have been developed especially for the purpose of international comparison and study. In previous cross-national studies, test items and styles of test construction tended to be specific to the country in which the instruments were constructed. The evaluation instruments developed in one country typically showed that country to be superior to the other countries included in the study.

International Evaluation Instruments

This concern with internationally validated evaluation instruments impelled IEA to create international as well as national committees in each subject. Both types of committees studied national curricula and examinations and attempted to identify subject-matter content and educational objectives of major significance in the different countries which participated.

The national committees criticized the specifications proposed by the international committee. In addition, they constructed test items and questionnaire procedures, criticized particular proposals of items, did pilot studies on particular features of the instruments, translated the material into the national languages, and conducted national tryouts of the items and procedures.

The international committees finally produced the major evaluation instruments, supervised the procedures for major cross-national studies in each subject field, and took major responsibility for the international report on the results.

Each of the IEA subject studies has taken about seven years to complete, with at least half of this time devoted to instrument construction, criticism, and revision. Every effort has been made to develop valid international instruments based on what the representatives of the countries regard as the most important subject content and educational objectives of the subject field. Nevertheless these instruments are more "fair" to some national curricula and syllabi than to others.

The emphasis on international evaluation instruments has resulted in the involvement of a large number of persons in each of the participating countries on the national committees, both as critics of the tests and questionnaires and as consultants at different stages in the development of the instrument. This way of working has resulted in a set of evaluation instruments which represent the variety of objectives and content included in the subject field for most of the participating nations. The IEA evaluation instruments give an excellent picture of the state of evaluation and education (objectives and content) in the countries represented in these studies. The evaluation instruments also represent an international consensus on the knowledge and objectives most worth learning.

Evaluation and Education
IEA has stimulated the development of more adequate evaluation procedures in a high proportion of the countries involved in these studies. There is an increased interest in modern evaluation methods, more concern about the subject-matter content and objectives of education, and greater sophistication in using and interpreting evaluation data. In each country, most teachers whose students were tested in the IEA study were asked to review each item in the tests and to judge it in terms of the students' opportunity to learn that idea or process. This procedure has introduced many teachers throughout the world to modern evaluation methods.

As a result of these studies there is a more realistic understanding of what education is accomplishing at present in each country, an awareness of what is being accomplished in other countries, and some grasp of the reasons for the international differences. There is also increased concern for the improvement of education and the schools in most of the IEA countries, including interest in more effective curricula and the training of teachers for these new curricula. While I do not wish to claim that IEA is the major force in encouraging new curriculum work, the IEA methods and instruments, the interaction of educators and evaluators, and the results of the IEA studies are powerful incentives for the development of more adequate curricula and improved teaching-learning approaches within and between IEA countries.

The IEA surveys provide baseline data for each country against which future changes in education may be appraised. The IEA instruments and the increased sophistication about evaluation in each of the countries provide methods and procedures for the systematic evaluation of the effectiveness of new approaches to education. They also make it possible to study alternative approaches on a small scale before major decisions are made to implement the most effective approaches on a larger scale.

Differences between Countries

Perhaps the most dramatic findings of all the IEA studies during the past decade and a half have to do with differences between countries. For highly developed countries there is a difference of about one standard deviation between the means of the highest scoring and lowest scoring of these countries. But, there are approximately two standard deviations between the means of the highest of the developed nations and the average of the developing nations.

One can translate these statistics in a number of ways.

If the mean of the highest-scoring nation is used as the criterion of what it is possible for students to learn, about 85 percent of the students in the lowest scoring of the developed nations would be below this mean while about 98 percent of the students in the developing nations would be below this point.

If school marks were assigned in the various nations on the basis of the highest nation's standards (where perhaps the lowest fifth might be regarded as failing), then almost 50 percent of the students in the lowest scoring of the developed nations would fail but about 85 percent of the students in the average developing nation would fail.

These results may also be considered in terms of grade norms. If judged by test results in the highest-scoring nation, the average student in the lowest scoring of the developed nations would be at about the eighth-grade norm after twelve years of schooling, while the average student in the developing nations would be at about the sixth-grade norm after twelve years of schooling. This would be true even when selectivity at the secondary level is held constant. Although one may have misgivings about such attempts to put schooling in terms of age or grade norms in the highest-scoring nation, it is evident that the attainment obtained in one year of schooling in the highest nation requires one and one-half or two years of schooling in less-favored nations. To put it in terms of time and human resources spent, it may cost twice as much for a particular level of learning in one place as it does in another.

The IEA studies may be viewed as demonstrating what education can accomplish under the most favorable conditions we can find throughout the world. In principle, any country which so desires may do for its youth what the most-favored national system does do for its students. Since there must be many trade-offs, each national system which attempts to do better for its youth must search for ways of accomplishing this—even though it may not necessarily attempt to duplicate the particular pattern of conditions in the other countries.

Opportunity to Learn

Perhaps the most important variable in accounting for the differences between national systems—even where they are equally selective—is the opportunity to learn as judged by teachers. Teachers were asked to evaluate each item in the IEA test as to the proportion of their students who had an opportunity to learn the idea or process underlying that item. When the results for particular groups of teachers and students across a nation are correlated, the IEA studies show a very high relation between these teachers' judgments and the overall performances of the students.

This variable—opportunity to learn—is essentially a description of the curriculum in the local schools and classrooms, perhaps a more direct measure of this curriculum than are the published versions of the official curriculum at the national or local level. The IEA tests were based on the official curriculum in the different nations, and this variable suggests what portion of the official curriculum has survived at the classroom level. Perhaps the most important curriculum implication is that beautiful curriculum plans have little relevance for education unless they are translated into what happens in the classrooms of the nation or community. Until curriculum plans and material affect the classroom they are little more than dead documents to be stored in libraries. If the curriculum is to be brought to life in the classroom, many of the nations will have to provide more preservice and in-service education for teachers. And such training programs will be effective only if they succeed in changing teachers' behaviors in the classroom. Some national curriculum centers have been experimenting with various approaches to these problems, and some of the approaches to in-service education of teachers have been effective. The nations may learn much from each other if they develop a cooperative approach to the study of such teacher training problems.

Teacher Competence

There is evidence that the competence of teachers in both subject matter and methods of teaching varies greatly between nations. In one developing country a sample of science teachers took the IEA science test and scored below the average secondary school student on the international norms. It is unlikely that students can learn much from teachers who do not thoroughly understand the subject they are teaching. Where the capabilities of the teaching staff are low, a nation which wishes to upgrade its students' learning must either attract more competent teachers, provide more adequate in-service education, or use mass media to supplement what the classroom teacher offers.

If Beeby is correct about the levels of teaching that can be provided by teachers with different levels of postsecondary education,[11] some developing countries must either wait decades before they can provide adequately trained teachers at all levels of schooling or they must find a way in which a small number of well-trained teachers can provide the bulk of instruction through the use of mass media in the classroom. There has been some excellent research on different ways of using radio and television for instructional purposes. Under favorable conditions a small number of very competent teachers can provide high-quality instruction for thousands of students through the use of such media.

Time

A third variable that appears to be important, a combination of curriculum and instruction, is time. Time has been studied in the IEA research in terms of number of years of instruction in a subject, the number of hours of instruction per week or year, and the number of hours of homework per week in a particular subject. Throughout the IEA studies there is a significant relationship between the amount of time the student devotes to a subject and learning in that subject.

Although there is little direct evidence in the IEA research, there is a strong likelihood based on other research that involvement, the percentage of time in class that the student is actively working on a subject, is also a significant element in learning. On the basis of simple observational studies it appears that in some countries students are actively engaged in learning for 90 percent or more of class time, while in other countries students are actively engaged in learning only about 50 percent of the time. Further studies in depth are needed to check these observations. While the amount of time students are actively engaged in the learning should be highly related to achievement on the IEA tests, the explanations for differences in degrees of involvement in school learning are more complex and probably include cultural differences, the importance of school learning to students and their parents, ways in which teachers use time available for teaching, the quality of instruction, and the extent to which students are helped to attain the prerequisites for particular learning tasks.

There are no simple suggestions for curriculum and instructional changes which will quickly and drastically alter the picture of national differences reported in the IEA studies. Each nation must decide whether it wishes to do anything about the results reported. If a nation decides to make changes, it is likely that in the short run changing some of the instructional strategies used in the classroom will be most effective. There may be need for changes in curriculum and instruction as well, but it should be recognized that these are costly long-term problems. Perhaps most will be gained in the near future if countries seeking change can find ways of exchanging experience, material, and personnel so that they may study basic ideas and approaches which have been found to be effective in other nations.

Verbal Education

The IEA studies typically consist of separate samples of students participating in each subject study. But a selected sample of students did participate simultaneously in the studies of literature, science, and reading. The median intercorrelations for these subjects in fifteen countries are shown in Table 1.

TABLE 1
Median Intercorrelations for Literature, Science, and Reading

	Students		
	Age 10	*Age 14*	*Final Year Secondary Education*
Science vs. reading comprehension	.68	.60	.44
Literature vs. reading comprehension	. . .	.68	.54
Science vs. literature	. . .	.41	.28
Science vs. literature (holding reading comprehension constant)	. . .	.00	.05

Several generalizations can be drawn from these correlations.
1. Learning in both science and literature is highly related to reading comprehension. This is true to such a degree that there is almost no residual relation between science and literature when the level of reading comprehension is held constant.
2. Reading comprehension is more highly related to literature than to science.
3. The relation between reading comprehension and science or literature declines with age or grade of school—probably because the schools drop the students who are less able in reading comprehension.

While the relation between subject-matter competence and word knowledge is somewhat lower, the same generalizations tend to hold.

These generalizations are true, almost without exception, in each of the nations included in this portion of the IEA studies.

If we view reading comprehension and word knowledge as two facets of what British psychologists term "verbal education," it is apparent that this type of learning tends to dominate and in large part determine what students learn in the schools in all the countries included in the IEA studies.

These two aspects of verbal learning are important because most teacher instruction and most of the learning materials in the schools are verbal. Unless the student can understand the teacher's explanations and instructions, he has difficulty in learning. Verbal skills enable students to learn from the instructional materials even when the teaching is less than adequate.

We might wish that instruction and instructional materials placed less emphasis on reading comprehension and word knowledge, but it will be a long time before this will occur to any significant degree in the schools as they are now organized. Learning in the schools is, now and for the foreseeable future, likely to be based on verbal instruction to groups of students using textbooks and other instructional materials which are largely verbal in nature, with judgments about the student largely based on evaluation procedures using questions and responses that are verbal in form. The early development of verbal ability (vocabulary and reading comprehension) appears to be necessary if the child is to learn well—or even to survive—in school.

Over the past decade studies in the United States, England, Israel, and other countries show that much verbal ability is developed in the home. In the IEA study of reading comprehension the three most important variables related to students' level of reading comprehension are reading resources in the home, socioeconomic status (father's occupation and parents' education), and parents' interest in the child's education and the encouragement they give the child to read.[12] Especially in the 10-year and 14-year populations, the home background accounts for more of the student variation than do the school characteristics. This is not true of the 18-year population—largely because of the selectivity of the schools at the older ages. (In the United States, where over 75 percent of the students are still in school at 18 years of age, the home background is still the most important variable in accounting for reading comprehension.)

Throughout the world there appears to be a curriculum and instruction in the home as well as a curriculum and instruction in the school. The effects of the home curriculum and instruction for reading comprehension and word knowledge appear to be so powerful that schools are not able to compensate adequately for the differences already present when children enter school. Differences in verbal ability developed at home before age 6 are exaggerated by the schools in the period between ages 6 and 10 and the school period between ages 10 and 14. By age 18, the schools' selective policies have weeded out all except the most able students in verbal ability.

Societies which wish to improve children's school learning have only two realistic policies to follow: increase the effectiveness of the early education of children and/or increase the effectiveness of verbal education in the schools, especially during the ages of 6 to 10.

Early Childhood Education

Many countries are exploring the possibility of providing early childhood education (ages 3–6) for children—especially for children who are likely to be deprived because of inadequacies in the home curriculum and instruction. Mass media appear to be quite effective for some kinds of instruction at this age level.

Research in the United States indicates that it is possible to find ways of helping parents to improve some of the learning conditions in the home.[13] When this is done, the results in verbal learning, attitude toward school, and ability to learn in school are likely to be as good as or better than the results obtained through the use of nursery schools alone. Even better results are obtained when parents and nursery schools collaborate in the effort to help the children. Schools may relate to parents in a variety of ways to increase the effectiveness of both the home curriculum and the nursery school curriculum and to strengthen the relations between these curricula in this period of great verbal development of the child.

The Primary School

Both the Coleman Report in the United States[14] and the Plowden Report in England[15] indicate that there is also great language development in the age period 6–10 but that there is an increasing amount of individual differences in verbal abilities during these years. That is, whatever differences there are between children at age 6 in verbal ability are considerably increased during the primary period of schooling. In the various attempts to provide "compensatory" education in the United States and elsewhere, a number of special curricula have been developed which apparently enable the lower third or half of the children to close much of the gap between them and their more favored peers. These curricula emphasize specific instruction in the particular features of language, thought, and reading on which these children appear to be most deficient. Many of these curricula require special techniques of patterned practice in the classroom, a great deal of success on the part of the children supplemented by frequent and varied rewards and reinforcements, and appropriate classroom evaluation and corrective procedures to insure mastery of each part of the learning process.

Some of the newer procedures stress a closer relation between the primary school and the home so that they mutually support each other. R. H. Dave and Richard Wolf[16] have identified some of the home environmental processes which may be improved when home and school collaborate in improving the child's learning as well as his attitude toward school and school learning.

While there is no point in the child's educational development at which it is too late to improve conditions, there is considerable evidence that the critical point for verbal education in schools as they are presently organized is before age 10. If home and school do a good job in this area by age 10, school is an exciting and interesting place for children. If they do not, then school is a frustrating place which can do great damage to the child's self-view and attitude toward learning and development.

It is to be hoped that many of the IEA nations will search for ways in which to improve the curriculum and instruction in this critical area and will concern themselves especially with methods of enabling all children to profit from school by providing them with the verbal tools they need to learn well and to enjoy learning.

Patterns of Objectives—Cognitive and Affective

The IEA tests have been developed to sample the content and objectives in each subject. The specifications for these evaluation procedures were provided by the national and international subject committees, and the various committees were involved in criticizing and validating the proposed evaluation instruments. In the final data processing, scores and other types of indices have been reported for each of the cognitive and affective objectives in each subject.

Cognitive Objectives

In reading, science, literature, and mathematics, test scores in the cognitive domain have been provided at different levels of complexity, varying from direct measures of remembered knowledge or information to higher-level objectives involving complex interpretations, applications, and inferences.

In each subject, in almost every country, students perform best on the lower mental processes involving knowledge, perform less well on items involving some interpretation or comprehension, and perform least well on test problems requiring applications, higher mental processes, and complex inferences. Students in the final year of secondary education—usually the most select group in each country—do slightly better on problems involving the higher mental processes (in terms of percentage of problems correct) than do students at the 14-year age group.

When one looks at the emphasis in the curriculum as indicated by syllabi and curriculum experts, or when one looks at the "opportunity to learn" as judged by teachers, it is evident that the pattern of decreasing scores from lower to higher mental processes reflects these emphases. Schools, teachers, and textbooks throughout the world are apparently largely directed toward filling a presumably "empty head" with things to be remembered. Although teachers, curriculum makers, and testers profess more complex objectives for education, the actual emphasis in the classrooms is still largely on the learning of specific information.

Education throughout the world is primarily concerned with the acquisition of information or the development of literal comprehension. While there is no doubt that such "lower mental processes" are of value, it is likely that increasingly throughout the world problem solving, inferential thinking, and various higher mental processes will be required if the student is to use what he learned in the school, if school learning is to be relevant to the problems individuals encounter, and if adults are to continue learning after the school years. These objectives are basic to some of the exciting ideas about education and the learning society developed in the UNESCO report *Learning to Be*.[17]

Textbook writers and curriculum makers find it easiest to make instructional material and curricula which emphasize lower-level cognitive processes. Testers find it easiest to design evaluation instruments that deal with factual knowledge and literal interpretation. However, the numbers of curriculum makers and evaluation specialists in each country are relatively small. The training of these specialists to make learning materials and evaluation procedures directed at more complex cognitive processes should not be difficult.

The real problem in every country is how to provide preservice and in-service education for teachers in inquiry skills, problem solving, and higher mental processes. Little progress in developing these higher processes in the schools can be expected until teachers develop the necessary capabilities and are helped to find ways of teaching higher intellectual processes to the students in their classes.

Affective Objectives

In the IEA studies, there was an attempt to secure evidence on such affective objectives as interest in the subject and attitudes toward the subject, school, and school learning. In each country there is a significant correlation between measures of the affective and cognitive objectives. For example, within each country interest in science and positive attitudes toward it are significantly related to cognitive achievement in science, and the number of hours spent reading for pleasure each week (as reported by students) is highly related to reading comprehension as well as to cognitive abilities in literature.

The scores on these measures of interest and positive attitude toward the subject and toward schooling increase from ages 14 to 18 in most countries. But it is not clear whether there is actual growth in these affective characteristics or whether the differences are attributable to selective policies.

The evidence collected in the IEA studies and other research summaries[18] suggests that the affective objectives are largely being developed as a by-product of the cognitive objectives. That is, students who master the cognitive objectives well develop positive interests and attitudes in the subject. Students who believe they are succeeding in school come to like school. Similarly, students who believe they are learning less well than their peers tend to develop negative affect toward school subjects and toward school. Research further indicates that the affective characteristics are more closely related to the students' perception of their standing relative to their peers within a particular school than to their measured progress on standard tests given on a national or international basis.

The affective domain has been given least emphasis throughout the world by curriculum makers, teachers, or the schools. Perhaps our limited knowledge of how to develop these qualities inhibits curriculum makers and teachers from dealing directly with them. For some time to come, we can expect these affective objectives to be developed by sheer exposure to the subject matter and by accidental forces—other than the student's tendency to like things that he does well. But it is likely that reading habits, interest (and disinterest) in particular subjects, and positive as well as negative attitudes toward school and school learning may become more stable characteristics of the individual in the long run than the cognitive abilities and capabilities developed by appropriate learning experiences. If individuals are to continue learning in the major subject fields and areas of interest introduced by schools, much will depend on the affective qualities that schools have developed in them, whether they were developed intentionally or not. This is an area that warrants cooperative research throughout the world.

The Most Able Students—and the Others

If only the developed nations in the IEA are considered it will be found that on most of the subject tests, the top 5 percent of students across the world are roughly equal in their achievement at age 14 and at the final year of secondary education. This will generally be true whether one is considering the upper 5 percent of the entire age group sampled —such as the 14-year level where typically 90 percent or more of the students are still in school—or the approximations to the top 5 percent of the age group at the final year of secondary education where the countries differ widely in the percent of the age group still in school (from 9 percent in one country to 75 percent in another country).

Thus, in spite of differences in curriculum, instructional procedures, and many other differences between countries, it appears that the upper 5 percent of students in these countries are roughly comparable in their achievement as measured by these tests.

While IEA does not provide precise data on these points, the relationships among the different variables studied suggest that these top students typically come from homes in which the parents have had a relatively high level of education (for the country), provide a great deal of interest in and support for learning in school, provide support and incentives for the development of verbal ability and reading skill, and share with their children expectations for tertiary education and entry into a learned profession.

These are students who typically have a high level of verbal ability, including word knowledge and reading comprehension, and who have had the maximum amount of years of study in each of the academic subjects. They tend to have the most favorable interests and attitudes toward the subject and positive attitudes toward school and school learning.

If education had to deal only with this small group of students the schools could do little wrong. Even when the curriculum is inadequate or outdated and teachers provide only mediocre instruction, these students would do well. What school cannot provide, many parents would. What teachers or parents cannot provide, these students could provide for themselves. One can wax eloquent about the learning achievements of such students when aided by schools and parents—or in spite of schools and parents—but this is hardly the group that the schools are supported to serve.

In principle, the resources of at least the highly developed nations are intended to support the education of all youth—not just the top 5 or 10 percent of students and not just the children of the best-educated and most-favored citizens.

Countries differ in their treatment of students below the top 5 or 10 percent of the group. In most countries in the IEA studies a high proportion of the remaining 90 percent are dropped from school somewhere between ages 14 and 18. In spite of differences in retention of students in school there is considerable evidence that very few countries do an "adequate" educational job for the majority of this age group—and especially for the lower 50 percent of students.

What are the implications for the schools if nations are to more adequately serve the entire population of youth rather than only the top students who survive relatively well because of or in spite of the schools as they are now? If we sketch a picture based on the bottom half of students, several suggestions may be made.

Characteristically these students are drawn from the part of the population with the least-favorable conditions for education in their homes. Their parents have had less education and typically are in the lower half of occupational and income distributions. There is less support for education in the home in terms of parent interest, books, or incentives to further education. These are students with the lowest verbal ability and least-adequate reading comprehension. They spend less time in reading on their own. They do not have positive attitudes toward school, and their interests in particular academic subjects are not high. They receive few favorable rewards and reinforcements in school from their learning, from their teachers, or even from their peers.

With this group of students, the school is largely on its own and must provide for instruction without counting on the home to provide supplementary instruction or to aid the student when he is having difficulty in school. If homework is required (and the IEA studies find this to be a variable favorable for learning) the school will need to provide conditions for it to be done in school with aides or teachers to provide help when these students are having difficulty.

The students are in special need of verbal education in the preschool years or in the primary period of schooling if they are to survive in schools as now organized. Schools must also provide the models of learning and incentives for education and learning—without counting on the home to do this. Such models might be provided if teachers were able to develop closer relations with their students and encouraged and helped them when needed.

One might also hope that teachers would develop instructional strategies designed to help most of the students achieve mastery of at least the tool skills and the required subjects. Some strategies have already been experimented with in a number of countries and characteristically have enabled about four-fifths of students to do as well as the upper one-fifth of students under more conventional approaches to instruction.[19] These instructional strategies make use of the existing curriculum but provide frequent feedback to students on their learning development or learning problems and follow the feedback with changes in instructional procedures and with help and correctives as needed. Such approaches might be expected to be less and less necessary as students gain confidence in their own learning capabilities and as they find ways of correcting their own difficulties.

Under present conditions in most countries, students become less and less interested in school learning as they find themselves doing relatively poorly and as they are frustrated by their difficulties. It is likely that some parts of the curriculum are difficult to relate to the life they lead outside school, and little of the curriculum relates to the expectations they have for work and adult life.

Curriculum makers have rarely had this group of students in mind as they attempted to formulate the specifications for the curriculum or the learning materials to be used in instruction. One might hope that in the future curriculum makers in each country would attempt to deal more directly with the learning of this group of students. National curriculum centers could profit greatly from an exchange of experiences and approaches with other nations on this problem.

IEA and the Future for Curriculum and Instruction

The IEA studies provide a glimpse of education in a large number of countries. While the emphasis is on the evaluation of student learning in each subject, the variety of data on the countries, the schools, the teachers, the students, and the students' home background provides the richest store of information on education that has ever been assembled. No one of us is fully adequate to the many ways in which these data should be analyzed and reanalyzed. Hopefully, scholars will become acquainted with the IEA data banks and the many possibilities for further investigation which they offer.

But educators throughout the world cannot wait for future reanalyses. They must act now on what they believe to be important and true, aided by whatever data they can assemble on the problems they regard as central. The IEA national reports will provide some of the data that policymakers, educational leaders, and teachers need. Since these reports are being written by educational research workers who are thoroughly familiar with their own national scene, it is to be hoped that interaction will be generated between educators and the IEA findings within each country and that these findings will serve as a basis for a constructive response to some of the educational problems posed by the evidence in that country.

An important new educational assest in many IEA countries is the availability of a small group of persons highly trained in educational evaluation, educational research methods, and data-gathering and analysis procedures. This means that educators can try a variety of new approaches to curriculum and instruction on a pilot basis and determine which are most promising. They can investigate the most successful approaches on a broader scale and at each step can appraise the effectiveness and consequences of this work. If educators will utilize the talents and methods at present available in each of the national research centers, they can move ahead with greater confidence that they are moving in the right direction. Furthermore, the network of communication provided by IEA and other international agencies makes it possible for each country to learn from the errors and the successes of others. While each country cannot use the work of other countries directly, it can learn from the experiences, ideas, material, and persons available throughout the world. Each country, school, teacher, and student is unique, but all can learn from the experiences of others.

In my efforts to learn from a decade and a half of experience with the IEA methods, data, and findings, I have attempted to point up some of the more obvious findings and their implications for curriculum and instruction. These implications are little more than suggestions of what appear to me to be constructive responses to this rich store of educational data.

The least costly of these suggestions in terms of time, resources, and change to the educational system is the use of mass media such as radio, television, films, and tapes to enable a country to utilize its best teachers and teaching to supplement what thousands of teachers can at present do for their students. Such efforts can be tried on a small scale and evaluated and improved before they are tried on a larger scale.

Slightly more costly is the development of teaching-learning strategies which use existing curriculum and instructional methods and materials but which, in some countries, have enabled larger proportions of students to learn effectively. The special virtues of such teaching-learning strategies is that their effectiveness can be determined in months (rather than years), and they require a minimum of change in the teachers, the teaching, or the curriculum. Such strategies have already been applied to reading comprehension, mathematics, science, second language, and many other subjects in the school program.

Much more costly is the improvement of teaching through changes in preservice and in-service education. Such efforts should, wherever possible, make use of what other countries have learned about the least effective and most effective approaches to these problems. Effort and resources spent on such problems do not automatically yield good results. Far from it, many of the approaches already tried have produced very little, and only a few approaches appear to be promising.

Even more costly are major curriculum reforms. While such reforms may be necessary and even required by local conditions, they depend on the availability of highly trained creative workers who use appropriate evidence and research at each step to insure that the new is really an improvement over what it is to replace. They also depend on a thorough retraining of existing teaching personnel.

We have learned from the IEA data as well as from other research throughout the world that the curriculum and instruction provided by the home are in many ways related to the curriculum and instruction provided by the school. The largest problem each country faces is to understand how these two educational forces may best relate to each other if the education of each child is to be in his best interests as well as in the society's best interests. The problem is even more complex in that it involves the school as one subsystem of a society. No longer can we think of the system of schooling as relatively insulated from other parts of the society. In the future, the schools of most nations will be under pressure to relate more clearly to the other parts of the social system. We will increasingly try to determine what can best be learned in the schools, what can best be learned elsewhere, and what can be learned only through an effective interrelation of different parts of the social system. This is the grand vision of the Edgar Faure UNESCO report.[20] Its implementation will involve all of us in education for many years to come.

References

This article was adapted from a paper presented at an IEA conference held at Harvard, November 1973. The papers and discussions at this conference were published in Purves, A. and Levine, D. (eds.) Educational Policy and International Assessment. Berkeley, Cal.: McCutchan Pub. Co., 1975.

1. The centers are located in Australia, Belgium, Chile, England, Federal Republic of Germany, Finland, France, Hungary, India, Iran, Ireland, Israel, Italy, Japan, Netherlands, New Zealand, Poland, Rumania, Scotland, Sweden, Thailand, and the United States.

2. A. W. Foshay, ed., *Educational Achievements of 13-Year-Olds in Twelve Countries* (Hamburg: UNESCO Institute for Education, 1962).

3. Torsten Husén, ed., *International Study of Achievement in Mathematics: A Comparison of Twelve Countries*, vols. 1, 2 (New York: John Wiley & Sons; Stockholm: Almqvist & Wiksell, 1967).

4. L. C. Comber and John P. Keeves, *Science Education in Nineteen Countries: International Studies in Evaluation. I* (New York: John Wiley & Sons; Stockholm: Almqvist & Wiksell, 1973).

5. Robert L. Thorndike, *Reading Comprehension Education in Fifteen Countries: International Studies in Evaluation. III* (New York: John Wiley & Sons; Stockholm: Almqvist & Wiksell, 1973).

6. Alan C. Purves, *Literature Education in Ten Countries: International Studies in Evaluation. II* (New York: John Wiley & Sons; Stockholm: Almqvist & Wiksell, 1973).

7. Carroll, John B. The Teaching of French as a Foreign Language in Eight Countries. International Studies in Evaluation, V. (New York: John Wiley & Sons, Stockholm: Almqvist & Wiksell, 1975).

8. Lewis, E. Glyn and Massad, Carolyn E. The Teaching of English as a Foreign Language in Ten Countries. International Studies in Evaluation, IV. (New York: John Wiley & Sons, Stockholm: Almqvist & Wiksell, 1975).

9. Torney, Judith V.; Oppenheim, A. N., and Farnen, Russell F. Civic Education in Ten Countries: An Empirical Study. International Studies in Evaluation, VI. (New York: John Wiley & Sons, Stockholm: Almqvist & Wiksell, 1976).

10. Wolf, R. M. Achievement in America. (New York: Teachers College Press, 1977).

11. C. E. Beeby, *The Quality of Education in Developing Countries* (Cambridge, Mass.: Harvard University Press, 1966).

12. Thorndike.

13. E. Kuno Beller, "Research on Organized Programs of Early Education," in *Second Handbook of Research on Teaching,* ed. Robert M. W. Travers (Chicago: Rand McNally & Co., 1973).

14. James S. Coleman et al., *Equality of Educational Opportunity* (Washington, D.C.: Government Printing Office, 1966).

15. Lady Beatrice Plowden et al., *A Report of the Central Advisory Committee on Children and Their Primary Schools* (London: Her Majesty's Stationery Office, 1967).

16. R. H. Dave, "The Identification and Measurement of Environmental Process Variables That Are Related to Educational Achievement" (Ph.D. diss., University of Chicago, 1963); Richard Wolf, "The Measurement of Environments," in *Testing Problems in Perspective,* ed. A. Anastasi (Washington, D.C.: American Council on Education, 1966).

17. Edgar Faure et al., *Learning to Be* (Paris: UNESCO; London: Harrap, 1972).

18. S. B. Kahn and Joel Weiss, "The Teaching of Affective Responses," in Travers.

19. James H. Block, ed., *Mastery Learning: Theory and Practice* (New York: Holt, Rinehart & Winston, 1971).

20. Faure.

Twenty-Five Years of Educational Research

3

Introduction

As President of The American Educational Research Association I have been trying to take stock of what we have accomplished during the past quarter of a century. Such stock taking tells as much about the person doing the inventory as it does about the field. Although the President (now Past President) of an organization may believe that this role gives him access to more information and a more objective perspective than is available to others, this is probably one of the delusions fostered by the office.

In any case, it is this writer's hope that each group of educational research workers will be sufficiently provoked by this paper to undertake a similar effort on their own to determine what has been accomplished over the past 25 years by our educational research. Such efforts should take into consideration the ways in which we have worked and should give some thought to the ways in which our efforts in the future can be increasingly effective. Each group will probably see the field from a different perspective, and it is to be hoped that sharing these perspectives and stock taking will enable us to find a better base for our work in the future.

Need for Stock Taking
This is the 50th anniversary of The American Educational Research Association. An anniversary provides a ceremonial occasion for stock taking, but it hardly warrants an effort to do more than engage in the appropriate sentimental reminiscences.

Somewhat greater motivation for the task may be derived from the rapid increase in federal funding of educational research and development. The increase from the level of support in 1960 has been on the order of 2,000 percent. This increase has been so rapid that few of us have had the opportunity to assess the overall effects of these funds on educational research, to say nothing about the effects they have had on education. We are all aware that the increases in support are in large measure based on faith in the "magic" of research. The power of

NOTE: Presidential address presented to the American Educational Research Association, Chicago, February 1966.

research has already been amply demonstrated in medicine, engineering, and agriculture. The effects of research in the natural sciences have also been clearly demonstrated. The case for educational research is yet to be demonstrated. The effects of the new funding on the quantity of educational research is already quite evident. We anticipate marked changes in the quantity and quality of students in educational training programs, and we have already seen the effects of funding in bringing new breeds of workers from many related fields to educational research and development. Stock taking is an inevitable consequence of new governmental funding—let us hope that the best minds in the field of education will share in the making of the inventory.

An even more telling reason for stock taking arises from the new faith in education and the new tasks thrust on it. Education is looked to for solutions to problems of poverty, racial discord, crime and delinquency, urban living, peace, and even for the problems arising from affluence. The new tasks thrust on education require new approaches, new understandings, and a closer relation between theory, research, and practice than has ever existed before. It is not likely that education will be able to provide all the solutions that are expected of it. However, if solutions are found, they are likely to be based on research and development. Compensatory education for the disadvantaged is a case in point. Educational solutions must be found for these children— solutions which depend on more than the dedicated teacher working by himself. The educational researcher cannot ignore such problems, and he must contribute to the creation of the solutions.

To put the matter in a larger setting, there is increasing evidence that many societies are repelled by the fruits of research in the physical sciences, which seem to create more problems than they solve. Each new development of energy, power, and speed appears to bring about greater means of destruction and more anxiety than existed before. As societies seek for more positive and optimistic areas in which to put their hopes and resources, they appear to be those concerned with man and his development. Most of us are of the view that education is the one area which is the hope of mankind. If educational research is able to respond effectively to the new order of problems, this field will probably come to occupy the position hitherto held by research workers in the natural sciences.

But enough of the future. As educational researchers we need to get a clearer picture of our recent past. We tend to veer from overoptimism about educational research and its effects on education and the schools to almost complete despair and pessimism. From time to time we wonder whether anything has been produced by our efforts. Have the schools been changed in any respect by our work over the past 25 years? It is probable that the truth lies somewhere between our most optimistic and our most pessimistic picture of the state of education and educational research. We all need to find the picture for ourselves if we are to have the courage and energy to go on.

Personnel and Research Output

There are many ways in which we might take stock of where we are and how far we have come. One is to look at personnel and research output quantitatively. The number of persons awarded doctoral degrees in education has gone from about 1,500 in 1954 to approximately 2,400 in 1964. While this increase in personnel presumably equipped to do educational research is relatively small compared with the great increase in funding, it does indicate that there are likely to be more people available for research.

Membership in AERA has been increasing at the rate of about 25 percent per year during the past five years. It is debatable whether this growth rate is an indication of increased interest in educational research or increased effectiveness of our Membership Committee.

Another indication of the strength of the field is the interest in education and educational research shown by scholars from other disciplines. An increasing number of scholars from the behavioral sciences, and especially psychology, sociology, anthropology, and economics, are turning to educational research, and many of them are making important contributions to the field. Some of them are doing much to help us see education in new terms. I am happy to report that many of these scholars from other disciplines are joining AERA. However, the significant point is that scholars from many disciplines are recognizing the central place of education in the scheme of things and are interested in making their contributions to educational research and development.

During the past three years I have had an opportunity to visit a number of schools and departments of education and to meet with many research workers through AERA activities, conferences, and summer institutes. Although my impressions are highly subjective, I am convinced that the young educational research workers are as able a group of research workers as can be found in any of the social sciences. These young people represent our most valuable asset, and, if properly encouraged and supported in their research, they are likely to make major contributions to the field.

Finally, there is no lack of research output. Educational research workers have no hesitancy about writing up their studies and publishing them. During the last 25 years approximately 70,000 titles were listed in the *Review of Educational Research.* While there is some overlap in that the same article or book may have been listed in several issues of the *Review,* it is clear that we are now annually publishing about 2,500 items that the authors of the reviews regard as contributions to educational research. From the increase in research completed under Office of Education grants, it is safe to predict that publications of educational research will increase rapidly in the near future.

Quantitatively there is no doubt that educational research is a lively and growing field. In terms of manpower and research output it is developing rapidly. There are also some indications that the quality of research personnel is improving, but this is only a highly subjective impression.

Another approach to stock taking is to make an estimate of the significant contributions to the field over the past quarter of a century. This is a highly controversial type of inventory and only the most daring or foolish individuals are likely to permit their summaries to be published. It is my hope that although I may find myself in the latter category, others will be stimulated to do the same in order to correct the record.

Methodological Contributions

In some ways education is one of the strongest fields in the behavioral sciences in terms of its contributions to research methodology and its use of complex techniques and technologies for research. With the possible exceptions of psychology and economics, educational research workers have contributed to and used stronger and more powerful research procedures than have other social scientists. Our colleagues in other fields have recognized this and occasionally accuse us of using "elephant guns to shoot at fleas." I do not mean to say that all of our research is characterized by precision and methodological elegance—far from it. What I am trying to say is that research workers dealing with educational problems have contributed to and used very powerful research methods and procedures and that our field does not lag behind other social science fields in this respect.

Especially with respect to *statistical methods,* educational researchers have pioneered, adapted, or used skillfully a great variety of complex procedures. Factor analysis, analysis of variance, multivariate procedures, sampling methods, and research design are some of the areas in which educational research workers have made major contributions during the past twenty-five years.

Educational researchers have contributed new computer programs and have made a great deal of use of *computers and computer technology* in their research. In the use of computers for statistical purposes, for research on learning, and for the simulation of individual and group processes of thought and behavior, workers in educational research have been in the forefront.

Advances have been made by educational workers in the *mapping of human characteristics.* The delineation of human aptitudes and abilities by factor analysis and other methods has progressed greatly in the past quarter of a century. Closely related to this have been the developments in the classification of the outcomes of education. These maps have been very useful as bases for further research, and they have helped greatly in the communication process. I regard such maps as methodological contributions because they enable us to specify some of our variables with greater precision and because they provide classificatory devices for some of our research findings.

Closely related to these maps of human characteristics have been the many contributions over the past 25 years in the development of *tests and testing procedures.* Workers in educational research have made many advances in the evaluation of student progress toward specific objectives of education. While much of the work has centered on cognitive outcomes of learning, including creativity, some developments have taken place in the evaluation of interest, attitudes, and values. A great deal of work has also been done by educational researchers in the development of more precise instruments for the measurement of a large number of aptitudes, abilities, and specific personality and emotional characteristics.

One more type of contribution that I would regard as methodological has been the development of *instructional procedures.* Programmed instruction and computer-assisted instruction are two of the more dramatic examples. Other instructional procedures such as those emphasizing inquiry and discovery may also be regarded as methodological contributions.

Undoubtedly, there have been other methodological contributions which might have been cited here. I leave it to my readers to amend this list and to point out important omissions.

Substantive Contributions

By substantive contributions I mean contributions to new ways of viewing a particular phenomenon, new understanding of a particular topic or problem, and new ways of stating the question or problem. Methodological contributions have to do with new procedures and techniques for research while substantive contributions have to do with research which has made a difference in the way we think about education and learning, in the view of a particular educational problem, and, we hope, in the way education goes on in the school or home.

This distinction does not embody a value judgment about which is the more important—methodological or substantive. It is likely that progress in one type is dependent on progress in the other. The development of the electron microscope (a methodological contribution) dramatically affected our understanding of cell tissue and disease (substantive contribution). The development of new measures and statistical techniques (methodological contributions) are likely to be basic to the development of new insights into particular areas of learning and development (substantive contributions).

In what follows, I propose to name a few areas in which I believe certain crucial studies have altered, or are likely to alter, our way of thinking about educational phenomena. I have emphasized those areas most directly concerned with the educational development of the student.

One group of studies has vitally affected our conceptions about the *development of the individual.* During the past 25 years we have gained a great deal in our understanding of developmental sequences through the work of such persons as E. Erickson, A. Gesell, R. Havighurst, and J. Piaget. These studies of developmental sequence, which have emphasized process, are in large part supported by longitudinal research of a more quantitative nature done by workers connected with the Harvard Growth Study, the Berkeley Growth Study, the Oakland Growth Study, and the Fels Institute. While these studies show great individual differences in growth, they do reveal an orderly sequence of development and the great importance of the early years of childhood for much of later development.

Another set of studies has shown us a great deal about the *effects of the environment* on the development of the individual. Perhaps one of the most fundamental distinctions that is emerging is the view of the home as an educative environment with its own curriculum, in contrast to an earlier view of the home as a unit in a socioeconomic or social-class status system. The role of parents as models has been studied in some detail by J. W. Douglas and J. Floud; the teaching style of mothers has been investigated by R. Hess and S. Stodolsky; while the language learning in the home has been studied in depth by B. Bernstein, D. McCarthy, and L. Vigotsky. The effect of the early environment on conceptual development and intelligence has been studied by M. Deutsch, A. Jensen, J. Mc V. Hunt, and R. Wolf. The effects of parents and the home on attitude formation in relation to the schools has been clarified for us by the work of J. A. Kahl, D. McClelland, and S. Smilansky. Another type of environment that has been studied is the peer group. The work of J. S. Coleman has enabled us to understand some of the effects of the adolescent subculture on the individual student.

Much research has been done on the *predictability of human characteristics*. It has become increasingly evident that school achievement and other characteristics particularly relevant to the work of the schools can be predicted with greater precision than was previously thought to be the case, especially when the home and school characteristics are put in as part of the predictor variables. The work of A. Payne, F. Peters, and L. Tucker bears directly on this problem.

Quite in contrast to the research on the prediction of human characteristics is the work on the *modifiability of human characteristics*. In one sense this is the central task of education and much of our research on education is concerned with this problem. Some of the more crucial studies which seem most pertinent to this problem as it relates to young children have been done by S. Kirk, S. Gray, M. Deutsch, and M. Smilansky.

During the past twenty-five years there has been a tremendous amount of research on a great variety of *teaching methods and instructional strategies*. It had been difficult to see any generalizations emerging from this research until models for the study of instruction, such as those developed by J. Carroll, J. Ginther, and L. Siegel, were available. What appears to be emerging is that a great variety of instructional methods yield essentially equal outcomes in terms of student achievement of lower mental processes, such as knowledge or simple skills. Large class, small class, T.V. instruction, audio-visual methods, lecture, discussion, demonstration, team teaching, programmed instruction, authoritarian and nonauthoritarian instructional procedures, etc. all appear to be equally effective methods in helping the student learn more information or simple skills. This does not mean that each use of an instructional approach is equally good with every other use of the same approach. There is still good and bad teaching, good and bad programmed instruction, etc. We need quality-control studies to insure that a particular example of an instructional strategy is of the appropriate quality. However, we are free to use a great variety of instructional methods—if the goal of instruction is the acquisition of information. In contrast to the evidence about the great variety of instructional approaches which are relevant to the learning of information is the lack of clear evidence about the instructional approaches which are effective in bringing about significant changes in the higher mental processes. While the work of P. Dressel, H. M. Chausow, E. M. Glaser, R. Suchman and others suggests that dialectic (rather than didactic) approaches appear to be more effective in producing changes in higher mental processes, the research evidence is far from complete and convincing on this point.

The effect of *individual differences in learners* has always been one of the central concerns of educators. Much of educational research attempts to bring in individual differences as a major variable in the investigation. Some especially pertinent research on the role of personality in learning has been reported by such workers as T. M. Newcomb, N. Sanford, S. B. Sarason, and G. G. Stern. Research on the effects of independence vs. dependence in learners has been carried on by C. Houle, C. McCollough, W. J. McKeachie, H. Thelen, and E. L. Van Atta.

During the past quarter of a century a great deal of work has been done on the *principles of learning.* The role of learning cues, student involvement and participation, and reward and reinforcement have been clarified by the work of J. S. Bruner, J. Dollard, E. Hilgard, N. E. Miller, B. F. Skinner, and R. W. White.

As a final area in which I believe crucial investigations have been reported during this period is the work on *sequence in learning.* Especially noteworthy in revealing some of the considerations involved in learning sequences is the research of N. A. Crowder, R. M. Gagné, and B. F. Skinner.

I am sure that any readers will take issue with my classifications of areas of research that have been most significant as well as with the particular work (or researchers) I have named.

In Retrospect

As I indicated earlier, approximately 70,000 studies were listed in the *Review of Educational Research* over the past 25 years. Of these 70,000 studies, I regard about 70 as being crucial for all that follows.

That is, about 1 out of 1,000 reported studies seem to me to be crucial and significant, approximately 3 studies per year. It is likely that a somewhat more relaxed criterion would increase the number of studies regarded as crucial by the order of 3 times the present list. I doubt if anyone would increase the list as much as 10 times. Even with the threefold increase, this would mean no more than 9 crucial studies a year (out of approximately 2,500 per year). Perhaps this is all that we should expect in educational research, and it may be about the level expected in any field of research. However, it is my opinion that we need much more in education, and I am confident that we can get a great deal more if we are willing to make the effort and if the proper research strategies are available to us.

Some Suggestions for the Future

One way in which we can get more and better research is to increase the amount of time available for research. Very few persons in the United States give the largest portion of their time to educational research. Administrative work, teaching, committee responsibilities, speaking engagements, etc. all conspire to reduce the time most of us devote to research. It is possible that the increase in funding of research will enable many of us to buy more time for research, but research is difficult, and there are many tempting distractions. We will devote more of our time to research as we become convinced of the need for research in education, and as we become more fully aware of the contributions that research can make to education. Perhaps this is only another way of saying that as the demand increases, we will find ways of increasing the supply.

Another way in which we can improve the quality of educational research is to improve the qualifications of educational research workers. All of us must constantly seek to upgrade our research competence and ways must be found to provide opportunities for each of us to secure further training as needed. The use of brief training sessions is wide-spread in most fields of research, and we must find better means of providing such opportunities in educational research. The pre-session workshops and conferences provided by AERA this year represent a small move in the right direction. We can also improve the quality of educational research workers by improving our graduate training programs. The new grants for training provided by the Office of Education give us an opportunity to attract the best students and to improve our training programs simultaneously. Let us hope that our schools of education will take advantage of both of these possibilities. The increased interest in education and educational research makes it possible to attract to educational research some of the outstanding scholars in other disciplines. We have already seen this taking place. We must find ways of involving our colleagues in other fields in the attack on educational research problems as well as in helping us in the training of our graduate students.

We need advances in our theoretical and conceptual schemes, but it is difficult to do anything directly which will result in improvements in theory and model building. We also need improvements in our research methodology and especially in the training of research workers in the use of research methods. As I have indicated earlier, it is my opinion that we do not lag behind other social sciences in this area. Advances in this area will be beneficial to us all, but I suspect that this is not the direction from which we will secure great increases in the production of crucial research contributions to education.

What is especially needed, in my opinion, is the development of basic new research strategies which are analogous to those which have resulted in the rapid strides made in such fields as medicine, biology, and physics. Some suggestions for this may be found in the article "Strong Inference" by John Platt in *Science,* October 16, 1964. Platt, in attempting to explain the rapid growth of crucial investigations in molecular biology and other fields, believes that it is the use of strong inference which is responsible. There are several features of the strong inference research strategy that I believe to be most important for educational research.

1. There is a need for a clear map of the present state of the field. Such a map should indicate the most promising alternative pathways for future research as well as the alternatives that have been found to be inadequate or incorrect. Platt points out that in molecular biology the different research groups appear to have worked up trees of knowledge in which they graphically represent the present state of the field and the branches show the pathways that have been most fruitful as well as the ones which have not. In such a scheme the research view of the home environment as a curriculum and instructional approach might be contrasted with the less adequate (for education) research view of the home as a sociological status unit. This paper represents one effort to sketch the nature of such a map (or tree).

2. There is a need for rapid communication throughout the coun-

try and world among the researchers dealing with a particular portion of the map. It is claimed that research workers throughout the world in medicine and in some areas of physics and biology are able to get word of important discoveries within twenty-four hours. I am of the opinion that it takes months for educational researchers to learn about what has been found by other workers and that it takes years before a "discovery" is recognized as such. We need to find procedures for speeding up the communication process and for developing "invisible colleges" in which educational researchers throughout the world can be in close touch with their colleagues working on closely related problems. We need communication at various stages of the research process, but especially at the stage where each new finding must be related to the overall picture or map.

It is likely that the development of maps and closer communication would do much to discourage research which is a mere repetition of something already clearly determined by previous research. The creation of R and D Centers and Regional Laboratories will probably result in improved maps of the field as well as better communication. The publication of lists of research in progress will help researchers find colleagues currently interested in related problems. The increased use of summer centers, training programs and conferences of educational research workers should do much to bring communication about educational research to the level now found in some of the other fields of research.

3. A major element in strong inference, according to Platt, is the search for crucial ways of asking the question and for research procedures which will yield clearer and more definitive results. He suggests the use of multiple hypothesis procedures and the use of research designs that permit the testing of several hypotheses simultaneously, in contrast with the slower method of taking one hypothesis at a time. Some of the newer developments in research design and multivariate statistical procedures (see Gage, *Handbook of Research on Teaching*, 1963) appear to me to be relevant to this feature of strong inference.

Some Possible Consequences

It is likely that one major result of the use of some of the elements of "strong inference" would be a reduction in the amount of redundant research. There is much repetition in educational research, and this is particularly apparent in any careful scrutiny of the research summarized in the *Review of Educational Research* over the past twenty-five years. It is this redundancy that in part explains why there are so few examples of crucial research in the period under consideration.

Another possible effect of strong inference approaches to educational research could be a greater emphasis on the research problems of education rather than the methods of research. Each of us becomes addicted to favorite methods of doing research, and we keep looking for problems to which our methods may be applied. Perhaps we should turn it around and seek the important problems of research and then select the methods we find to be relevant.

It is possible that this way of looking at educational research would help us to view educational research as something which is important in itself. Research would be for "real" rather than for the gaining of points in a rating system related to academic rank, salary, prestige, etc.

Finally, it is to be hoped that the use of strong inference approaches would result in a rapid sequence of fundamental discoveries which could then be supported by further replication and demonstration under a wide range of conditions.

Let us hope that more powerful research strategies will enable us to produce in the next five years at least as many crucial substantive pieces of research as we produced in the last twenty-five years.

HOME
AND
SCHOOL

Early Learning in the Home[1]

$\mathbf{T}$he importance of the early years of childhood for all development that follows it has long been recognized by parents, by therapists, and by various specialists who have been actively concerned with the study of or the teaching of young children. More recently a number of educational research workers, including myself, have attempted to analyze the evidence on the relations between childhood development and growth and development in later years. In particular, the evidence of the effects of childhood development on later educational achievement has been given a great deal of attention by the educational and scholarly community as well as by the popular press.

Undoubtedly these research reports—which are rather dry in their contents and style—have been seized upon because of their timeliness in relation to the educational problems of culturally and socially disadvantaged students. Here is a social problem of long duration which has come to the center of public interest because it is so evident in the large urban areas as a result of changing residential patterns. Furthermore, this is a social problem which has enormous implications for the long-term welfare of submerged groups, and this has been recognized by the leaders of these groups as well as by political and community leaders. Impetus for vast educational and social reform is now emerging as a result of the social and political dynamics at the federal as well as the local level.

When the American public recognizes the existence of an important problem, it quickly converts the problem into dollars and funding programs. Such economic solutions to social problems are rapid but not necessarily effective. However, there is no doubt that the dollars do attract persons and organizations and that a great deal of energy becomes available as a result of the availability of resources. It is to be expected that many of the initial attempts to attack the educational problems of cultural deprivation will be ineffective. However, I am convinced that within a decade this problem will be effectively solved for a sizeable proportion of our children—and especially so by the efforts at preschool education.

There is a rapidly accumulating body of evidence that special programs of nursery school and kindergarten can do much to overcome some of the educational deficiencies commonly found in culturally deprived children (Bloom, Davis, & Hess, 1965). While considerable

[1]The First B. J. Paley Lecture, University of California at Los Angeles, July 18, 1965.

effort must be invested at all stages of the educational system to reduce the ravages of cultural deprivation, it is likely that the highest rate of "pay-off" will come from preschool programs specially devised to meet the educational needs of socially disadvantaged children. Furthermore, such programs will be attractive to school systems because success at the preschool level will enable the schools to maintain their present curricular and teaching practices with a minimum of alteration for these children. The tendency for educational systems to maintain stability at all costs is likely to mean that preschool programs will become exceedingly popular. So popular, that I expect every urban school system to develop a rather elaborate preschool program, especially for culturally deprived children in the inner-city area. Please remember that I am not advocating preschool programs as the only way of attacking the educational problems of cultural deprivation. I am merely predicting that preschool programs will become the most popular (and, I suspect, effective) method of dealing with the educational problems of these children.

Until World War II, nursery schools were relatively rare, and with few exceptions were available only to children whose families could pay the relatively high fees. During the war years, publicly supported nursery schools were available where mothers were working and needed day-care provisions for their young children. Such programs were largely abandoned after the war. At present, about 2 percent of 4-year-old children are in nursery schools. Kindergartens have been more common and have generally been publicly supported or are a regular part of the school system whether it be private or public in support. However, even in 1964, only about 50 percent of 5-year-olds were enrolled in kindergartens.

As the federal government seeks its role in educational support, it is likely to find needs and areas of interest that have not been fully developed through local and state educational support. One such area is the preschool program for the culturally disadvantaged and poverty groups. Here is a program that is obviously needed but for which the community has not hitherto provided resources or facilities. It would appear to me that the federal funds will give heavy support to the creation of preschool educational programs. I am not sure whether the continuation of these programs will depend on local, state, or federal programs. However, I am convinced that these preschool programs will become a permanent part of the educational system, and that not only will they serve the culturally deprived, but they will also, in the near future, be available to all groups of children.

As we contemplate the rapid and I believe, inevitable encroachment on the "freedom" of the child by institutional arrangements, we must begin to ask ourselves a number of difficult questions. What is to be gained by providing preschool experiences for culturally deprived children? What should be the goals of preschool programs for culturally deprived children? What is to be gained by providing such experiences for all children? What is likely to be lost? What should be the goals of such programs for all children?

My own concern for these problems, in part, arises from the varying interpretations drawn from my own work on *Stability and Change in Human Characteristics* (Bloom, 1964). In part, I am concerned about some of the directions preschool education is beginning to take. Finally, I am concerned that the powerful and desirable effects of preschool education may be lost if our efforts are not systematically related to the achievement of what seem to me the desirable goals of such programs.

Let me point out a few features of emerging preschool programs which I hope will not be continued too long.

What seems to me to be the most misdirected effort is the attempt by some parents and some preschool programs to teach children to read, write, and do simple arithmetic in the nursery school and kindergarten. I do not doubt that it is possible to teach something of these school subjects to four- and five-year-old children. I have no evidence that the learning of these subjects so early in the child's development will be harmful. What I do believe is that the learning experiences of these critical years should be directed to more important goals. These are the years in which the child should "learn to learn" rather than learn the particular skills usually taught in the first or second grade of school. It is too simple to take the position that all that needs to be done in the cognitive domain is to take the curriculum of the first years of school and introduce them earlier. That it is good for children to learn to read at ages 6 and 7 does not mean that it is better to learn this skill at younger ages. I do not think we can justify taking over the precious years of childhood to give the children an earlier start on the three "Rs."

Another type of program which appears to be emerging is the brief crash program in which culturally deprived children are to be prepared for school by a seven- to ten-week summer program. Again, I do not believe this will be harmful to the children involved, but I have no evidence on this point. I suspect that very little is likely to emerge that is useful for these children. Even the best of these programs under the best of instructors is likely to be too little and too late. The major danger is that it may become a diversionary procedure which could get in the way of more carefully developed longer programs of a year or two. Who can argue against the possibility that eight weeks of instruction can do the work of two years of preschool instruction? What taxpayer would not prefer the shorter and cheaper solution? If projects such as "Headstart" are regarded as emergency efforts to be replaced by longer and more systematic efforts at preschool education, then one cannot argue against a *little* in preference to *nothing*. What can be opposed is the attempt to find quick and cheap solutions to the serious problems of cultural deprivation.

Another effort that appears to me to be misguided is the notion that anyone can teach in these new nursery school programs. Because of their "crash program" quality, there will be a great shortage of qualified teachers. Voluntary workers, elementary school teachers, and anyone who has had some higher education may be used as teachers in these new programs. While I am convinced that to do something is usually better than to do nothing, it doesn't seem to be much of a solution to regard any available adult as an appropriate preschool teacher. We must begin to recognize that preschool education is an exceedingly complex process and that the teachers at this stage must be very well prepared for this very important task. Furthermore, the teachers must be prepared in terms of the special goals and curriculum necessary for the stimulation of the cognitive and emotional development of these children. This is no place for the temporary volunteer or the well-meaning but poorly prepared amateur. What may be justified as a temporary measure must not be continued on a permanent basis.

One other type of solution which is likely to seem to be attractive for schools working with culturally deprived children is to use the typical nursery school–kindergarten program with little or no alteration. Such preschool programs have been relatively effective socializing agencies for middle-class children. The play and social activity which are central in the typical nursery school and kindergarten build on middle-class child-rearing patterns, and they have been so effective because of the congruence between the values and efforts of the home and of the school. It is unlikely that these programs will be of great benefit to children who have come from homes which are very different from the typical middle-class home. In my view, the nursery school–kindergarten will be effective to the extent to which its methods and procedures take into consideration the prior development of these children and their special needs.

But it is easy to criticize present efforts and to find fault with the many efforts to attack the very real and complex problems of cultural deprivation. How does one go about the process of finding more adequate solutions? And why should we expect any effective solutions to emerge from preschool programs for these children?

Some answers to these questions are available from several types of research: longitudinal studies, other theoretical and empirical studies of development, research on the home environment, and research on the processes involved in intellectual development.

Evidence from Longitudinal Studies

In the book, *Stability and Change in Human Characteristics* (Bloom, 1964), I attempted to summarize the results of approximately 1,000 longitudinal studies. These are studies in which the same individuals have been repeatedly measured or observed at different points in their development. A special advantage of these studies is that each measurement or observation can be made without being influenced by the previous observations or measurements. Furthermore, the precision of each measurement can be estimated and the level of error can be taken into consideration when one attempts to summarize the evidence on a particular child or on a group of children.

One major finding that emerges from the longitudinal analysis of each characteristic is that the results of many studies are in very close agreement. When appropriate allowances are made for the sampling variations and the errors of measurements, longitudinal data gives such similar patterns of relationship for a particular characteristic that we can begin to think in terms of *laws* rather than trends. A single curve of development for each characteristic can be used as a very close approximation to the results found in many different studies. The major point is that the congruence of the many different quantitative findings permits us to draw powerful generalizations in what have hitherto been regarded as the "soft" sciences. This consistency of the data gives great promise that investigations of the underlying variables and determinants will yield increased understanding of the ways in which growth and development take place and of the forces which may affect these developments.

This work also reveals the typical growth curve for each characteristic. These curves differ from characteristic to characteristic, but for the most part the curves reveal that growth or change at some stages of development is much more rapid than at other stages. For some characteristics there is as much growth in a single year at one period in the individual's development as there is in eight to ten years at other stages in his development. It is especially noteworthy that for some of the most significant human characteristics the most rapid period of development appears to be in the first five years of life.

A major proposition which is tested throughout this book is that the environment in which the individual develops will have its greatest effect on a specific characteristic in the most rapid period of change and will have least effect on the characteristic in its least rapid period of change. This proposition, supported by a considerable amount of data and research, helps us to understand why the home and family are so important for the characteristics which develop most rapidly during the first five years of life. The evidence, as well as theory, makes it clear that change in many characteristics becomes more and more difficult with increasing age or development, and that only the most powerful environmental conditions are likely to produce significant alterations in a stable characteristic at later stages of life.

Longitudinal evidence makes it very clear that the child does not come to the first grade of school as a *tabula rasa* on which teachers will indelibly imprint the educational values and competencies prized by the culture. Quite the contrary, the child enters first grade after having gone through perhaps the most rapid period of development which will take place throughout his life. In this book, the early development is described quantitatively with regard to about 30 human characteristics.

With regard to academic achievement, it is estimated that at least one-third of the development at age 18 has taken place prior to the child's entrance into the first grade of school. Educational growth is clearly not limited to what takes place in the school in grades one to twelve. The schools build on a foundation which has been largely developed in the home in the early years of life. Much of the variation in children at the beginning of first grade can be attributed to variations in the home environment. While hereditary influences undoubtedly are of significance in determining individual variation when environment is held constant, it is very clear that social class, ethnic, and racial differences in learning are, for the most part, to be accounted for by environmental differences.

Evidence from Other Empirical and Theoretical Investigations

The early environment is of crucial importance for three reasons. The first is based on the very rapid growth of selected characteristics in the early years and conceives of the variations in the early environment as so important because they shape these characteristics in their most rapid periods of formation. I have already referred in brief detail to the evidence for this.

However, another way of viewing the importance of the early environment has to do with the sequential nature of much of human development. Each characteristic is built on a base of that same characteristic at an earlier time or on the base of other characteristics which precede it in development. Hebb (1949) has pointed out the differences in activity and exploratory behavior of animals reared in very stimulating environments in contrast to those reared under very confining conditions. Such differences in initial behavior are of significance in determining the animal's activity and intelligence at later stages in its development. Erickson (1950) has described stages in the development of human beings and the ways in which the resolution of a developmental conflict at one stage will in turn affect the resolutions of subsequent developmental conflicts. The entire psychoanalytic theory and practice is based on a series of developmental stages (Freud, 1933; Freud, 1937; Horney, 1936; Sullivan, 1953) with the most crucial ones usually taking place before about age 6. The resolution of each stage has consequences for subsequent stages. Similarly, other more eclectic descriptions of development (Gesell, 1945; Havighurst, 1953; Piaget, 1932; Murray, 1938) emphasize the early years as the base for later development. All these theoretical as well as empirical descriptions of development point up the way in which the developments at one period are in part determined by the earlier developments and in turn influence and determine the nature of later developments. For each of these viewpoints, the developments that take place in the early years are crucial for all that follows.

A third reason for the crucial importance of the early environment and early experiences stems from learning theory. It is much easier to learn something new than it is to stamp out one set of learned behaviors and replace them by a new set. The effect of earlier learning on later learning is considered in most learning theories under such terms as habit, inhibition, and restructuring. Although each learning theory may explain the phenomena in different ways, most would agree that the initial learning takes place more easily than a later one that is interfered with by an earlier learning. Observation of the difficulties one experiences in learning a new language after the adolescent period and the characteristic mispronunciations which tend to remain throughout life are illustrations of the same phenomena.

Several explanations for the difficulties in altering early learning and for the very powerful effects of the early learning have been advanced. Schachtel (1949) and McClelland (1951) believe that the learning which takes place before language development is so powerful because it is not readily accessible to conscious memory. Others, such as Dollard and Miller (1950), Mowrer (1950), and Guthrie (1935), would attribute the power of early learning to the repeated reinforcement and over-learning over time such that the early learning becomes highly stabilized. More recently, the experimental work on imprinting in animals by Hess (1959) demonstrates the tremendous power of a short learning episode at critical moments in the early history of the organism. Hess has demonstrated that ducklings at ages of 9 to 20 hours may be imprinted to react to a wooden decoy duck as a mother duck in a ten-minute learning experience and that the duckling will thereafter respond to the decoy duck in preference to real mother ducks.

Although it is possible that each type of explanation is sound, especially as it applies to different learning phenomena, all three tend to confirm the tremendous power of early learning and its resistance to later alteration or extinction.

The power of early learning must still, for humans, remain largely an inference drawn from theory, from descriptive developmental studies, and from quantitative longitudinal studies. In many respects, the attempts to describe the learning process as it takes place in the first few years of life are still far from satisfactory. We know more about the early learning of experimental animals than we do about human infants. In this writer's opinion, the most vital research problems in the behavioral sciences are those centered around the effects of early learning and early environments on humans.

Research on the Home Environment

Much of the research on the relation between home environments and learning have been sociological in nature. These studies have grouped children on the basis of the education or occupation of the parents, social class or socioeconomic status, race, or ethnic background, and then related these classifications to the educational achievement of the children in school. Most of these studies reveal significant differences between extreme groups and correlations on the order of +.30 to +.50 between these sociological indices and measures of school achievement. While such studies do demonstrate some overall effects of the home environment, they are not very helpful to the schools because of the very weak statistical relations and because they do not give specific clues as to what the schools and parents can do to improve the situation for particular children.

A somewhat different approach to the study of the effects of home environment on intelligence and school learning was undertaken by Dave (1963) and by Wolf (1964). They began with the premise that it is what parents *do* rather than what they *are* that accounts for the learning development of children in the early years. Through interviews and observational techniques they attempted to investigate the environmental process variables in the homes—that is, the interactions between parents and their children.

Dave hypothesized on the basis of the literature that the home environment relevant to educational achievement might be studied in terms of six process variables:

1. *Achievement press*—the parents' aspirations for the child and their interest in, knowledge of, and standards of reward for the child's educational achievement.
2. *Language models*—the quality of the parents' language and the standards they expect in the child's language.
3. *Academic guidance*—the availability and quality of academic guidance and help provided in the home.
4. *Activity in the home*—stimulation provided in the home to explore various aspects of the larger environment.
5. *Intellectuality*—the intellectual interests and activity in the home.
6. *Work habits*—the degree of routine in home management and the emphasis on regularity in the use of space and time.

These six variables were broken down into more specific process characteristics and ratings were made on interview and observational data. When an overall index of the home environment was correlated with the results of a fourth-grade battery of achievement tests, the correlation was found to be +.80. In general the correlations were highest with tests of word knowledge and reading, and they were lowest with spelling and arithmetic computation. These results suggest that the home has greatest influence on the language development of the child and his general ability to learn, and least influence on specific skills primarily taught in the school.

This approach makes it clear that parents with relatively low levels of education or occupational status can provide very stimulating home environments for educational achievement. Dave's and Wolf's research demonstrates that it is what the parents *do* in the home rather than their *status* characteristics which are the powerful determinants in the home environment. They find that the relationship between these interactive processes and the parent's status is relatively low.

This approach is also suggestive for the division of labor between the home and the school. Three of the characteristics are likely to be highly modifiable in the home (achievement press, activity in the home, and work habits). That is, it is quite likely that parents can be encouraged and helped to alter these aspects of the home environment and, in turn, these are likely to affect the child's achievement in school. The other three characteristics (language models, academic guidance, and intellectuality in the home) are less likely to be modifiable in adults who are thirty years of age or older. It would seem that the school, and especially the preschool, can do a great deal to supply these aspects of the environment where they are at a relatively low level in the home environment.

A related type of research on the home environment has been carried out by the Henrietta Szold Institute in Israel under the direction of Dr. M. Smilansky. Observational and interview studies of the parents and their interactions with their children reveal many differences between the homes of European origin and the homes of "Oriental" origin. This research makes it clear that the learning stimulation of the European children is at a much higher level than it is for the Oriental children. The differences are most extreme with regard to the use of language, stimulation of questioning and thinking, and in the structuring of space and time.

The work of Bernstein and Hess emphasizes the role of communication and language as it affects the young child. They take the position that the behavior which leads to social, educational, and economic poverty is socialized in early childhood, that is, it is learned in the home. Bernstein (1961, 1962) has studied the way in which language structures and conditions what the child learns and how he learns. He finds that the forms of communication are related to the types of social interaction and that these determine not only the verbal behavior of the child but also the nature of his thinking and learning and his social behavior with authority figures as well as peers. Hess, Shipman, and Jackson (1964) have followed up this work by observing the ways in which mothers teach their four-year-old children how to solve or understand selected problem tasks. Their research is beginning to reveal the ways in which the language interaction and the control system, which relates parent to child, restrict the number and kinds of alternatives for action and thought that are open to the culturally deprived child. This constriction reduces the child's tendency to reflect and to consider and choose among alternatives for speech and action. Hess and his colleagues believe that this constriction eventually leads to modes for dealing with problems which are impulsive rather than reflective, which emphasize the immediate rather than the future, and which handle ideas in disconnected rather than sequential patterns.

These types of research reveal the aspects of the home environment which seem to be most significant in affecting the level of measured intelligence of the child as well as his school learning. The research makes it clear that there is a curriculum and a teaching style in each home and that it is the variations in this home curriculum and teaching which accounts for much of the differences in children's preparation for the learning tasks of the schools. In most general terms this curriculum may be analyzed in terms of its provisions for general learning, the models and help it provides for language development and social interaction, and the stimulation and concern it provides for achievement and learning on the part of the child. It is the adults in the home who serve to stimulate the child's intellectual development, and it is the adults in the home who determine the basic preparation of the child for later learning in the school.

The Process of Early Development

While such empirical research does reveal some of the characteristics of the home environment which relate to and which influence the intellectual development of the child, it does not reveal the dynamic process by which the interaction between the child and the world about him takes place. Theoretical analyses and clinical types of investigations help to reveal something of the process by which intellectual development takes place in early childhood.

Beginning very early, the child comes to perceive many aspects in the world about him. This perceptual development takes place through the sensory modalities such as vision, hearing, touch, and even taste and smell. This development continues in more and more complex ways as the child approaches the beginning of formal schooling at age six. Perceptual development is stimulated by environments which are rich in the range of experiences available; which make use of games, toys, and many objects for manipulation; and in which there is frequent interaction between the child and adults at meals, playtimes, and throughout the day. At the beginning of the first grade there are differences between culturally deprived and culturally advantaged children in the amount and variety of experiences they have had and in their perceptual development. Although differences in perceptual development are less evident by age nine, it is likely that the differences present at age six make for differences in school learning in the first few grades. The typical middle-class home provides a very complex environment for the child's early perceptual development, and this gives these children some advantage in the early years of school (Deutsch, 1963; Hunt, 1964; Jensen, 1965).

Linked to this perceptual development of the child is his linguistic development. As the child comes to perceive the world about him, he is able to "fix" or hold particular objects and events in his mind as he is given words or other symbols to "attach" to them. "Mama" and "Dadee" become representations of the important adults in his life. "Bottle," "cup," and "dog," become symbols for appropiate objects in the environment. The adults in middle-class homes characteristically tend to use words so freely and easily that they teach them to the child at almost every opportunity. They encourage the child to say the word aloud, correct him when he says it incorrectly or applies it to the wrong object or event, and reward him when he uses the word or symbol correctly. This corrective feedback, which seems to be essential for the learning of language in relation to experience, is more readily available to the culturally advantaged child than it is to other children.

As the child attempts to communicate with others, and especially with his parents, he uses a relatively crude and limited language. In many middle-class homes, the child's language is extended by the parent's responses to his statements and questions. In culturally deprived homes, the parent is more likely to respond to the child with a monosyllable or to nod the head without using any words. The point of this is that one major difference between culturally deprived and more advantaged homes is the extension and development of the speech of children. Such differences have become very evident as a result of the studies done in various homes where parents are observed interacting with their children (Bernstein, 1961; Casler, 1961; Hess et al., 1964; John, 1963).

As a child develops more complex language, he becomes more able to perceive aspects of his environment, to abstract such aspects and to fix them in his memory, and to gain considerable control over his environment through the use of language. The frequent use of language in relation to his environment and the people in it enables the child to use words and language as tools for thought. Furthermore, the child becomes able to use language to express his own emotions, intentions, and desires. He is able to consider alternatives with regard to his emotions and to develop ways of delaying the gratification of his desires. Finally, the child develops his ability to compare, differentiate, and abstract aspects of his environment as well as his own thoughts and emotions (Berlyne, 1963; Carroll, 1960; Jensen, 1965; Luria, 1960; Vigotsky, 1962). Here again the child in the culturally advantaged home is given a great deal of opportunity to use language in these more complex ways, while the child in the disadvantaged home has less opportunity to develop in this way.

Put in other terms, the child in many middle-class homes is given a great deal of instruction about the world in which he lives, to use language to fix aspects of this world in his memory, and to think about similarities, differences, and relationships in this very complex environment. Such instruction is individual and is timed in relation to the experiences, actions, and questions of the child. Parents make great efforts to motivate the child, to reward him, and to reinforce desired responses. The child is read to, spoken to, and is constantly subjected to a stimulating set of experiences in a very complex environment. In short, he "learns to learn" very early. He comes to view the world as something he can master through a relatively enjoyable type of activity, a sort of game, which is learning. In fact, much of the approval he gets is because of his rapid and accurate response to this informal instruction in the home.

"Learning to learn" should not be confused with the early teaching of the child to read, to spell, and even to do simple arithmetic. Such coaching in the home is merely trying to do the school's task before the child enters public education. "Learning to learn" is a far more basic type of learning than coaching the child on school learning. It includes motivating the child to find pleasure in learning. It involves developing the child's ability to attend to others and to engage in purposive action. It includes training the child to delay the gratification of his desires and wishes and to work for rewards and goals which are more distant. It includes developing the child's view of adults as sources of information and ideas, and also as sources of approval and reward. Through such development the child changes his self-expectations and his expectations of others.

While all of this is not absent in the culturally deprived home, it does not play such a central role in child rearing in such homes. The size of the family, the concern of the parents with the basic necessities of life, the low level of educational development of the parents, the frequent absence of a male parent, and the lack of a great deal of interaction between children and adults all conspire to reduce the stimulation, language development, and intellectual development of such children. (Ausubel, 1963; Deutsch & Brown, 1964; Goldberg, 1963; Keller, 1963; Milner, 1951).

If the home does not and cannot provide these basic developments, the child is likely to be handicapped in much of his later learning and the prognosis for his educational development is very poor. Such a child is likely to have difficulty and to be constantly frustrated by the demands of the typical elementary school program. His frustrations and disappointments in school are likely to have an adverse effect on his view of himself and his main desire must be to escape from the virtual imprisonment which school comes to represent for him.

The Task of the Schools

Ideally, the early intellectual development of the child should take place in the home. Efforts should be made to help parents learn how to teach their children. It is likely that parents can learn to develop higher and more realistic aspirations for their children's educational and vocational careers. Undoubtedly parents can be helped to stimulate their children to explore aspects of the environment and to raise questions about it. Here it is likely that television and neighborhood libraries can do a great deal. Parents can also be helped to develop better work habits in their children and to better organize the environment with regard to space and time. This is likely to have some value for many parents and their children. However, the results of such efforts are not likely to be very effective when the total syndrome of poverty, broken homes, slum living, large families, and illiteracy all conspire against the intellectual development of the child.

All later learning is likely to be influenced by the very basic learning which has taken place by the age of five or six. If the intellective training of the child cannot be done adequately by the home and by the parents, it is the responsibility of the schools to insure that the culturally deprived children have as good a set of initial skills and intellectual development as children from more culturally advantaged homes. This position may be taken in the interest of the individual child. But also, this position may be taken to insure that the work of the schools for the next ten years will not be largely wasted because of what has taken place in the previous two or three years.

Careful but small-scale studies in the U.S. and in other countries demonstrate that it is possible to bring culturally deprived children up to satisfactory stages of readiness for regular school learning (Brazziel & Terrell, 1962; Hess et al., 1964; Gray & Klaus, 1963; Smilansky, 1964). If this can be done on a broader base, then the regular learning procedures of the schools which are now quite effective for the advantaged children are also likely to be effective for the culturally disadvantaged children.

Nursery schools must be organized to provide culturally deprived children with the conditions for their intellectual development and for the learning-to-learn stimulation which is found in the most favorable home environments. This would mean that such nursery schools would need to be created to take care of approximately one-third of the children at ages 3 and 4. Since this would involve about 3 million children and about 100,000 teachers (assuming that each teacher worked a double shift with 15 children in each shift), it would require an additional school expenditure of approximately 1 billion dollars per year.

Such a large-scale addition to the work of the schools must involve financial and other help from the federal government if it is to be started at the level required and if it is to be accomplished without undue delay. The problem of cultural deprivation cuts across state lines and, in part, arises from migrations of people across state lines. Support for preschool education must come from federal as well as other sources.

However, the problem of financial support is dwarfed by the problems of teacher training and by the problems of creating a nursery school which will provide the learning-to-learn stimulation so needed by culturally deprived children. These nursery schools cannot be patterned after the nursery schools commonly used for middle-class children. They must systematically provide for the intellectual development of the child. In these new types of nursery schools much of the learning can take place through games, concrete materials (blocks, toys, objects), and dramatic play. Teachers must be selected who can provide a supportive structured environment in which being read to, music, and art are enjoyable social experiences for the children.

While much must still be learned from the educational experiments being conducted, it is possible to outline some of the major objectives for these special types of nursery schools. These objectives may be derived from the studies of home environments, from the theoretical and empirical literature on child development, and from the analysis of the differences observed between culturally deprived and culturally advantaged children in the early years of school. Some of the major objectives of nursery schools for culturally deprived children should be:

1. *Stimulation of children to perceive aspects of the world about them and to fix these aspects by the use of language.*

   Every effort must be made to increase the range of perceptions of these children and to increase the range of their experiences. First-hand experiences, books, pictures, including films and television, and carefully selected objects and other material must be part of the learning experiences of these children. These experiences and materials must be fixed in the child's memory by the use of language.

2. *Development of more extended and accurate language.*

   There must be a great deal of language interaction between the children and the teacher. Much of this must be on an individual basis in which the child's comments are extended by the teacher's responses. The language patterns of the child should be developed at every opportunity and this should emphasize increasing mastery over standard speech forms as well as precision, complexity, and variety in the use of language.

3. *Development of a sense of mastery over aspects of the immediate environment and an enthusiasm for learning for its own sake.*

   While particular types of competence must be developed, the staff of the nursery school must not lose sight of the primary goal, which is an interest in learning for its own sake. Every effort must be made to help the children enjoy the learning process and to develop skill in learning. Children will need to have learning tasks which they can master; they will need opportunities to explore an increasingly complex environment, and they will need much feedback and reinforcement.

4. *Development of thinking and reasoning and the ability to make new discoveries for oneself.*

   Language and thought must be continually interrelated in the nursery school. Children must have many opportunities to make new discoveries and to be rewarded for making them. Problem tasks must be provided at the appropriate levels of difficulty, and the children should be given help and encouragement to attack and solve them. Insofar as possible, the problem tasks should be in the form of games and play which are pleasant and nonthreatening.

5. *Development of purposive learning activity and ability to attend for longer periods of time.*

As the child develops in the nursery school his activity should become more purposive, and he should be able to attend for longer and longer periods of time. In part, this objective will be a by-product of successful problem solving and language development. In part, this will emerge from a highly rewarding environment which continually encourages the child and which provides feedback and reinforcement as he engages in various activities.

It is to be hoped that the materials and methods for this new type of nursery school will in large part be developed out of the pilot programs now being tried in various parts of the U.S. (Hess, 1965). What would be especially helpful in developing new nursery-school programs would be the creation of a national commission of teachers and other specialists to coordinate and to develop curricular guidelines, materials, and methods for this special type of nursery school. This commission should be charged with responsibility for experimenting with alternative approaches to these problems and for evaluating the effectiveness of such curricula with different groups of children.

The teachers for this new type of nursery school should be carefully trained for the specific set of teaching tasks they must assume. Essentially these teachers should be trained to do for many children what very good parents can do for a small number of their own children.

The parents must be sufficiently involved in the nursery school to understand its importance for their child and to give support and reinforcement to the learning objectives and tasks of these special schools. The parents should be so committed to this type of school that they are willing to do everything possible to insure the continuity of the child's school experiences. Ideally, the parents should learn the appropriate communication and instructional patterns so that they can do much of this on their own with their own children. One might foresee the time when most parents can provide such stimulating home environment for the cognitive development of their children that special nursery schools will not be widely needed. To this end, every effort should be made to have parents serve as parttime assistants and observers in these schools.

It is likely that these cognitively oriented nursery schools will do much to give culturally deprived children many of the intellective and language competencies and attitudes which they would otherwise not develop. However, if the regular primary school program is frustrating and punishing in its approach, it is quite likely that these children will regress to a lower level of school learning. Care must be taken to reinforce and support these children, especially in the early years of primary school. The point of this is that no one approach to the problems of cultural deprivation is likely to "solve" the learning problems of these children. In our work (Bloom, Davis, Hess, 1965) we have stressed the need for modification of educational procedures and curriculum at all levels. While this is a task of great magnitude, it is our view that only through such a multi-faceted approach can the educational problems of cultural and social deprivation be effectively attacked. The emphasis in this paper on the preschool program should not lead the reader to regard the nursery school as the sole method of attacking these problems.

Nursery Schools for All Children

The development of special nursery schools for culturally and socially disadvantaged children will, if successful, result in nursery schools becoming an integral part of our educational system. From a program which at present reaches only about 2 percent of the children, it is likely that nursery schools will in the near future reach a third or more of the 3- and 4-year-old children.

It is to be expected that gradually these nursery schools will become available to all social and economic groups, since I cannot imagine a permanent system of publicly supported nursery schools which will be confined to any single group in our society. If preschool programs for child education do, in fact, become a regular part of the educational system, one might expect a variety of programs to result. The special needs of culturally deprived children can be met by a nursery school deliberately created for this purpose. However, for children who are given adequate intellectual stimulation in the home, quite another type of nursery school may be needed.

One can only speculate about the nature of such nursery schools. My own work on stability and change, and a vast body of theoretical and empirical literature, makes it clear that major personality characteristics are largely developed in the early years of childhood. The accidents of family and home conditions play a large role in determining these personality characteristics for good or evil. There are few social and environmental forces outside the home which directly influence personality development of young children.

It would seem to me that in these critical years of childhood, a system of nursery schools dedicated to the social and emotional development of the child could help each child get a good start toward mental health. Such an approach could do much to provide each child with the environment and adult support needed at these critical years.

The creation of such nursery-school programs and the selection and training of the teachers for these nursery schools is an exceedingly complex task. We can only dimly see the outlines of such a program. Much more research is needed before we can have any assurance about exactly what will be necessary. In spite of the difficulties, I am convinced that a system of nursery schools to provide for the mental health of each child is possible. I am further convinced that it is in this direction that we will find the Great Society—rather than in our search of outer space.

References

Ausubel, D. P., 1963. How reversible are the cognitive and motivational effects of cultural deprivation? Implications for teaching the culturally deprived child. Paper read at Conference on Teaching the Culturally Deprived Child, Buffalo, New York. March 28–30, 1963.

Berlyne, D. E., 1963. Soviet research on intellectual processes in children. *Monogr. Soc. Res. Child Developm.*, 28, No. 2.

Bernstein, B., 1961. Social class and linguistic development: a theory of social learning, in Halsey, A. H., Floud, J., and Anderson, C. A. (Eds.), *Education, economy and society.* Glencoe: Free Press.

Bernstein, B., 1962. Linguistic codes, hesitation phenomena and intelligence. *Language and Speech*, 5 (1), 31–46.

Bloom, B.S., 1964. Stability and change in human characteristics. New York: John Wiley and Sons, Inc.

Bloom, B.S., Davis, A., and Hess, R., 1965. Compensatory education for cultural deprivation. New York: Holt, Rinehart, and Winston.

Brazziel, W.F., and Terrell, Mary, 1962. An experiment in the development of readiness in a culturally disadvantaged group of first grade children. *J. Negro Educ.*, 31, 4–7.

Carroll, J.B., 1960. Language development, in Harris, C.W. (Ed.), *Encyclopedia of educational research.* New York: Macmillan.

Casler, L., 1961. Maternal deprivation: a critical review of the literature. *Soc. Res. Child Developm. Monogr.*, 26, No. 2.

Dave, R.H., 1963. The identification and measurement of environmental process variables that are related to educational achievement. Unpublished Ph.D. dissertation, Univ. of Chicago.

Deutsch, M., 1963. The disadvantaged child and the learning process, in Passow, A.H.

(Ed.), *Education in depressed areas.* New York: Teachers College, Columbia University, 163–180.

Deutsch, M., and Brown, B., 1964. Social influences in Negro-white intelligence differences. *J. Soc. Issues,* 20 (2), 24–35.

Dollard, J., and Miller, N.E., 1950. *Personality and psychotherapy.* New York: McGraw-Hill.

Erickson, E. H., 1950. *Childhood and society.* New York: Norton.

Freud, A., 1937. *The ego and mechanisms of defense.* London: Hogarth Press.

Freud, S., 1933. *New introductory lectures on psychoanalysis.* New York: Garden City.

Gesell, A., 1945. *The embryology of behavior.* New York: Harper.

Goldberg, Miriam L., 1963. Factors affecting educational attainment in depressed urban areas, in Passow, A.H. (Ed.), *Education in depressed areas.* New York: Teachers College, Columbia University.

Gray, Susan, and Klaus, R. A., 1963. Interim report: early training project. George Peabody College and Murfreesboro, Tenn., City Schools, mimeo.

Guthrie, E. R., 1935. *The psychology of learning.* New York: Harper.

Havighurst, R.J., 1953. *Human development and education.* New York: Longmans, Green.

Hebb, D.C., 1949. *The organization of behavior.* New York: Wiley.

Hess, E., 1959. Imprinting. *Science,* 130, 133–141.

Hess, Robert D. 1965. Inventory of Compensatory Education Project. Mimeo. Urban Child Center, University of Chicago, Chicago, Illinois.

Hess, R.D., Shipman V., and Jackson, D., 1964. Experience and the Socialization of Cognitive Modes in Children. Paper read at Symposium of the Amer. Assoc. for the Advancement of Science, Montreal, Canada.

Horney, K., 1936. *The neurotic personality of our time.* New York: Norton.

Hunt, J. McV., 1964. The psychological basis for using pre-school enrichment as an antidote for cultural deprivation. *Merrill-Palmer Q.* 10, 209–245.

Jenson, A.R., 1965. Social class and verbal learning in Deutsch, M., and Pettigrew, T. (Eds.), *Social class, race, and psychological development.* Society for the Study of Psychological Issues (in preparation).

John, Vera P., 1963. The intellectual development of slum children: some preliminary findings. *Amer. J. Orthopsychiat.,* 33, 813–822.

Keller, Suzanne, 1963. The social world of the urban slum child: some early findings. *Amer. J. Orthopsychiat.,* 33, 823–831.

Luria, A.R., 1960. *The role of speech in the regulation of normal and abnormal behavior.* U.S. Dept. of Health, Education and Welfare, Russian Scientific Translation Program.

McClelland, D.C. et al., 1951. *Personality.* New York: William Sloane Associates.

Milner, Esther, 1951. A study of the relationship between reading readiness in grade one school children and pattern of parent-child interactions. *Child Develpm.,* 22, 95–112.

Mowrer, C.H., 1950. *Learning theory and personality dynamics.* New York: Ronald Press.

Murray, H., 1938. *Explorations in personality.* New York: Oxford Univ. Press.

Piaget, J., 1932. *The moral judgement of the child.* New York: Harcourt, Brace.

Schachtel, E. G., 1949. On memory and childhood amnesia, in Mullahy, P. (Ed.), *A study of interpersonal relations.* New York: Hermitage Press.

Smilansky, Sarah, 1964. Progress report on a program to demonstrate ways of using a year of kindergarten to promote cognitive abilities, impart basic information and modify attitudes which are essential for scholastic success of culturally deprived children in their first two years of school. Jerusalem, Israel: Henrietta Szold Institute.

Sullivan, H.S., 1953. *The interpersonal theory of psychiatry.* New Haven: Norton.

Vigotsky, L.S., 1962. *Thought and language.* New York: Wiley.

Wolf, R.M., 1964. The identification and measurement of environmental process variables related to intelligence. Unpublished Ph.D. dissertation, Univ. of Chicago, Chicago, Ill.

The Effect of the Home Environment on Children's School Achievement

5

In separate national studies of education in seven countries as well as in international studies involving twenty-two nations it has become clear that the home environment is a most powerful factor in determining the level of school achievement of students, student interest in school learning, and the number of years of schooling the children will receive. While the effects of the home are slightly different from country to country, there is no doubt that the home environment accounts for more of the student variation in learning than does the school curriculum or the quality of the instruction in the schools.

During the past decade and a half, many countries throughout the world have been experimenting with early childhood education, new curricula, and new instructional methods. Some of these new approaches have worked well, while others have not been very effective. Whatever the long-term effects of these new approaches to education, it is likely that for some time it will be the parents and the home environment that hold a major key to the learning of the children.

National and International Studies

During the past two decades, the educational research leaders in twenty-two nations have engaged in a cooperative study of the learning, teaching, and curriculum of the schools in their national educational systems. They have also compared the countries in terms of the achievement, interest, and attitudes of the students. These studies, which have been reported in great detail, have found great educational differences between the countries as well as within each country. These differences within and between countries are related to the curriculum of the schools and the opportunity they give students to learn the major ideas and skills in each of the school subjects (mathematics, science, reading, literature, social studies, and a second language). These differences are also related to teacher competence and the way in which time in the classroom is used by both teachers and students. In some countries, the average student is actively engaged in learning for over 50 percent of the classroom period while in other countries the average student is actively engaged in learning for over 50 percent of the classroom period.

However, no matter how we analyzed the data, the major factor in explaining the differences among students *within each country* was the home environment. Differences among teachers and differences among schools were relatively small in comparison with the differences in the homes of the students (Bloom, 1974; Walker, 1976).

In recent years, large national studies of the schools have been made in seven nations. In each of these studies, the one variable that explains much of the variation in the learning of the students is their home environment. Here again, the differences among the schools are relatively small when compared to the differences among the home environments (Coleman, 1966; Plowden, 1967).

Early Childhood Education

The research on home environments at the national as well as at the international level has led many nations to create special programs of nursery school and kindergarten education. Some of these programs have been very effective in ensuring that many of the students get a good start for elementary educations, while other programs have been less effective. In the United States, it has been found that programs which help the parents to provide support and encouragement for their children *in addition* to the early childhood education in the schools have been especially effective. Early childhood education programs which emphasize language development "learning to learn" skills, and motivation to learn have also worked well, but not as well as similar programs which also include parent support (Bronfenbrenner, 1974). All of this is to say that any hopes that the early childhood programs in the schools could give children what was lacking in the homes have not been supported by the work so far.

It was also found that even when the early childhood education program was effective over the short run, the effects wore off in the next few years in the primary school. Many reasons are offered for this gradual wearing off of the effects of the "head start." My own speculation is that parents are still the key in the learning of their children because they are likely to be a constant factor in their children's lives. When parents are very effective (or when they can learn to be more effective) in supporting the child's learning, they remain with the child over his or her years of schooling. In contrast, no matter how effective a particular teacher is, each teacher interacts with the child only over a particular school term and is then replaced by a succession of other teachers in later school terms.

Primary Education

In recent years, there has been a great deal of research on the effectiveness of different learning conditions in the primary grades. Mastery learning and a number of so-called direct instruction methods have proved to be very successful in raising the learning level of most of the students. These methods appear to do in the school what some of the parents are able to do in the home for their own children. These include the *setting of appropriate learning standards, providing feedback periodically* on what the child has learned and what he still needs to learn, *individualized corrective procedures* to help the child learn what he has missed, and *support and encouragement* of the child's learning efforts.

The reports on these new instructional methods in a number of countries make it evident that the large majority of students can learn to a very high level, they can develop very positive attitudes toward school learning, and they do develop very positive views about their own learning capability. Similar findings are beginning to emerge in some of the large urban school systems of the United States (Bloom, 1978; Bloom and others, 1979; Block and Burns, 1976).

However, in most instances these new programs are limited to a small number of classrooms and schools. Parents may take some initiative in getting their local teachers and schools to try these more effective methods. However, school systems in the United States move slowly; even when there is parent pressure for innovations, the changes may come too late to be of benefit to the children now in a particular school grade or school subject.

Each parent has a special concern for his or her own children. If the parents wish to improve the learning of their children, the home environment is the only place where they are likely to have some degree of control. *An understanding of the home environmental factors that affect children's learning in the school and what the parents can do to encourage and support their children's learning* may give parents some start on this.

It is clear that when the home and the school have similar emphases on motivation and learning, the child has little difficulty in his later school learning. But, when the home and the school have divergent approaches to life and to learning, the child is likely to be penalized severely (by both the school and the home)—especially when school attendance is required for ten or more years.

During recent years there have been a large number of studies which attempt to alter some of the home environment processes. These studies have made use of home visitors, special courses for parents, parent involvement in the schools for brief periods of time, and the provision of special materials and games to be used by the parents with their children. This research has established that many of the home environment processes can be altered by parents—if they choose to do so—and that the effects of such alterations on the children's school learning are very great (Bronfenbrenner, 1974).

In the next section of this paper, there is a brief review of the research on the home environment in relation to school learning. This is followed by a discussion of each of the aspects of the home environment that have proven to be most important in influencing school learning—especially at the elementary school level.

Research on the Home Environment

Much of the research on the relation between home environments and school learning has been sociological in nature. These studies have grouped children on the basis of the education or occupation of the parents, their social class or socioeconomic status, and their race or ethnic background and then related these classifications to the educational achievement of the children in school. Most of these studies reveal significant differences between extreme groups and moderate relationships between these sociological indices and measures of school achievement. While such studies do demonstrate some overall effects of the home environment on school learning, they are not very helpful to the schools or the parents because they do not give specific clues as to what the parents or the schools can do to improve the learning of particular children. It is obvious that little can be done by the schools (or the parents) to change the educational or occupational level of the parents, their ethnic characteristics, or their economic level.

A somewhat different approach to the study of the effects of the home environment on school learning was undertaken by Dave (1963) and by Wolf (1966). They began with the premise that it is what the parents *do* rather than their *status* that accounts for the learning development of their children. Through interviews and observational techniques they attempted to investigate the environmental process variables in the homes—that is, the interactions between parents and their children.

Dave hypothesized on the basis of the literature that the home envi-

ronment relevant to educational achievement might be studied in terms
of the following process variables:

1. Work habits of the family—the degree of routine in the home
   management, the emphasis on regularity in the use of space and
   time, and the priority given to schoolwork over other pleasura-
   ble activities
2. Academic guidance and support—the availability and quality of
   the help and encouragement parents give the child for his or her
   schoolwork and the conditions they provide to support the
   child's schoolwork
3. Stimulation in the home—the opportunity provided by the
   home to explore ideas, events, and the larger environment
4. Language development—opportunities in the home for the development of correct and effective language usage
5. Academic aspirations and expectations—the parents' aspirations for the child, the standards they set for the child's school
   achievement, and their interest in and knowledge of the child's
   school experiences

These variables were broken down into more specific process characteristics, and ratings were made on the basis of interview and observational data. When an overall index of the home environment was related
to the result of a battery of school achievement tests on the children, the
relationship was found to be very high (+.80). It is clear that an index of
the home environment is far more predictive of school achievement
than is the best intelligence or aptitude test. The results suggest that the
home has greatest influence on the language development of the child
and his or her general ability to learn. It has least influence on specific
skills primarily taught in the school such as spelling and arithmetic
computation.

The Dave and Wolf studies have been replicated in a number of other
countries with very similar findings (Marjoribanks, 1979). These methods have also been used to some extent in the international studies. This
approach to the study of the home environment makes it clear that
parents with different levels of education, income, or occupational
status can provide very stimulating home environments which support
and encourage the learning of their children. The research of Dave and
Wolf demonstrates that it is what the parents *do* in the home rather than
their status characteristics which are the powerful determinants in the
home environment.

Home Environment Processes That Influence School Learning

The specific parent-child interactions that have great effect on the child's school learning are discussed in some detail in this section. In these discussions, the most positive characteristics of this interaction are emphasized. In the Dave study and the other studies which followed his, the parents who emphasized these interactions were the ones with children who were highly successful in their school learning. The parents who rarely emphasized these interactions were the ones with children who were least successful in their school learning.

As you read about each of the major home environment processes and the more detailed aspects of each of these, try to determine whether this characterizes your home and your interaction with your children. Decide for each of the lettered characteristics whether this is *usually true* of your home or whether it is *seldom true* of your home.

The readers of this section should *not* view these ideas as a list of rules to be followed mechanically. If these ideas are to be applied in a specific home they must be reinterpreted in relation to the home circumstances, the history of the parents and children, and the relations between the schools and the homes. Ideally, small groups of parents might use these ideas as a basis for considering alternative ways in which they can be used and adapted to fit particular circumstances. Even more ideal situations would involve parents and teachers meeting periodically to discuss these and related ideas in order to work out more effective ways in which the children could be encouraged and supported by *both the school and the home.*

1. Work habits of the children (and parents)
Some degree of structure and routine in the home is essential for good work habits in the school as well as out of it. Children need to have a time to study, a time to work, a time to eat, a time to play, and a time to sleep. Ideally, there should be some allocation of space in the home to various activities—including a place to study in relative quiet. The Dave study found that children from homes with clear structure, shared responsibilities, and set routines learned better in school than children from homes where each one did what he wanted to do whenever he wanted to do it.

It is likely that parents and children can discuss and plan some of the ways in which the activities and habits of members of the family can be improved. The major aspects of this might include the following:

*A. The degree of structure, sharing, and punctuality in the
home activities*

This includes clear plans for work and play, the sharing of duties and household chores among family members, and an emphasis on tasks being done on time. While it is to be expected that younger children will not be required to do the same tasks as older children, each one should have some share in the home activities.

*B. Emphasis on regularity in the use of time and space in the
home*

This includes an allocation of time for members of the home to eat, to sleep, to play, to work, and to study or read. Some balance among these activities may need to be worked out so that TV and play should not take precedence over other activities. It is also important to provide a place for study and reading at least at those times when members of the household are expected to engage in such activities.

*C. Priority given to schoolwork, reading, and other educative
activities over TV and other recreation*

Schoolwork and reading should be done, ideally, before play, TV, or even other work. A sufficient amount of time needs to be given to school work, reading, and other educative activities, even if it reduces the time for play, TV, or other recreational activities.

2. Academic guidance and support

School learning is a long and difficult process for most children. Unless there is a great deal of support and encouragement, children will find it difficult to maintain their interest in and commitment to the learning. Almost every child encounters some very difficult problems in particular aspects of the learning or in some of the learning tasks. Unless there is someone to help the child over these special difficulties, he may despair of his ability to learn. It is typically in the home that children get the encouragement they need and it is usually someone in the home that helps children over very difficult learning problems when they are encountered.

Dave found that homes differ greatly in the amount of encouragement and support they give the children. However, unless there is someone (in the home, school, or the community) who can provide the support each child needs at some times, the child may find school to be a difficult and unrewarding place to be. Some of the kinds of guidance and support that homes may give are:

*A. Frequent encouragement of the child for his or her
schoolwork*

This includes frequent praise and approval for good schoolwork. It may include speaking approvingly to others about what the child has accomplished, and drawing the attention of the family and friends to some accomplishment of the child in school. It may also include small gifts and rewards related to something the child has done well. As someone has put it, "It is catching the child when he has done something good and giving recognition for it."

B. Parental knowledge of strengths and weaknesses in the child's school learning and supportive help when it is really needed

This includes detailed knowledge by the parents of what the child is learning in each school subject, the child's special strengths and weaknesses in each subject, and encouragement of the child to do his or her best. It would also include giving the child help on learning problems when it is necessary. It may include some supervision over the child's homework, study, or schedule of activities—if needed.

C. Availability of a quiet place to study with appropriate books, reference materials, and other learning material

Each child needs a quiet place in which to study, a desk or table at which to work, and books, a dictionary, or other reference material. However, the emphasis is on the use of these rather than on their quality or their mere presence in the home. While all homes may not be able to supply a separate room and a great variety of learning material, almost all homes can provide a place for children to work and a quiet time during which the children can devote themselves to study or reading.

3. Stimulation to explore and discuss ideas and events

There is much learning that takes place outside of the school. While some of this learning may be related to the learning that takes place in the school, it is not organized by school subjects and is less formal. It is usually related to the activities of other members of the family; to conversations and other interchanges within the family; to the games, hobbies, and special interests of family members; and to shared activities of the family in play, reading, and visits to libraries, museums, concerts, and other cultural activities. It should be kept in mind that these are different from the teaching in the school in that they take place as the occasion arises and they rarely involve the deliberate teaching by one member of a family to another.

A. Family interest in hobbies, games, and other activities which have educative value

It is important for family members to share their interest in hobbies, games, and other activities which have educative value. Where possible, preference should be given to activities which have educative value over activities which are primarily recreational. However, what should be emphasized is that the activities are shared among members of the family and that each member of the family finds the activity interesting in its own right.

B. Family use and discussion of books, newspapers,
magazines, and TV programs

Ideally, members of the family should share in, jointly participate in reading activities, and discuss the ideas, views, and subjects included in the reading. Also daily events, news, and selected TV programs can have great value to stimulate members of the family to explore and discuss matters which may be of great significance. It is especially valuable if all members of the family are able to take part in these discussions and exchanges. What is most essential is that each member of the family have an opportunity to express and share his or her ideas and views with others. Also, the discussions should take place frequently and in an informal way.

C. Frequent use of libraries, museums, and cultural activities
by the family

Ideally, each member of the family should have a library card which is used frequently to secure books to read. The family should plan visits to museums, zoos, historical sites, and other places of interest. In addition, music, art, plays or films, and other cultural activities should be shared by the family and discussed. Even if the family members cannot visit such centers and activities, they may select and discuss particular TV programs which serve the same purpose.

4. Language development in the home

Much of the learning in the school or outside of it is based on the use of language. It is largely through listening, reading, talking, and writing that one learns the subjects in schools. These same language skills are also the means by which one learns about and uses ideas, topics, and events outside the school. Language is used to store ideas in the mind and to recall them when one needs them. Language is also the means by which one shares ideas and feelings with others. All individuals (at any age) need to constantly improve their language and to use it more and more effectively. The home is where the child learns much of his "mother tongue" and it is the one place where he may have the greatest opportunity to enlarge and enrich his language. The learning of language and its use in the home include the following:

*A. Family concern and help for correct and effective
language usage*

The family can give great support for the child's development of correct and effective language usage through its help or emphasis on good speech habits. Family members can help the child to use the correct words and phrases needed to communicate with others. Where possible, family reading should be emphasized and the dictionary should be one of the most frequently used books in the home. Each child should have a constantly changing list of words to be learned and used correctly.

*B. Opportunities for the enlargement of vocabulary and
sentence patterns*

All members of the family should have some opportunity to talk about the day's events at the dinner table or at some other daily occasion when the family gathers together. Each one should have some opportunity to speak and be listened to by the other members of the family. The emphasis should be on ways in which each individual can communicate thoughts and feelings through an expanding and accurate use of the spoken language.

5. Academic aspirations and expectations

The home is usually the place in which the child secures the motivation to learn well and to aspire to an education and life-style which will serve him or her well in the future. Typically, it is the parents who support and encourage each child at the different stages in his educational and cultural development. Almost no one can make it on his own—each needs the support and encouragement of others to reach for higher goals in education and personal development. While it is usually the parents who are most central in this support, other members of the family may also provide some of this encouragement. Some of the ways in which this can be done are in the following:

*A. Parental knowledge of the child's current schoolwork and
school activities*

The parents should know the child's current teacher(s), what the child is doing in school, the subjects being studied, and the learning materials being used. The parents should be interested in knowing about and sharing current school learning with their child. Also, the parents need to know how well the child is doing and the subjects in which progress is good as well as the subjects where special support may be needed from time to time.

*B. Parental standards and expectations for the child's
schoolwork*

It is usually the parents who set the standards for the child's learning in and out of the school. This includes the quality of the work the child is expected to do as well as the grades or marks he or she should seek to secure. However, parents should not only set the standards but also provide the support and even the direct help the child needs when he or she doesn't meet these standards. This typically requires constant attention and communication, rather than only a monthly or yearly review of how well the child is doing in school.

C. Parental education and vocational aspirations for the child

It is the parents who help the child aspire to a high level of education and vocation. They communicate the level of education and occupation they would like the child to aspire to in frequent discussions and plans for the future. They help the child make plans for high school and college and help him or her see the present learning in relation to such future goals. Frequently, parents encourage the child to make friends with other children who are serious about education and who have similar long-term goals and aspirations. It is also the parents who make the sacrifices of time and money for these aspirations.

What About Our Home?

Parents wishing to review the areas in which their home environment encourages and stimulates the children—especially during the elementary and secondary school years—should read each of the foregoing sections and decide for each of the lettered qualities whether it is

0   something that is rarely done or emphasized in your home

+   something that is frequently done or emphasized in your home

++   something that is given great emphasis or is especially emphasized in your home

These fourteen selected qualities of the home are listed briefly in the following table. The 0, +, or ++ marks should be put on this table. After you have marked the following table, count the number of + marks you have indicated. (A ++ should be counted as two plus marks.)

If you have marked 11 or more plus marks, your home is among the top 25 percent of homes in the encouragement and support you give to your children for school learning.

If you have marked 9 or more plus marks, your home is among the top 50 percent of homes in the encouragement and support you give to your children for school learning.

If you have marked 7 or fewer plus marks, your home is among the bottom 25 percent of homes in the encouragement and support you give to your children for school learning.

If you have a lower level of support and encouragement than you desire or believe possible, you may wish to reread the points at which you have marked a zero (0) to determine which of these you believe can realistically be given more emphasis in your home. You may find it useful to discuss these with other parents and friends to determine how they do these and the special ways they have of encouraging and helping their children in these areas. Teachers may also be very helpful in making suggestions about ways in which the home may be supportive of the children's learning.

If you do make major changes in these areas, you should find that over a six-month period there should be some improvement in your child's attitudes and interest in school learning. Also, there should be a noticeable gain in the child's level of school learning as indicated by teacher's marks and test scores.

References

Block, J. H., and Burns, R. B. Mastery Learning. See: L. S. Shulman, ed. *Review of Research in Education 4.* Itasca, Ill. F. E. Peacock Publishers, 1976.

Bloom, B. S. Implications of the IEA Studies for Curriculum and Instruction. *School Review* 82: 413–35, 1974.

Bloom, B. S. New Views of the Learner: Implications for Instruction and Curriculum. *Educational Leadership* 35: 563–76, 1978.

Bloom, B. S., and others. "Mastery Learning," *Educational Leadership* 37: 104–161 1979.

Bronfenbrenner, U. Is Early Intervention Effective? See: H. J. Leichter, ed. *The Family as Educator.* New York: Teachers' College Press, 1974.

Coleman, J. S., et al. *Equality of Educational Opportunity.* Washington, D.C.: Government Printing Office, 1966.

Dave, R. H. *The Identification and Measurement of Environmental Process Variables That Are Related to Educational Achievement.* Ph.D. dissertation, University of Chicago, 1963.

Majoribanks, K. *Families and Their Learning Environments.* London: Routledge & Kegan Paul, 1979.

Plowden, Lady Beatrice, et al. *A Report of the Central Advisory Committee on Children and Their Primary Schools.* London: Her Majesty's Stationery Office, 1967.

Walker, D. A. *The IEA Six Subject Survey: An Empirical Study of Education in Twenty-One Countries.* New York: John Wiley and Sons, 1976.

Wolf, R. The Measurement of Environments. See: A. Anastasi, ed., *Testing Problems in Perspective.* Washington, D.C.: American Council on Education, 1966.

CHECKLIST OF HOME ENVIRONMENTAL PROCESSES RELATED TO ELEMENTARY SCHOOL ACHIEVEMENT[*]

1. Work habits of the children (and parents)

———— A. The degree of structure, sharing, and punctuality in the home activities

———— B. Emphasis on regularity in the use of time and space in the home

———— C. Priority given to schoolwork, reading, and other educative activities over TV and other recreation

2. Academic guidance and support

———— A. Frequent encouragement of the child for his or her schoolwork

———— B. Parental knowledge of strengths and weaknesses in the child's school learning and supportive help when it is really needed

———— C. Availability of a quiet place to study with appropriate books, reference materials, and other learning material

3. Stimulation to explore and discuss ideas and events

———— A. Family interest in hobbies, games, and other activities which have educative value

———— B. Family use and discussion of books, newspapers, magazines, and TV programs

———— C. Frequent use of libraries, museums, and cultural activities by the family

4. Language development in the home

———— A. Family concern and help for correct and effective language usage

———— B. Opportunities for the enlargement of vocabulary and sentence patterns

5. Academic aspirations and expectations

———— A. Parental knowledge of the child's current schoolwork and school activities

———— B. Parental standards and expectations for the child's schoolwork

———— C. Parental educational and vocational aspirations for the child

————————Total number of + marks

*Adapted from the Dave (1963) study.

Stability and Change in Human Characteristics: Implications for School Reorganization

6

In response to a request from the editors of the
Educational Administration Quarterly, *Professor*
Bloom has suggested some policy implications
growing out of his research on the development
and change of human characteristics. Professor
Bloom discovered that a fundamental order
characterized his data, and from these
regularities he outlines some specific implications
for school reorganization.

The book *Stability and Change in Human Characteristics*[1] represents an attempt to understand the development and alteration of human characteristics over time. Using almost 1,000 longitudinal studies of selected characteristics, this work summarizes what we now know about the quantitative development of these characteristics from as near birth as possible to the adult manifestations of these same characteristics.

This research reveals the high degree of comparability of the results of many longitudinal studies. There is a fundamental order such that a large number of longitudinal studies on a particular characteristic can be summarized by a single equation or descriptive curve. The results of earlier longitudinal studies may be used to anticipate the results which will be found in new longitudinal studies.

This work also reveals the typical growth curve for each characteristic. These curves differ from characteristic to characteristic, but for the most part the curves reveal that growth or change at some stages of development is much more rapid than at other stages. For some characteristics there is as much growth in a single year at one period in the individual's development as there is in eight to ten years at other stages in his development. It is especially noteworthy that for a number of the most significant human characteristics the most rapid period of development appears to be in the first five years of life.

A major proposition which is tested throughout the book is that the environment in which the individual develops will have its greatest effect on a specific characteristic in its most rapid period of change and will have least effect on the characteristic in its least rapid period of change. This proposition, supported by a considerable amount of data, helps us to understand why the home and family are so important for the characteristics which develop so rapidly in the first five years of life.

The evidence, as well as theory, makes it clear that change in a characteristic becomes more and more difficult with increasing age or development, and that only the most powerful environmental conditions are likely to produce significant alterations in a stable characteristic at later stages in life.

Finally, the longitudinal data reveal the extent to which each characteristic may be predicted from one age (or grade) to any other. In general, these predictions are far higher than previous research has revealed. The longitudinal data are used in this book to show the levels of prediction that are possible and to suggest the methods and techniques of research and data analysis required to reach these levels of prediction.

In the book, the theoretical as well as practical consequences of these findings are considered for child rearing, for education, as well as for other fields. In this paper the author will attempt to make explicit some of the policy and organizational implications of this research for the schools. While the findings of the book will be referred to briefly, it is likely that the interested reader will need to use the book for a more detailed documentation of these findings.

Early Childhood Education

The child does not come to the first grade of school as a *tabula rasa* on which teachers will indelibly imprint the educational values and competencies prized by the culture. Quite the contrary, the child enters first grade after having gone through perhaps the most rapid period of development which will take place throughout his life. In the book this early development is described quantitatively with regard to approximately thirty characteristics.

With regard to academic achievement, it is estimated that at least one-third of the development has taken place prior to the child's entrance into the first grade of school. Educational growth is clearly not limited to what takes place in the schools in grades one to twelve. The schools build on a foundation which has been largely developed in the home in the early years of life. Much of the variation of children at the beginning of the first grade can be attributed to variations in the home environments as well as to hereditary influence.

The research summarized in this book reveals the very early development of the child's language and cognition. It also reveals the aspects of the home environment which seem to be most significant in affecting the level of measured intelligence of the child as well as his school learning. In most general terms, the preschool environment may be described in terms of its provision for general learning, the models and the help it provides for language development, and the parental stimulation and concern for achievement and learning on the part of the child. It is, for the most part, the adults in the home who serve to stimulate the child's intellectual development.[2]

The differences in home environments are most dramatic in the contrasts between culturally deprived children and those who come from more culturally advantaged home backgrounds.[3] The child in many middle-class homes is given help in dealing with the world in which he lives, in using language to fix aspects of this world in his memory, and in thinking about similarities, differences, and relationships in his environment. Parents in many middle-class homes make great efforts to motivate the child, to reward him, and to reinforce desired responses. The child is read to, spoken to, and is constantly subjected to a stimulating set of experiences in a very complex environment. In short, the culturally advantaged child learns to learn very early. He comes to view the world as something he can master through a relatively enjoyable type of activity—learning. Much of the approval he gets is because of his rapid and accurate response to this informal instruction in the home.

Although some of the same type of stimulation and learning takes place in culturally deprived homes, it does not play such a central role in child rearing in such homes. The size of the family, the concern of the parents with the basic necessities of life, the low level of educational development of the parents, the frequent absence of a male parent, and the lack of a great deal of interaction between children and adults all conspire to reduce the stimulation, language development, and intellectual development of the children in such homes.

Since all later learning is likely to be influenced by the very basic learning which has taken place by the age of five or six, it increasingly will become the responsibility of society and the schools to find ways of insuring that all children begin the regular public school with as good a set of initial skills and intellectual development as possible. This social responsibility will become most urgent for children where the home cannot provide for these functions at an adequate level. Although some efforts can be made to help parents do a more adequate job of child rearing in this area, it is likely that special nursery schools and kindergartens will need to be organized to provide culturally deprived children with the conditions conducive to their intellectual development and the learning-to-learn stimulation which is now found in the most favorable home environments.

Such nursery schools and kindergartens are likely to be very different from the nursery schools and kindergartens commonly used for middle-class children. They must systematically provide for the intellectual development of the child. Specifically, the primary task of these nursery schools and kindergartens should be to stimulate the child to perceive aspects of the world about him and to fix these aspects by the use of language. They also should provide for the development of more extended and accurate language, a sense of mastery over aspects of the immediate environment, an enthusiasm for learning for its own sake, and the ability to make new insights and discoveries for oneself. Finally nursery schools and kindergartens should foster the development of purposive learning activity and the ability to attend for longer periods of time.

While the schools will develop programs of preschool education with great reluctance, it is likely that various economic and social pressures will lead to a large scale development of these programs of early education. Perhaps the most compelling reason for developing such programs is the increasing evidence that early childhood education is the key to insuring that the following ten or twelve years of required public education are not largely wasted. Undoubtedly it would be best if the intellectual training of the child in the early years could be done in the home and by the parents. If they cannot do it adequately, it would appear that the schools are the most logical social institution to do it.

Importance of the First Three Grades of School

The evidence from longitudinal studies makes it clear that much of the development of the child with regard to basic learning prerequisite to later learning has been completed by the end of the third grade of school. By this time approximately 50 percent of the variation at grade 12 can be accounted for.[4] This basic learning includes language competence; such basic characteristics of "learning to learn" as the ability to receive instruction from adults, deferring gratification of reward, and the more generalized motivation to learn. It also includes the basic attitudes toward school and teachers.

While much of this development takes place in the home and is reinforced by the home and kindergarten during the preschool years, it is apparent that the school does have its major impact during the first few grades. If learning has gone very poorly during this period, much of the work of the schools thereafter must be disciplinary or remedial. If learning goes very well during this period, the task of the schools in the later years is at higher and higher levels of learning and school learning is as enjoyable for the children as school teaching is for the staff.

There is a growing recognition of the vital importance of the first few years of primary education. As educators come to realize more fully the key quality of these first years of school, we are likely to see major changes taking place. Some of the changes in policy, organization, and practice for grades one to three suggested by our present knowledge are the following.

In the past, the major resources of the school were put in the later years of public education rather than at the beginning stages. It would take little effort for many school districts to determine the extent to which their expenditures per student increase from the first grade to the twelfth grade. It is likely that at one time the rationalization for such policies was based on the pyramidal character of school enrollment, with smaller and smaller numbers of students at the higher levels. However, with increased emphasis on education, it is likely that at present most K–12 school districts have little variation in the number of students enrolled at each grade level through the tenth grade. In many school districts the enrollment should be approximately equal at all grades through the twelfth grade. Thus, a rationalization based on a selective system of education is no longer tenable when completion of high school is regarded as a necessary goal for almost all youth. What is implied in the following suggestions, however, is not equality of resource allocation at the different levels of school. If the early years of education are fundamental to all that follows, then it is in these years that the allocation of resources should be greatest.

The teachers in the first three grades should be the best-trained and most carefully selected teachers in the system. The qualifications of the teachers should be, if anything, higher during the first three grades than at other stages in the school. These are the teachers who play the key role in each child's educational (and vocational) career. If salaries of teachers reflect the training and experience of the candidates, then it is here where the higher salaries should be allocated.

Because of the vital role of individualization of learning and instruction during these first few grades, the ratio of teachers and assistants to students should be higher at these grades than at the later levels of school. Although any ratio must be justified in more precise terms than is possible here, it would seem that a ratio of one adult to fifteen children might be regarded as optimal for grade one with slightly higher ratios for the next two grades. Furthermore, the ratio of teachers to children should be greatest for children having difficulty in learning.

It is at this level where the in-service education of teachers should be most intensive and should keep in step with new research and curriculum developments. Here is where the major problems of learning must be solved, and no effort or expense should be spared in finding more effective and productive solutions.

At this level one should find the most highly developed diagnostic and evaluation techniques. The diagnostic analysis of each child's skills, interests, and attitudes should be followed by appropriate instructional strategies. It is apparent from much of the research that no one educational approach will be equally effective for all children. Ideally each teacher in the first grade should be a specialist in a particular approach to a range of learning problems and should be assigned a group of children who are most likely to be helped by that approach. Each teacher should be helped by specialists who can identify and analyze problems at a deeper level than most teachers are able to do. Thus reading and language specialists, school psychologists, and testing and evaluation specialists should be available to help the teachers as they work with the children in these first years of school.

The work of the pupils in these early years must be one of constant success. This will probably mean that great care must be taken in planning learning tasks which children can successfully complete. Failure of children to succeed with learning tasks should be regarded as a failure of the curriculum and instruction rather than as a failure of the children. It is likely that some children will need more time and assistance to complete a specific learning task than will others. However, the repeating of a grade or year of work at this level would seem to be an inappropriate procedure. In contrast, the ungraded school[5] has much merit if this plan is accompanied by teaching methods and curriculum programs which encourage each child to move to his highest level of capacity and continually rewards him for his accomplishments.

Most of the learning in the first three years of school should be enjoyable for the children. Drill work and repetitious types of learning tasks should be in the form of games and play. Ideally the child should get his rewards from the task itself or from improving his own performance. Competition among children should not be a primary motivational force if learning is to become a major drive in its own right. A basic goal of this initial period of education should be to develop a need for learning in such a way that learning becomes a highly satisfying and rewarding activity for each child.

This is quite in contrast with what prevails in many schools where children who are not adequately prepared for school by their parents are frequently punished so much by the first few years of school that their own image of themselves deteriorates.[6] The frustration that these children (and the teachers) experience with a curriculum not addressed to their needs and development gives these children a sense of failure and inadequacy that makes it difficult for them to engage in later school learning with confidence or enjoyment.

Sequence in Learning

One of the conclusions based on the longitudinal research on educational achievement is that there must be an increasing concern for a picture of educational development over time. All too frequently, the age-grade division of the school focuses attention on what happens within a particular term or grade. Furthermore, the specialization of teachers by grades or subject fields means that no one follows the educational development of an individual over time (at least more than a term or year). In fact, the tendency is for a teacher to feel she has gotten rid of her problems when the students are passed on to the next teacher in line.

Much can be said for the division of school effort by grades, term, and subjects in that it provides highly specialized teaching competence at each stage of the school program. However, it does not provide the continuity and sequence of learning so vitally needed by many students.

One of the major problems posed by longitudinal evidence is that there appear to be particular grades in which there is great emphasis on a particular type of learning, while at another grade this type of learning is almost completely neglected. More research is needed on this, but it is evident that the sequence of learning tasks from grade to grade is not given the same kind of attention that is now given to the sequence of learning tasks within a grade. This undoubtedly is an organizational problem arising from the asembly-line notion of education in the graded system of education. Sequence in learning is not just the avoiding of unnecessary repetition or overlap from grade to grade. It is the planned movement of learning from one level of complexity or mastery to another. The development of sequence in learning requires not only the planning of subject matter and materials over time; it also requires the development of continuity in teacher-student relationships over time. Probably the simplest method of establishing sequence and continuity would be for the same teacher to work with a particular group of students over long periods of time—perhaps as much as two or three years. This would require great effort on the part of the teacher as he moves from one level of teaching to another, but it would do much to keep a teacher alert and learning—perhaps paralleling the new learning expected of the pupils from year to year.

Another aspect of sequence is posed by the newer research on academic prediction. Payne[7] has demonstrated that appropriate use of cumulative school records makes it possible to predict academic achievement over a five-year period at a level of precision that was formerly possible over a single year. This means that by the middle of the first grade one can forecast achievement levels at grade six with as much precision as was hitherto possible from grade five to grade six. This type of "tracking" and prediction is based on the cumulative data in the students' folders and can be handled rather simply by improved methods of graphing the student's records or by the use of computer analysis of data. Payne's work is rather easy to verify in any school that maintains cumulative records since all that is required is the appropriate analysis of data already accumulated in the records of a school on students who have completed six to eight years of school. It can also be verified for different groups completing a program (say Kindergarten-6) in different years. Thus, the high level of academic predictability is not an abstract theoretical or research conception—it is a fact which is easily verified in each school with minutes of computer time or a few hours of computation on a calculator.

What is at issue, however, is not the repeated verification of the predictability of academic achievement. If a particularly low level of achievement at grade eight is predictable at grade one or two, what can be done in the intervening six to seven years to alter the predictions? What this new level of predictability offers to education is *time*—time in which to introduce more powerful educational procedures to overcome the predictions. What is required is the early identification of individuals who are likely to have difficulty in learning and the development of more effective learning experiences for these students. Such effort must begin with careful diagnoses of the students' competence and the analysis of the sources of difficulty. On the basis of appropriate evidence, an educational prescription for the students must be written, followed by appropriate teaching strategies and learning materials. If these problems can be treated as early as possible, it is likely that a great deal of frustration and difficulty can be avoided at later stages in the education of the student—frustration for teachers as well as students.

What is suggested here is not necessarily individual educational therapy. The new levels of predictive accuracy give time to the school in which to prevent forecasts from coming true. Changes in curriculum practices, special groupings of children with common problems, new strategies of learning, more adequate techniques for defining the problems in educationally meaningful terms—all are possible ways in which the time made available to the school can be used to avoid consequences which can be anticipated long in advance.

But all the attention need not be placed on remedial measures. The accuracy of prediction applies to children at all levels of competence and mastery and includes many educationally important characteristics. Time is made available through these forecasts for more appropriate educational planning for *all* children. Special talents such as creativity and originality, artistic and musical aptitudes, and the like can be identified very early and nurtured by the schools—and at least the impairment of these talents by adverse practices in the school (and home) may be prevented.

The major point to be made is that the child's development over time is the responsibility of the school and that someone in the school (the school psychologist, the curriculum director, or the school principal) should assume special responsibility for observing this development and initiating appropriate action within the school as needed. The careful maintenance and frequent analysis of the cumulative records should enable the school to take appropriate measures at the optimum time for such measures. The proper maintenance of these records should give abundant evidence of particular educational needs long before the forecast becomes hardened into irreversible reality.

Decision Making—A Cumulative Process

Longitudinal evidence reveals the orderly progression in the development of particular characteristics in individuals. Although there are many short-term fluctuations, the long-term developments are, in general, characterized by pronounced trends which can be in large part predicted from the early developments of the individual and from the nature of the environment with which he interacts over a period of time.

This orderly progression and the increasing stability and predictability of many human characteristics is in sharp contrast to our present practice of attempting to make vocational and educational decisions at fixed times. Decisions about college attendance and the choice of a college are usually made on the basis of the student's high school record and a set of tests administered during the junior or senior year of high school. Vocational guidance is in many high schools given in a particular year. If guidance and decision making are to open, as well as close, doors and if they are to be based on increasing probabilities, they should begin much earlier than is customary in the public schools and should be developing parallel with the development of appropriate individual characteristics.

Among the most orderly developments are scholastic aptitude and school achievement (as measured by grades or achievement tests). The student's potential for higher education is clearly established long before the junior year of high school—perhaps as early as the fifth or sixth year of school. If educational guidance is to be useful both for decision making as well as for motivating and guiding the individual, it should begin long before the high school level.

Educational guidance beginning during the elementary school years should encourage pupils to higher levels of aspiration and should give them some notion of long term goals. Such guidance should hold up possibilities for the student and it should not close doors or make adverse decisions about the individual's long term potential. As further evidence is gathered, one might expect further educational guidance at the junior high school level, which again is encouraging wherever possible. At this level, there should be provided a thorough review of the individual's educational development and guidance should take into consideration the effects at remediation and special help at earlier stages. Further educational guidance should be provided at the high school level until a firm decision can be made at the junior or senior year of high school.

What is suggested here is that educational guidance should take place at many stages in the individual's development and that this guidance should start out with broad possibilities and gradually become more specific and firm. Early efforts at educational guidance should be positive rather than negative and should help both the pupil and his parents become aware of educational potentials for which economic and other types of planning might be begun. Educational guidance should be a gradual process which should help students begin long-term planning to be corrected at various stages as further evidence becomes available from the student's record, from his performance on tests, and from the observations and reports of teachers and other school personnel. Educational guidance should help the individual become aware of the full range of possibilities available to him at each stage in his development.

The primary purpose of educational guidance should be motivational —to help individuals plan for their fullest development and to take maximum advantage of the educational opportunities available to them as they proceed through the different levels of school. A secondary purpose of continuous educational guidance should be to avoid the worst features of anxiety and trauma associated with the efforts to make major decisions at a single point in time—the junior or senior year of high school. The consequences of continuous educational guidance are likely to be fewer dropouts at the end of the compulsory education period, less delinquency and other aberrant behavior while in school, and a greater use of the educational opportunities which are available. Perhaps, also, this emphasis on continuous educational guidance could help the school staff become more fully aware of the ways in which the school may be of help to the individual in the process of his educational development. This could be a healthy antidote against policy and practice stemming from the use of the secondary school as a selection and certifying agency for colleges and industry.

Vocational guidance is, of course, intimately related to educational guidance. While it is unlikely that vocational choices and decisions are as clear in their development as are educational choices and decisions, it should be possible for vocational guidance to be a continuous process in which the individual begins to consider long-term possibilities as early as the elementary school level. Such long-term vocational plans must be thought of in the most tentative of ways but must be available for further exploration. As the individual tries various possibilities in his mind as well as explores the nature of vocations through reading and observation, he is in a better position to entertain possible vocational goals as well as to discard some of these goals. One might hope that a continuous process of vocational guidance would help the individual to explore many possibilities and slowly reduce the possibilities to those which are both attractive to him as well as realistic.

The one great danger in such a process of continuous vocational guidance and decision making is that doors may be closed prematurely or that firm choices may be made too early. If the vocational guidance is a gradual one which permits full exploration of interesting possibilities, it will help the individual to keep his vocational choices interrelated with his own development of relevant characteristics. Such vocational guidance can also be more clearly attuned to the relations between general education and more specialized education.

The School As An Environment

The school is frequently seen as only one of many agencies involved in the development of the students. Furthermore, the task of the school is all too frequently viewed as a series of subtasks and responsibilities which can be divided among the staff who have specialized competence and roles. For the most part, each subtask is viewed as separable from the other subtasks and only minimal communication is needed among the specialists in the school.

Longitudinal evidence makes it clear that human characteristics are strongly influenced by the environment with which the individual interacts and that the influence of the environment is greatest in the most rapid periods of normal change in the characteristic. In our studies of environments (especially the home environment) it is evident that highly consistent environments have more powerful effects on specific relevant characteristics than environments which are not so consistent.[8]

Where the home and the school are mutually reinforcing environments, the child's educational and social development are likely to take place at higher and higher levels. Where the home and the school are contradictory environments, it is likely (although our evidence is not very systematic on this point) that the child's development will be slower, more erratic, and, perhaps, with a good deal of emotional disturbance for the child.

This would argue that the schools must seek ways of bringing about greater consistency in the two environments—home and school—at least insofar as they both influence the educational development of the child. Thus, one might expect that schools will need to be more alert to the definition of the school environment and to the collection of evidence on the home environments—at least in these cases where there is marked conflict between the two. In the early years of preschool and elementary education, it is likely that special efforts will need to be made in the school to help the child in those areas where the home has not done its part, such as language development, motivation and study habits.

However, the problems of relating the school and the home environments are still matters for further research, and they raise very fundamental value questions about what the ideal relationship should be between the two. A more immediate problem is that of determining ways of increasing the internal consistency of the school environment. This is essentially a curricular question and has to do with the extent to which the overall objectives of the school are consistently implemented in all phases of the school program.

If the extracurricular program of the school has goals and objectives which are fundamentally different from the goals and objectives of the curricular program, then one of the two programs is likely to be considerably weakened. Thus, Coleman[9] has shown that the status system of student groups in a high school may emphasize values which are at great variance with the intellective development of youth. Under such conditions it is likely that only a minority of the students will fully accept the demands of the classroom learning or prize the rewards and approval connected with such learning. Such an inconsistent environment within a school will have weakened effects on the students' cognitive development, unless the school can bring the extracurricular aspects of its program in harmony with its curricular program.

But another way of viewing the environment is to determine the consistency of its curricular program. If problem solving is emphasized in certain courses, are these weakened by the lack of emphasis on problem solving and inquiry in other courses? Is competition among students for grades and prizes the major reward system in some courses, while more intrinsic rewards are emphasized in other courses? Are some courses characterized by discussions and the explorations of alternatives while other courses are characterized by lectures, recitations, and other teacher-centered modes of instruction?

The point of all this is that a highly consistent environment is likely to produce marked effects on the students while a highly inconsistent environment is likely to have only a negligible effect on the students' development both in the cognitive as well as the affective domain.[10]

It is likely that very few schools in the United States constitute consistent and powerful educational environments. In the near future, it is probable that schools will increasingly attempt to determine the nature of the environment they have created and will take steps to determine ways in which they can become more nearly the educational environment which will promote particular types of educational development in the students. This will require that administrative and other educational leaders take steps to assess the present environment as well as help the faculty in its efforts to promote a more powerful and consistent educational environment.[11]

Conclusion

Longitudinal research yields a picture of individual development over time. If we conceive of education as a powerful force in determining much of this development, then we must find ways of relating the findings of longitudinal research to the work of the schools. Perhaps the most important implication of relating the two is that education, and the work of the schools, must find ways of dealing with the child's development over both the preschool as well as the school stages.

The longitudinal evidence summarized in the book, *Stability and Change in Human Characteristics,* makes it clear that much of education takes place outside the schools and that the schools must take this into consideration if they are to deal with the very real problems posed by the out-of-school environments. Furthermore, a major task of the school is to provide an educative environment which can be appropriately related to the out-of-school learning on the part of the students.

The implications for the schools that have been spelled out in this paper, on the basis of the findings of this book, call for major changes in resource allocation, major changes in the organization of school personnel and curriculum, and major changes in the conceptual framework for teaching, learning, and guidance. While these changes will probably require additional resources, these are not likely to be as important as the quality of educational leadership. It is likely that changes of the type suggested here will take place only where there is a well-informed and enthusiastic educational leadership. It is to be hoped that this paper and the suggested readings will make a small contribution toward informing educational administrators about the problems and the needs.

References

1. Benjamin S. Bloom, *Stability and Change in Human Characteristics* (New York: John Wiley and Sons, Inc., 1964).

2. Richard M. Wolf, "The Identification and Measurement of Environmental Process Variables Related to Intelligence," (unpublished Ph.D. dissertation, Dept. of Education, University of Chicago, 1964), and R. H. Dave, "The Identification and Measurement of Environmental Process Variables That Are Related to Educational Achievement," (unpublished Ph. D. dissertation, Dept. of Education, University of Chicago, 1963).

3. Benjamin S. Bloom, Allison Davis, and Robert Hess, *Compensatory Education for Cultural Deprivation* (New York: Holt, Rinehart, and Winston, 1965).

4. Benjamin S. Bloom, *Stability and Change in Human Characteristics,* Chapter 4.

5. See John I. Goodlad and Robert H. Anderson, *The Nongraded Elementary School,* Rev. ed., (New York: Harcourt, Brace and World, Inc., 1963).

6. Sarah Smilansky, "Evaluation of Early Education," UNESCO, *Education Studies and Documents,* No. 42, 8–17.

7. Arlene Payne, "The Selection and Treatment of Data for Certain Curriculum Decision Problems: A Methodological Study" (unpublished Ph.D. dissertation, Dept. of Education, University of Chicago, 1963). See also Payne's article entitled "Early Prediction of Achievement" in *Administrator's Notebook* (Midwest Administration Center, The University of Chicago, September 1964).

8. Benjamin S. Bloom, *Stability and Change in Human Characteristics,* Chapter 6.

9. James S. Coleman, "The Adolescent Subculture and Academic Achievement," *American Journal of Sociology,* LXV (January, 1960), 337–47.

10. Benjamin S. Bloom (Ed.). *Taxonomy of Educational Objectives, Handbook I, Cognitive Domain* (New York: David McKay, 1956) and David R. Krathwohl, Benjamin S. Bloom and Bertram B. Masia, *Taxonomy of Educational Objectives, Handbook II: Affective Domain* (New York: David McKay, 1964).

11. C. Robert Pace and George G. Stern, "An Approach to the Measurement of Psychological Characteristics of College Environments," *Journal of Educational Psychology,* XLIX (October, 1958), 269–77.

INSTRUCTION AND CURRICULUM DEVELOPMENT

Introduction to Instruction and Curriculum Development

LORIN W. ANDERSON
College of Education
University of South Carolina

I n the eyes of many educators, curriculum and instruction are virtually synonymous. Other educators see the two concepts as being so closely related as to be inseparable. In contrast, Bloom believes that important differences exist between curriculum and instruction. These important distinctions form the focus of the four papers that comprise this section.

These four papers were written over a period of fifteen years. Two papers, "Learning for Mastery" and "The Role of the Educational Sciences in Curriculum Development," represent the beginning of new developments in instruction and curriculum, respectively. These two papers, written in the latter part of the 1960s, describe somewhat radical ideas concerning curriculum development and instructional effectiveness. A third paper, "New Views of the Learner," represents Bloom's attempt to summarize both educational research and educational progress with respect to the ideas he stated some fifteen years earlier. As the reader will notice while reading this paper, Bloom's earlier ideas were not as radical as they may have seemed. The fourth paper, "Peak Learning Experiences," also written in the late 1960s, is not as directly comparable with the other three papers in this section. Nonetheless, the paper describes Bloom's concern for the range of outcomes that can result from the instructional process.

Since, as has been said earlier, the distinction between curriculum and instruction form the focus of this chapter, let us begin with a consideration of Bloom's conception of these two terms. A curriculum, according to Bloom, consists of the goals and objectives of a course, program, or school and the learning materials and planned learning experiences which appear to be related to those goals and objectives. The tasks of a curriculum specialist, therefore, are (1) to identify those goals, objectives, learning materials, and planned learning experiences, and (2) to define the interrelationships among those goals and objectives. While the identification of goals, objectives, materials, and experiences is difficult enough, the interrelationships among the goals and objectives are even more difficult to describe. Crucial questions such as, "What objectives should precede what other objectives?" and, "How can the objectives of a mathematics curriculum be integrated with the objectives of a social studies curriculum so that the goals of the school are adequately met?" need to be answered. Finding answers to these questions is extremely time-consuming and difficult. As a consequence, curriculum changes must be viewed as long-term endeavors and must be approached in a systematic fashion.

In contrast with curriculum, instruction is seen by Bloom as consisting of the implementation of teaching-learning activities. These activities need to be selected so as to make use of the curricular materials and prescribed learning experiences in such a way as to achieve the curricular goals and objectives. Given this conception of instruction, the major task facing an instructional specialist would be the identification of those teaching-learning activities which are to be used. An additional task would be the sequencing of these activities. Examples of instructional activities would include informing students of goals and objectives, providing learners with cues to guide their learning, providing incentives and reinforcement, providing feedback concerning student progress relative to the goals and objectives, and providing for supplementary instructional activities in order to help students overcome poor initial learning.

As can be seen by examining this partial list of instructional activities, instructional changes can take place rather quickly. For example, the major instructional change suggested by Bloom in his "Learning for Mastery" paper is the inclusion of feedback and correctives for the purpose of monitoring student progress and correcting errors and misunderstandings as they occur. This change in instruction requires a relatively brief orientation of teachers to the use of test results and other evidence to identify student errors and the use of additional instructional activities which will help students to correct their errors before they accumulate.

Given the separateness of curriculum and instruction, two important points must be made. First, the effects of changes in curriculum require a long period of time to realize. That is, educators must wait patiently for several years before they will see the effects of curricular changes. On the other hand, the effects of instructional alterations can be seen almost immediately. Research indicates that it is possible to see the learning effects of the use of the feedback-corrective mechanism within a few weeks.

Second, instructional changes can be made without making curricular alterations. That is to say, it is possible to suggest *different* teaching-learning activities and teaching strategies for use with *existing* materials in order to attempt to achieve *existing* goals and objectives. In a similar vein, curricular changes can be made without altering instructional methods. If instruction is *not* altered, however, the goals and objectives of the "new" curriculum will be achieved *no more effectively than* the goals and objectives of the "old" curriculum. The reason for this equality of effectiveness stems from the fact that instructional activities are the determiners of learning effectiveness regardless of the curriculum. In an attempt to maximize curriculum effectiveness, therefore, curriculum centers throughout the world have begun to incorporate learning-for-mastery instructional strategies into the redesign of their curricula.

Bloom's distinction between curriculum and instruction can be seen quite clearly in two of the papers in this section. In "The Role of the Educational Sciences in Curriculum Development," he sets out the tasks of curriculum development. Throughout this paper he emphasizes the enormity of the task, in part by posing the type of questions that must be answered in order to accomplish it. The reader is urged to consider the magnitude of these questions. "What contribution [should] the study of the subject . . . make to other more general aims of education? What are the essential ideas, content and principles of the field which should, as a minimum, be included in a study of the subject? What are the aspirations of the people [who are supposed to benefit from the educational system]? Do these [aspirations] differ for different groups of the population? Which objectives of learning are most likely to be achieved at one level of education and which are more likely to be achieved at a later stage of education? Which objectives can be achieved over a relatively short period of time and which objectives must be emphasized over a number of years before significant growth is likely to take place? Which objectives are dependent for their attainment on their being emphasized in both the school as well as out of school environment?"

After posing these questions in 1966, Bloom reflects on the state of curriculum development in the United States in his paper entitled "New Views of the Learner," which was published in 1978. In general, his assessment is not very positive. "Little careful work is done in the U. S. about integration or sequence of learning experiences for a given group of students. Each subject is thought of as having little or no relation to other parts of the curriculum. And almost no concern is expressed in our published textbooks about local conditions or circumstances. Also, there is little or no concern for revision of the curriculum over time—except to introduce features that will 'sell well' or that reflect our current fads'' (p. 145).

The counterpart of his "Role of the Educational Sciences" paper, which sets out Bloom's ideas concerning curriculum development, is his "Learning for Mastery" paper, which sets out his ideas concerning instructional improvement. The reader is urged to consider the basic instructional changes recommended by Bloom in this paper. First, the learners should be informed of what they are to learn. Second, the learners should be made aware of the standard(s) of acceptable performance. Learners must attain these standards in order to demonstrate that they have, in fact, mastered the learning goal or objective. Third, errors and misunderstandings on the part of the learners should be identified and pointed out to the student. Finally, supplementary instructional activities should be prescribed for those learners whose learning is replete with errors so that these errors and misunderstandings are not allowed to accumulate over time.

These instructional alterations can be implemented quite rapidly, even within an existing curriculum. In fact, Bloom often advocates instructional changes within the existing curriculum. Consider his now famous statement: "Most students (perhaps over 90 percent) can master *what we have to teach them*" (p. 153; italics mine). The implication of this statement is that *whatever* goals or objectives are included in the curriculum, a high quality of instruction, such as that approached by the Learning for Mastery strategy, can help the vast majority of learners to achieve them.

When instructional changes, such as those inherent in mastery learning strategies, are made, the results are extremely positive (as noted by Block and Burns, 1976; Bloom, 1976). So positive, in fact, that Bloom has been led to develop some new views of the learner. Briefly, the evidence suggests that not only can most students learn to a high level the curricular goals and objectives, but also that "most students become very similar with regard to learning ability, rate of learning, and motivation for further learning when provided with favorable learning conditions" (p. 135).

This new view of the learner suggests that some fundamental questions must be addressed by educators at various levels of the educational system. These questions have to do with the role and responsibility of schools in educating our youth. Can schools remain content with their current roles of selecting out talented students? Or must schools confront their responsibility for the development of talent in all students? How much alteration in schools are we willing to make to ensure that all students do, in fact, learn those things that are deemed to be important? Or, are schools not responsible for making the necessary alterations? Clearly these are not easy questions to answer. But the point is, they must be asked (and answered) if Bloom's conception of the learner is accurate.

Despite the mounting evidence, many people are skeptical about Bloom's ideas. This skepticism will continue as long as we fail to gather evidence concerning what really is possible for instruction to accomplish in terms of current curricular goals and objectives. We continue to be content to make comparisons between "new" instructional programs and "old" instructional programs rather than to seek out the possibilities of some "ideal" instructional program. We would benefit considerably as educators if we were to begin to examine the limits of instruction, that is, the maximal learning that can result from a planned instructional program.

Bloom has frequently suggested that the use of tutoring by a trained tutor be used as an approximation to an "ideal" instructional program. Research can be conducted using this tutorial model to estimate the limits of educability. Since the purpose of this research is to determine the limits, cost should be unimportant. Once the effects of this "ideal" instructional program have been estimated, attempts should be made to modify this "ideal" so that the cost of implementing the program is not prohibitive.

What would we gain by pursuing an investigation into the limits of instructional effectiveness? We would attain a second perspective which could be used in evaluating proposed instructional programs. In addition to the now routine comparisons of proposed instructional programs with currently employed instructional programs, comparisons could be made between proposed programs and the "ideal" program. Consequently, instructional effectiveness could be examined from both perspectives and instructional improvement is more likely.

The necessity of separating curriculum and instruction is clearly seen in the fourth paper of this section, "Peak Learning Experiences." In general, the purpose of instruction is to facilitate the attainment of curricular goals and objectives through the proper use of the curricular materials and planned learning experiences. Put in another way, instruction most frequently is seen as a means to an end. According to Bloom, however, instruction also can be viewed as an end in itself. This occurs through what Bloom refers to as peak learning experiences, a term which he borrows from Maslow's conception of peak experiences.

Peak learning experiences are those experiences of students which occur in the instructional setting. These experiences are "so vivid that students will recall them in great detail many years later" (p. 149). During peak experiences, students tend to be almost totally involved in the learning situation. Interviews conducted by Bloom and his students indicated that students recalling peak learning experiences saw the "experience as *valuable in its own right* rather than as a means to some learning task or useful for other purposes" (italics mine).

When peak learning experiences were viewed as a means to an end, the end was typically global or abstract in nature. That is, the outcome resulting from the peak learning experience was apart from those goals specifically contained in the curriculum. Many students reporting peak learning experiences said they were stimulated to explore in greater detail the ideas being presented or to apply the ideas to other situations and material.

These two views of instruction (one as a means to an end, the other as an end in itself) are possible only if instruction and curriculum are seen as somewhat separate entities. When this differentiation is made, it seems clear that both aspects of instruction are valuable and worthy of consideration.

Bloom, however, paints a rather dim picture of the frequency of peak experiences in schools today. In his "New Views of the Learner" paper he states: "I am sure students in our schools do have occasional peak learning experiences—but they are rare indeed. Our students tend to seek these memorable experiences outside the classroom in sports, social events, and even in illegal and violent activities" (p. 150). In the context of this dismal view of the presence of peak learning experiences in schools, Bloom identifies the task of schools in this regard. "Perhaps we too may learn how learning in the schools can be vivid and one source of fulfillment for most of the students in our schools" (p. 150). Although curriculum and instruction are seen by Bloom as independent entities, the influence of one on the other is evident in his writings. As mastery-learning strategies continue to produce more and more capable learners, it becomes increasingly necessary to examine more closely what is to be learned. Given the time, effort, and material resources available, we must ask ourselves the following questions. Are the goals and objectives currently included in our curricula the most important goals and objectives that can be learned, or are important goals and objectives being excluded from the curricula? What are the most important goals and objectives that can be included? Let us briefly consider the answers to some of these questions within the learning-for-mastery framework.

Mastery learning as an instructional strategy falls into the category of so-called "adaptive instructional strategies." That is to say, alterations are made within the strategy in order to accommodate (or adapt to) learner differences. The major alteration within the learning-for-mastery strategy which produces this accommodation is the feedback-corrective component. The feedback-corrective component tends to provide the learners with skills and confidence which permit them to learn from the instruction typically presented in classrooms.

Adaptation is a double-edged sword, however. The positive aspect of adaptation is the increasing number of students who learn to a high level what the schools have to teach. The negative aspect of adaptation may be that students become accustomed to such adaptation; if so, they may begin to require ever increasing amounts of adaptation. One way of eliminating the potential negative aspect is through the development of what Bloom (1978) calls "independent learners." Put simply, the conception of "independent learner" is predicated on the idea that one of the most important goals of education is to provide learners with abilities and affective dispositions which will permit them to adapt to a wide variety of situations.

What kinds of characteristics must learners possess to be classified as "independent learners?" Bloom suggests several. First, they can engage in so-called higher-level thinking (e.g., they can analyze situations, make and defend decisions, solve problems). Second, they possess a certain degree of confidence in their ability to learn and to solve problems. They believe that they can alter their ways of thinking when necessary. Third, they are *intrinsically* rather than *extrinsically* motivated. That is, they are motivated more by learning and the attainment of the learning goal than by rewards that may be derived from the attainment of the goal. Finally, they possess a degree of social responsibility and can cooperate with (and benefit from) others in order to achieve some goal.

If we are to develop such independent learners, the implications for curriculum and instruction are quite clear. The curriculum must contain goals and objectives which are "beyond the knowledge level." These goals and objectives should include the higher-level thinking skills mentioned above. Although Bloom's cognitive taxonomy has been with us for almost a quarter of a century it is a sad fact that most of our goals and objectives still are concerned with the acquisition of knowledge by the students.

From an instructional perspective, the concept of independent learner has several implications. Intrinsic motivation, self-confidence and the possession of social skills seem to be aligned with a type of instruction similar to the learning-for-mastery instructional strategy.

When students are informed of what they are to learn and the standard they are to achieve, intrinsic motivation becomes possible. Students tend to become goal-oriented; they can gather evidence for themselves concerning their attainment of the goal. If students cannot see whether or not they have achieved the goal (or if they do not even know what goal they are pursuing), they must wait until someone else judges their performance. They must wait until some type of external reinforcement (knowledge of results, praise/criticism, or *M* & *M*s) is presented. This process of waiting for the judgment of others must lead to extrinsic motivation since the learner is *dependent* on others for reinforcement. On the other hand, if people are aware of the goal and the standard of success, they can inform themselves of their progress toward the goal. This process of self-informing would tend to lead to the development of intrinsic motivation.

When students are helped to overcome their weaknesses and achieve success through the use of supplementary instruction, they develop self-confidence. They learn to benefit from, rather than avoid, errors and mistakes. As a consequence, they tend to persist on future tasks since success is possible even if it isn't achieved "right away."

Finally, when a peer-tutoring or small-group-study approach to correctives is used (as is done in the majority of learning-for-mastery classrooms), students tend to develop a cooperative attitude and a degree of social responsibility. The fact that all students can learn and can "win" undoubtedly contributes to this development.

The importance of the development of independent learners cannot be overly stressed. One often overlooked point made by Bloom in several of his papers is that learning-for-mastery strategies are effective to the extent that they eventually become unnecessary. Bloom phrases this point as follows. The research on mastery learning demonstrates that while " . . . special and very favorable conditions may be needed at some stages of learning. . . over time these [favorable conditions] may be gradually discarded" (p. 136).

Despite the distinctions made by Bloom in terms of curriculum and instruction, one common thread weaves throughout his writings, both those in this section and those in the other sections of this volume. This thread is Bloom's concern for the use of evidence to examine the effectiveness of curricula and instructional programs and to make modifications in both curricula and instructional programs as is deemed necessary. Anyone following Bloom's writings over the past quarter century certainly could not have been surprised that the major element of the mastery-learning instructional strategy was the feedback-corrective component. Translated into everyday language the feedback-corrective component says that we should get information on how we're doing and make modifications if we find that we're not doing as well as we had expected or desired. As has been said, this theme runs through each of the articles in this section. Let us consider a sampling:

With respect to independent learners: "They develop skills in providing feedback to themselves in determining what they have learned well and what they need to do to improve their learning where they have learned less well" ("New Views," p. 137).

With respect to the essence of mastery learning: "Group instruction supplemented by frequent feedback and individualized help as each student needs it" ("New Views," p. 140).

With respect to new curricula: "New curricula are not acts of faith — they represent new hypotheses which should be empirically tested before they become part of the educational program" ("Role," p. 190).

With respect to curriculum development: "The third stage in curriculum development is essentially the problem of quality control and feedback of evidence to insure that the curriculum plans are being effectively realized" ("Role," p. 191).

With respect to operating procedures in mastery learning: "The operating procedures we have used are intended to provide detailed feedback to teachers and students and to provide specific supplementary instructional resources as needed" ("Learning for Mastery," p. 169).

With respect to instructional strategies: "It is hoped that each time a strategy is used, it will be studied to find where it is succeeding and where it is not. . . . Hopefully, the results in a particular year can take advantage of the experience accumulated over the previous years" ("Learning for Mastery," p. 172).

With respect to peak learning experiences: "The careful teacher will note which one of these efforts produces the intended effect and repeat it with another group" ("Peak," p. 199).

It is this emphasis on basing curricular and instructional decisions on empirical evidence that most clearly separates Bloom from many educational psychologists (who tend to use theory as a basis for decision making). Further, it is this emphasis on gathering and using evidence that threatens the "innocence" of educators. The papers in this section truly threaten one's innocence. What you, the reader, do once your innocence is threatened can have profound effects on the future of curriculum and instruction in our schools.

New Views of the Learner: Implications for Instruction and Curriculum

7

I f you can be moved to try these ideas with a few teachers in your school for even as short a period as three months, you can determine the validity and limits of these ideas where they really belong—in your classrooms and with your teachers and students. Even more important, I hope this conception of education and of the enormous potentials of our students and schools will inspire you and your teachers to strive toward a renewed and attainable dream of American education during the remainder of this century.

No other country in the world has succeeded in providing learning opportunities for its youth to the extent of the United States. We now have almost 80 percent of youth completing high school (in contrast with an average of about 33 percent in the other highly developed nations). Approximately 50 percent of our youth enter some form of higher education (in contrast with an average of 25 percent in the other highly developed nations of the world). In no other country has the level of financial support of the learners and the schools reached the level of the U.S. We now contribute about one-sixth of our Gross National Product to education when we count both the funds contributed to the support of the students and the support of the schools and colleges (National Center for Educational Statistics, 1976).

However, neither further opportunity for education nor increased financial support for education will do much to improve the education of each of our students. The answer does not lie in additional funds, new fads, or major and sweeping changes in the organization of our educational system. As I see it, the solution lies in our views about students and their learning. These views have grown out of our practices and they will not be changed until we alter these practices. When the changed practices succeed in promoting more effective learning, both teachers and students will change their views. It is these views and practices that are central in the following presentation.

NOTE: This paper was presented as a General Session address at the ASCD 1978 Annual Conference, San Francisco.

New Views About Learners

In my recent book, *Human Characteristics and School Learning* (Bloom, 1976), I have developed a theory of school learning that attempts to explain individual differences in school learning as well as to determine the ways in which such differences may be altered. The basic ideas in this book are not matters of abstract theory or faith. They depend on easily observed evidence readily obtainable in most of the classrooms of the world.

I find that many of the individual differences in school learning are man-made and accidental rather than fixed in the individual at the time of conception. My major conclusion is: "What any person in the world can learn, almost all persons can learn if provided with appropriate prior and current conditions of learning." However, I would qualify this by stating that there are some individuals with emotional and physical difficulties who are likely to prove to be exceptions to this generalization (perhaps 2 or 3 percent of the population). At the other extreme are 1 or 2 percent of individuals who learn in such unusually capable ways that they may be exceptions to the theory. At this stage of the work it applies most clearly to the middle 95 percent of a school population.

I will try to summarize some of the ideas in this book by relating them to three different constructs about students and their learning capabilities.

The first construct is that *there are good learners and there are poor learners.* When I began my career in the field of educational research and measurement, the prevailing view was that the normal distribution describes the quantitative differences in students' ability when measured by an intelligence test, an aptitude test, or an achievement test. Learning ability was regarded as a highly predictable characteristic and intelligence or aptitude tests were widely used to predict school achievement. It was also believed that good learners could learn the complex and abstract ideas in a school subject, while the poor learners could learn only the simplest and most concrete ideas.

Learning ability was regarded as a highly stable or permanent trait of the individual. Theoretically, at least, it was believed that it would remain stable throughout the life of the invididual. That is, learning differences found very early in the students' school career would be present not only throughout their school career, but also throughout the remainder of their lives. Evidence in support of this stability is found in longitudinal studies where the same students are repeatedly measured throughout their school career. For example, the correlation between measures of school achievement at grades 3 and 11 is about +.85, demonstrating that over this 8 year period the relative ranking of students in a class or school remains almost perfectly fixed.

If we fully accept this construct, there is little or nothing the schools can do about learning ability. Some have it while others lack it, and the causes are not to be found in the school. There are different views about the basic causes of differences in learning ability—the Lord, genetics, the home environment, or luck. To accept this construct is to believe that the task of the schools is to constantly weed out and eliminate the poorer learners while encouraging the better learners to get as much education as possible.

This construct is the basis for grading students, streaming practices, and selective systems of education. Most school systems in the world are based on it and school authorities, examining bodies, teachers, parents, and finally, the students themselves come to accept it. In most countries this construct influences guidance practices, the amount of education individual students get, and the careers and occupations made available to individuals. The results are reflected in an economic and social hierarchy in many countries.

The second construct is that *there are faster and there are slower learners.* In 1963, John Carroll (Carroll, 1963) presented a model of learning that postulated that learners differed in their rate of learning, and this rate could be predicted from an aptitude or intelligence test. While there was some ambiguity about the permanence or stability of rate of learning, this model was the basis for the idea that most learners could achieve equally high levels of learning in a school subject—if each student is provided with the time and help he or she needs, when it is needed.

This construct, as Carroll presented it, suggested that if all learners are given the same instruction in a subject and the same amount of time to learn it, the resulting scores on an achievement test over the subject will be normally distributed. If, however, the instruction and time are adapted to each student's needs, the achievement distribution will be highly skewed (most of the scores would pile up on the high end of the achievement measure). Under these conditions, the achievement scores at the end of the term cannot be predicted from an aptitude or intelligence test given at the beginning of the term.

However, the students are expected to need different amounts of time and help, with the slower students initially needing perhaps as much as five times the amount of time required by the faster students. The aptitude test, which no longer can predict the final achievement scores, does predict the amount of time each student needs to learn the subject to a high level.

Using the concept of mastery learning, my students and I sought to find ways by which the slower learners could be given the extra time and help they needed (outside of the regular classroom schedule). From this research, in both educational laboratories as well as classrooms, it has become evident that a large proportion of slower learners can learn to the same achievement level as the faster learners. When the slower learners do succeed in attaining the same criterion of achievement as the faster learners, they appear to be able to learn equally complex and abstract ideas, they can apply these ideas to new problems, and they can retain the ideas equally well, in spite of the fact that they learned with more time and help than was given to others. Furthermore, their interest and attitudes toward the subject in which they attain the achievement criterion are as positive as those of the faster learners.

Research on mastery learning has been done in many countries and at all levels of education including primary schools, secondary schools, junior colleges, four-year colleges, and advanced professional schools such as medicine, nursing, and engineering. Most of the different subject courses at each level have been shown to yield excellent results under mastery methods (Block, 1974; Block and Anderson, 1975; Bloom, 1971).

The typical result of the mastery learning studies in the schools is that about 80 percent of students in a mastery class reach the same final criterion of achievement (usually at the A or B+ level) as approximately the top 20 percent of the class under conventional group instruction. Much of this research contrasts a mastery group of students taught the same subject as a control group of students by the same teacher with as nearly as possible the same instructional methods and instructional material. The two groups of students are roughly equivalent in terms of previous levels of learning, aptitude, or intelligence measures.

As would follow from the Carroll model (Carroll, 1963), the achievement of the upper 20 percent of the control students is predictable from the aptitude tests, intelligence tests, or previous achievement tests; while the achievement of the upper 80 percent of the mastery students is not predictable from these earlier measures.

In general, the students in the mastery classes need about 10 percent to 15 percent more time than the students in the control classes—however, the extra time and help is used only by those students who need it. It should be pointed out that the control and mastery classes have the same schedule of instruction and that the corrective work of the students who need it in the mastery class is usually done outside of the classroom schedule.

One unexpected effect of this research is the extent to which the students in the mastery classes become cooperative in helping each other, while the control students become increasingly competitive. This could have been anticipated if we had recognized that under mastery learning all students may earn equally high grades if their achievement warrants it, while under control conditions there are scarce rewards— only a small percent may earn grades of A. Under the usual normal-curve grading conditions, if one student helps another in the learning process he or she may do so at his or her own expense. That is, one student can earn a high grade only at the expense of other students receiving lower grades.

Mastery learning is one of several teaching-learning strategies that can succeed in bringing a large proportion of students to a high level of achievement and to high motivation for further learning. Fast and slow students become equal in achievement and affect if given the extra time and help when they need it. This approach challenges our grading, streaming, and selection systems, it forces curriculum workers to ask new questions about what is worth learning well, and it threatens some societies with more able and highly motivated students than they may know how to deal with.

During the past decade, my students and I have done research that has led us to a third construct. *Most students become very similar with regard to learning ability, rate of learning, and motivation for further learning when provided with favorable learning conditions.* This research questions the first two constructs, especially about the necessary permanence of such traits as good-poor learning ability or fast-slow learning characteristics. However, the research does demonstrate that when students are provided with unfavorable learning conditions, they become even more dissimilar with regard to learning ability, rate of learning, and motivation for further learning.

The book provides theoretical support for this construct and brings together some of the contrasts between favorable and less favorable conditions of learning. However, direct evidence for this third construct can be derived from the many mastery learning studies that contrast the learning of two comparable groups of students under *more* and *less* favorable conditions of learning.

Under favorable learning conditions, the level of learning of students tends to rise over a series of learning tasks. In the mastery-learning studies, we typically find that on the first learning task of a new series the mastery and control classes do equally well. However, the mastery group tends to improve in learning on each subsequent learning task, while the control group of students tends to remain the same or decline over the subsequent learning tasks. The comparison of the results on the early and later learning tasks in a series demonstrates that two groups of students who were very similar at the beginning become very different in their levels of learning as well as in their affective qualities. These differences are most dramatically reflected in the final cognitive and affective measures. These differences are also reflected in the learning of subsequent related courses. Students who have learned the first course in a subject to a high level (by mastery or other procedures) tend to learn the subsequent courses in the same subject to a high level with less and less in the way of extra time or help needed.

We have already mentioned the variation in rate of learning for students at the beginning of a series of tasks as approximately five to one. That is, some students may take as much as five times as much time to learn a particular learning task as do others. In the mastery-learning studies where the same students are followed over a series of learning tasks, we find that the students who are given feedback and corrective individualized help as they need it do become more and more similar in their learning rates. Under such favorable learning conditions, students become more and more similar in their learning rate until the difference between fast and slow learners becomes very difficult to measure except by the most exact measurements of time.

This third construct, then, takes the position that learning characteristics such as good-poor and fast-slow are alterable by appropriate school conditions. The research demonstrates that under appropriate conditions almost all can learn whatever the schools have to teach. It indicates that special and very favorable conditions may be needed at some stages of the learning, but that over time these may be gradually discarded.

It is this research that underlies the theory of school learning developed in the book. This research calls into question some of the prevailing views about human nature, human characteristics, and school learning. Evidence in support of this third construct has far-reaching implications for the training of teachers, instruction in the classroom, the organization of systems of school and college education at the local and national level, selection systems, grading procedures, and the development of new curriculum and instructional systems.

Implications for Students

Favorable learning conditions have profound effects on student learning, student attitudes and interests, and student self-view and mental
health. These topics are treated briefly in the following pages.

1. Increased Learning Effectiveness of Students

The use of mastery learning and related teaching-learning strategies at
all levels of education from the primary school to the graduate and
professional schools typically results in about four-fifths of students
achieving at the same level as the upper one-fifth of students typically
taught by the same teacher. Not only do these students evidence high
levels of cognitive achievement on the tests used for grading purposes,
they also do very well on measures of retention and higher mental
processes when compared to the top one-fifth of the control group of
students. Furthermore, almost all of the mastery-learning students, who
make use of the corrective procedures, achieve above the average of the
control students (Block and Burns, 1976; Bloom, 1976).

If the mastery-learning procedures are utilized in the introductory
courses in a subject field (arithmetic, science, reading, mathematics,
social studies, second language, and so on), the students tend to maintain these new learning approaches in subsequent courses in the same
field with less and less need for further special help or extra time.

Since the cost of mastery learning for the students who need it is about
10 to 15 percent more time spent in learning the subject, it is a relatively
small cost for the individual student. This is especially true when the
student needs less and less corrective work and time as the course or
subsequent courses proceed.

If mastery learning is used on a wide scale (that is, in the major
academic courses or subjects), students appear to show major gains in
that elusive quality termed "learning to learn." The students devote
more of their classroom time to active learning, and they appear to be
enjoying the learning. They develop skill in providing feedback to
themselves in determining what they have learned well and what they
need to do to improve their learning where they have learned less well.
They become skillful in seeking answers and securing help from books,
friends, and teachers where they need to overcome special and detailed
learning difficulties in a subject.

Whether or not we wish to provide such approaches at all levels of
education, it is clear that providing favorable learning conditions should

be almost mandatory at the primary school level. Since the student is legally required to attend school for at least ten years, effective learning in the first three or four school grades is the very least the schools can do to ensure that the remaining six or seven years of school attendance are not dismal learning experiences for a sizeable proportion of students.

However, at least three-fourths of the students in the schools are no longer in these early primary grades. We find that students are prepared to learn in a new way at each new school level—primary grades, junior high school, and high school. The students tend to believe that a new school situation is one in which they can start afresh—no matter how poorly they did before. This new set of expectations enables the mastery learning procedures to work much better than we had anticipated when they are introduced at the beginning of the primary school, the beginning of the junior high school, or at the beginning of the high school.

In summary, if favorable learning conditions are provided at the beginning of new subjects or new school situations, less and less need will be found for these procedures in subsequent courses in a subject—although the new learning abilities may need to be supported to some extent in these later subjects or terms until they are strong enough to be self maintaining.

2. Confidence of Students in Their Learning Capabilities

Repeated evidence of success in learning is likely to lead to a greater interest in the learning and improvements in the student's self-concept as a learner. School learning becomes more attractive and the student has fewer problems of distractability. With the improvement of achievement, students find that the external rewards for good learning—good grades—are very satisfying. However, even more important is that the students find more intrinsic rewards in the learning itself.

Everyone has difficulties in learning. Students with little confidence in their ability to learn are unlikely to persevere very long in any efforts to solve the difficulties. Increased confidence in the self enables the student to secure the necessary energy and motivation to find solutions where otherwise he or she would give up very quickly.

Schools provide a very demanding set of situations for almost all students. If school learning is or can be made to be effective and successful, the student gains confidence in his or her own ability to cope with the school demands. As the student gains this confidence, his or her self-concept as a learner improves and success at one level of schooling almost assures success at a subsequent level of schooling. This, in turn, further increases one's self-confidence (Bloom, 1976; Kifer, 1973).

3. Improvements in Mental Health of Students

Evidence is accumulating that repeated success in school over a number of years (especially at the primary school level) appears to increase the likelihood that an individual can withstand stress and anxiety more effectively than individuals who have a history of repeated failure or low marks in school. To put it bluntly, repeated success in coping with the academic demands of the school appears to confer upon a high proportion of such students a type of immunization against emotional illness. Similarly, repeated failure in coping with the demands of the school appears to be one source of emotional difficulties and mental illness. Thus, while this research is beginning to draw parallels between immunization against physical diseases, such as polio or smallpox, and immunization against emotional diseases, it is also helping us to understand how schools may actually infect children with emotional difficulties (Dolan, 1978; Stringer and Glidewell, 1967; Torshen, 1969).

Associated with some of this research is the finding that most of the positive or negative emotional consequences are associated with teachers' marks and judgments rather than with the results of standardized achievement tests. Perhaps the explanation has to do with the fact that most of the evidence of success or failure in the schools is in terms of teachers' marks and judgments which the students receive daily. Standardized tests are given rarely and with little interpretation to students or parents. It is the perception of how well one is doing day after day relative to one's classmates that appears to be a key link between school achievement and its personality effects.

Research on the relations between school achievement and mental health is far from complete or satisfactory. I believe that when it is more fully established, it will have powerful effects on how we run our schools, mark our students, and even teach them. It will surely lead to a more complex view of education and our responsibilities for both the learning of our students and the more basic personality consequences of this learning.

Implications for Teachers and Instruction

1. Equality of Opportunity To Learn

Each teacher consciously strives to provide equal learning opportunities for all students in the class. However, the actual situation under group instruction is far from this ideal. Observations of teacher interactions with students in the classroom demonstrate that teachers (quite unconsciously) direct their teaching and explanation to some students and ignore others. They give much positive reinforcement and encouragement to some students but not to others, and they encourage active participation in the classroom discussion and question-and-answer periods from some students and discourage it from others. Typically, the students in the top third or fourth of the class are given the greatest attention and encouragement by teachers, while the students in the bottom half of the class receive the least attention and support. These differences in the interaction between teachers and students provide some students with much greater opportunities and encouragement for learning than is provided other students (Brophy and Good, 1970).

Teachers need to find ways of securing a more accurate picture of the extent to which their ideal of equal opportunity for learning is negated by their own teaching methods and styles of interaction in the classroom. Teachers need help if they are to provide favorable learning conditions for most of their students—rather than just for the top third or fourth of students. They need to be helped in developing methods of teaching that will result in a more effective realization of their own ideal of equal learning opportunities for all.

2. Feedback and Corrective Help

Group instruction produces errors in learning at each stage of a course or school term—no matter how effective the teacher is. These errors in learning are compounded with later learning errors. The errors resulting from this system of group instruction determine each student's final achievement, and only rarely is the individual able to recover fully from them.

A major thesis of my book is that a system of feedback to teachers and students can reveal the errors in learning shortly after they occur. And, if appropriate correctives are introduced as needed, the instruction can be self-correcting so that the learning errors made at one time can be corrected before they are compounded with later learning errors.

This is the essence of mastery learning strategies: *group instruction* supplemented by frequent *feedback and individualized help* as each student needs it. The *group instruction* is the same as the regular instruction presently provided by the teacher. The *feedback* is usually in the form of brief, diagnostic, formative tests, which indicate what each student has learned and what he or she still needs to learn before the learning task has been mastered. These are used at the end of each week or two of instruction.

The *individualized help* is provided to enable each student to learn the important points he or she has missed. This help may be provided by an aide, by other students, by the home, or by referring the student to the appropriate places in the instructional material. When this is done well, most students can be brought to mastery of each learning task.

When this process of group instruction, supplemented by feedback and individualized correctives, is used for each learning task, we find that almost all students gradually become similar in their learning effectiveness and in their interest and motivation for further learning. For most students, the extra time and help (in the classroom or outside) needed at the end of each two-week period is typically only an hour or so.

Since so little extra time and help are needed to bring most students to mastery the overall implication is that teachers have been doing a far better job of teaching than is usually demonstrated on the achievement tests given at the end of the term. If students start each new learning task with the prerequisite knowledge and skills, they gradually need less and less additional corrective time and help. The major change for teachers is that they do less in the way of judging and grading students on what they had learned by a particular date and do more to see to it that each student learns what he or she needs as preparation for the next learning task.

Mastery-learning techniques ensure that students have the necessary knowledge and skills for each new learning task and that they have confidence that they can learn each new task, since they have mastered the previous one. Over a period of time, students develop a positive view of their own learning capabilities. They become more active and involved in the learning process, and they participate more fully in the classroom interaction. Under these conditions equal opportunity for learning does become a reality in the classroom for most students.

3. Teacher Belief in the Learning Capabilities of the Students

Teachers begin a new term or course with the view that some of the students will learn well, some will learn very poorly, and some will learn only moderately well. Usually, by the end of the first month of the term the teachers have sorted their students into some such categories as these, and it is quite likely that this sorting process will remain much the same throughout the term or course. The teacher is very effective in conveying these categories to students through relatively subtle techniques in the interaction that takes place during the course or term.

Teachers rarely expect most of the students to learn well—and the students come to accept the teacher's view of them and their learning capabilities.

Research findings, lectures, and injunctions to teachers to have greater faith in the learning potential of their students are not very effective. Each teacher can and will change his or her belief in the learning capabilities of each student only by discovering this in the classroom.

In our work on mastery learning in the schools, we have insisted that teachers compare student learning under the mastery condition with learning under conventional procedures in a control class. The teachers using the mastery learning procedures find that the majority of students become very successful in their learning. Most teachers note the differences in student learning between the mastery and control class within the first four or six weeks—others may take longer to discover this. As one teacher put it, "My classroom suddenly became overpopulated with good students."

It is of interest to note that teachers who have found mastery-learning procedures effective continue to use such procedures thereafter on their own—without administrative urging. Also, such teachers refuse to use control classes (their conventional procedures) thereafter, even if it is suggested as a basis for further study about the process. They view the request to continue using control procedures as immoral or indecent—would you deny the use of a health-giving drug like penicillin to those who need it just for research purposes?

4. No Teacher Can Provide the Supplementary Help Needed by Each Student—Other Allies Are Needed

Teachers frequently feel isolated from all support in their job of teaching 30 or more students. And no teacher can provide the supplementary help each student needs, even if it is only an hour or so for each student every week or two. There just aren't that many extra hours of teacher time. Where teachers have tried to provide each student with all the individualized help, it required so much extra time and patience that the teachers, who got excellent results, refused to use mastery learning procedures thereafter.

The major point brought out in *Human Characteristics and School Learning* is that, while the teacher is responsible for group instruction, there are many allies to provide the supplementary help that almost all children need at one time or another. The use of peer tutoring (S. Bloom, 1976), the use of aides, the use of supplementary instructional material, and encouraging the students to do the necessary corrective work on their own or in small groups may all be used by the teacher to provide favorable learning conditions in the school for all the children (Bloom, 1976).

The home also can be a major ally of the teacher and the school—if teachers wish this to be true. This may involve periodic meetings of parents and teachers, detailed reports on the children's progress, reminders to parents about the support and encouragement each child needs, and suggestions to parents about help on specific learning tasks when the child needs it. Favorable learning conditions in both the school and home can provide almost ideal conditions for good learning (Dave, 1963; Marjoribanks, 1974; Wolf, 1966).

Implications for the Curriculum

Our building blocks for the curriculum have remained relatively constant over the past seventy years—so many years of arithmetic, so many courses in reading, literature, science, social studies, mathematics, and so on. Although the content of these curriculum building-blocks may change from time to time, we rarely entertain new notions about what the total curriculum should be. These courses were originally constructed with the view that only a fraction of students would learn them well, while most of the remaining students were expected to drop out of the schools at various ages or grades. We have held on to the view that only a fraction of students will learn them well, but no longer do our students drop out, most of them now complete high school.

Now we have to confront the possibility that almost all of the students can learn well whatever the schools have to teach. But what is worth learning well? Our immediate answer is likely to be the basic tool subjects such as reading, writing, and arithmetic. Even if we do agree on this, is there anything more on our list? Is it imperative that anything else should be learned well? If so, what should it be and who should learn it—all or only some students?

What is worth learning well will change for each society and for each individual over time. While no one can provide a complete list, some perspective on this can be secured from the work of some of the national curriculum centers in different parts of the world. Although conditions vary and each curriculum center strives to answer these questions from its own point of view, I will stress what I believe to be some of the more positive and general approaches to this question.

Who is responsible for the planning of the entire curriculum? In most countries, this is believed to be a cooperative task involving teachers, scholars, educational planners, citizens, various national groups, and a great variety of specialist groups. Curriculum centers are charged with the responsibility for developing the overall curriculum (including plans and instructional materials) with the aid and assistance of many subgroups in the society. The centers recognize that the curriculum must be continually modified and brought up to date with the changing conditions in the society, with the changing aspirations of both the society and the learners, and with long-term views about the central role that education plays in the life of the society and the people. The curriculum centers have learned, after much frustration, that no major curriculum change can be effectively introduced in the schools until many groups in the society have had some opportunity to understand the changes and express their views about these changes. Each center is charged with the task of tryout of the curriculum and systematic evaluation of the proposed curriculum changes to make sure that they work well before they are to be used on a national scale.

Each of the centers is concerned with the integration and sequence among the parts of the entire curriculum. However, they do recognize that local conditions may call for special alterations in the curriculum. They designate some portion of the curriculum that is basic and should be emphasized by all teachers, and they indicate which portions of the curriculum may be optional or adapted to meet local conditions. While teacher groups have considerable voice in the original planning and development of the curriculum, each teacher is not expected to be a curriculum expert who can make his or her own curriculum. Each teacher is given some voice in adaptations to fit local conditions and to add specific features within given limitations. In-service training for the new curriculum is provided the teachers. This in-service training includes the new subject matter of the curriculum as well as new teaching strategies to ensure that all students will learn well.

Contrast this with our own views of each school or teacher being given considerable freedom to determine which of several textbooks or curricular packages to use. In spite of this freedom, ours is a system dominated by a small number of publishers who provide the textbooks and instructional materials used by the majority of teachers. In most subjects, three or four textbooks or series account for 75 percent or more of the classrooms in that subject. When we examine these three or four textbooks, they are as alike as "peas in a pod." While we appear to have many choices, in fact we make few major curriculum decisions.

Contrast this also with the work of publishers or curriculum projects in which each part of the curriculum is developed separately without reference to the relations among the parts. Little careful work is done in the U.S. about integration or sequence of learning experiences for a given group of students. Each subject is thought of as having little or no relation to other parts of the curriculum. And almost no concern is expressed in our published textbooks about local conditions and circumstances. Also, there is little or no concern for revision of the curriculum over time—except to introduce features that will "sell well" or that reflect our current fads.

This method of curriculum planning in the United States rarely looks to see what is happening in the other educational agencies of the country —home, church, peer group, mass media, museums, and so on. In some other countries, there is a careful appraisal of these other agencies, and the school curriculum is planned as one part of a larger educational system.

In general, I believe our curriculum making and our curriculum choices are disastrously behind the times. We have much to learn about ways of improving these processes. Perhaps a small start might be a series of trips to look into the processes elsewhere. What can we learn from our own successes and failures in curriculum development, and what can we learn from the work in other countries?

But, so much for structure and curriculum planning. What is worth learning well in some of these national curriculum centers in other countries? I will confine my remarks to a few special groups of ideas that I believe to be important and that appear to me to be more emphasized in the schools of other countries than in our own.

1. Higher Mental Processes

While there is much of rote learning in many countries of the world, in some curriculum centers I find great emphasis on problem solving, application of principles, analytical skills, and creativity. Such higher mental processes are emphasized because the centers believe that this type of learning enables the individual to relate his or her learning to the many problems he or she encounters in day-to-day living. These abilities are stressed because they are retained and utilized long after the individual has forgotten the detailed specifics of the subject matter taught in the schools. These abilities are regarded as one set of essential characteristics needed to continue learning and to cope with a rapidly changing world. Some centers believe that these higher mental processes are important because they make learning exciting and constantly new and playful.

In these countries, subjects are taught as methods of inquiry into the nature of science, mathematics, the arts, and the social studies. The subjects are taught as much for the ways of thinking they represent as for their traditional content. Much of this learning makes use of observations, reflections on these observations, experimentation with phenomena, and the use of firsthand data and daily experiences as well as the use of primary printed sources. All of this is reflected in the materials of instruction, the learning and teaching processes used, and the questions and problems used in the formative testing as well as on the final examinations.

In sharp contrast, we make use of textbooks that rarely pose real problems. Our textbooks emphasize specific content to be remembered and give students little opportunity to discover underlying concepts and principles and even less opportunity to attack real problems in the environments in which they live. Our teacher-made tests (and standardized tests) are largely tests of remembered knowledge. After the sale of over one million copies of the *Cognitive Taxonomy of Educational Objectives* (Bloom, et al., 1956) and 20 years of use of this domain in preservice and in-service teacher training, over 95 percent of test questions that our students are expected to answer deal with little more than information. Our instructional material, our classroom teaching methods, and our testing methods rarely rise above the lowest category of the taxonomy—knowledge.

You as supervisors of teachers and as curriculum makers have great responsibility for helping teachers provide higher mental process learning experiences for all students. Do not accept the prevailing view that such processes can be developed only in the minority of students with unusually high intelligence and aptitude scores. Research has demonstrated that almost all students can attain very high levels of cognitive abilities if these are stressed in the teaching, in the instructional materials, and in the testing procedures used in the schools.

2. The Arts

In many countries of the world music, dance, poetry, painting, and the other arts are a central part of the curriculum at each stage of schooling. All students are regularly and systematically helped to develop a strong interest, enjoyment, as well as considerable competence in some of these humanistic arts. The curriculum and instruction in these fields move from simple interest and appreciation of these works to the development of a high degree of skill in performing and even creating such works. The underlying thesis appears to be that such interests and competence are essential to the good life for all.

In our schools, it is usually believed that everyone should be introduced to the arts, but that only a small percentage of students have the aptitudes or special qualities needed to develop competence in one or more of the arts. Furthermore, we tend to regard the arts as special frills or luxuries to be encouraged when the schools have extra funds, but to be put aside when the funds are needed for other areas of the schools. Even when we find a place for the arts in the schools, the amount of time and emphasis given is only a fraction of that devoted to the "more important" parts of the curriculum.

In a society dominated by TV and where satisfactions are primarily centered on material possessions and comforts, the arts can provide a basis for an alternative life style that is more than a luxury. Our schools must search more seriously for ways in which the arts may provide one source of comfort, satisfaction, and enjoyment for all—both during the learning process and throughout life.

3. Social Interaction

In many countries of the world, social processes among students are highly emphasized. The school (much smaller than ours) and the classroom (much larger than ours) are regarded as a special environment in which students learn that they are part of an extended family. They are expected to care for each other, to help each other, and to cooperate with each other in the learning process. The students assume responsibilities for each other in supporting, caring, sharing, and respecting each other. Learning goes on among and between students.

In contrast, our schools and classrooms emphasize competition for grades, teacher attention, and whatever other scarce rewards are believed to be available. Our teachers devote so much time to controlling, teaching, and judging students that our students are given little opportunity for either independence or the assumption of responsibilities for each other. Our schools are rather lonely places for many students, even though they are surrounded by so many other students.

Rarely do our teachers, students, and school authorities develop a school code of behavior that is consistent from year to year and from classroom to classroom. As a result, our teachers devote more time and attention to discipline and managing classroom behavior than appears to be the case in many other countries of the world.

There is a latent curriculum in each country that is reflected in the interactions between teachers and students, and between students and students. The latent curriculum is implicit in what we do (rather than what we say) in the school and it is probably better learned and longer remembered than the explicit objectives of the manifest curriculum. In our schools, this latent curriculum emphasizes punctuality, neatness, docility, and competition (Dreeben, 1968; Henry, 1965; Overly, 1970).

You as leaders in your schools must ask yourself whether these are the major qualities that your school now does and should emphasize. Are these the central qualities for the citizens of a democracy like ours? Until you and your teachers face these problems more directly, the latent curriculum will emphasize only the qualities teachers regard as important in managing the students. The central goals of the latent curriculum (as well as for the manifest curriculum) should be concerned with the learning of students. Social interactions and social qualities should be included among the major objectives and learning in your schools.

4. Continuing Learning

Throughout the world, the instruction and curriculum in the schools is being studied to determine its long-term contribution to continuing learning throughout life. The Edgar Faure (UNESCO) report "Learning To Be" has had great influence on this thinking. The Faure report (Faure, 1972) stresses the many changes taking place in all societies and the difficulties individuals have in adjusting to rapid change in the society, in their work, and in their lives. Since, the report continues, it is virtually impossible to anticipate and plan for the changes that will take place, the only adaptive mechanism people have to adjust to and cope with these changes is their ability and interest in continuing learning throughout life.

If schools weaken or destroy this potential for further learning, the individual will lose the basic tools for adapting to rapid change, and there will be serious negative consequences for the individual and the society. The schools, from this point of view, must develop a strong positive interest in learning and some of the basic skills in "learning to learn." These include skills in the use of libraries, skills in independent learning from books and "real" situations, and skills in developing knowledge and learning from a variety of sources, including other persons. It also includes the development of many of the problem-solving skills stressed under the higher mental processes in an earlier section of this paper.

There is considerable evidence from adult education studies in this country that we do much to develop these continuing learning attitudes and skills in our "best" students. However, it is likely that for a sizeable proportion of our students, schooling and further learning (in or out of the schools) is painful or dull and to be avoided as soon as one has reached school-leaving age or has completed high school or college. Only rarely do we look at the curriculum in terms of what it is likely to contribute to continuing learning for all students. Nor do we deliberately search for methods of teaching and learning likely to enhance the individual's skills in "learning to learn." We tend to believe that some students have the ability to learn while others lack it, and we do not regard it as a major goal of the schools to develop learning ability.

We, who are responsible for the learning of our students for a ten- to sixteen-year period, must extend our sights beyond the period that our students are in the schools or colleges. Until we do this and until it becomes a part of our curriculum planning, we will neglect those objectives of education that relate to the entire life of the individual. It is the long-term objectives of education that will give new meaning to what we do in the schools.

5. *Peak Learning Experiences*
In a number of curriculum centers, there is considerable thought given to providing a small number of memorable learning experiences that will serve to highlight some of the crucial ideas taught in the schools. These centers have been stimulated by A. H. Maslow's descriptions of peak experiences and the qualities such experiences are reported to possess (Maslow, 1959). Peak learning experiences (which share some of the qualities contained in Peak Experiences) tend to be so vivid that students recall them in great detail many years later (Bloom, 1966). Such experiences form landmarks in the student's later school recollections. They were, typically, the source of new interests in a subject, the stimulus to major attitude and value changes, and they serve to make school learning truly exciting.

The research done on this subject finds that peak learning experiences are typically very rare, and only a few students can report or recall such experiences after twelve to sixteen years of school attendance. The curriculum centers believe that in each school subject there should be a small number of such peak experiences for most of the students, and they are developing ways in which this can be realized. They are attempting to relate such experiences to major new ideas or concepts, the most important principles and generalizations in the subject, and also to some of the truly great works of literature, music, and the arts. The centers believe that such dramatic and vivid learning can be experienced by the majority of students if they are deliberately introduced as moments of great insight, discovery, awareness, vast implications, beauty, and truth. They are trying to secure such dramatic intensity by the use of specially constructed television or film units to be used at selected points in the course. They are also providing suggestions to the teachers about how selected ideas or materials in a subject can lend themselves to the creation of peak learning experiences.

Peak learning experiences are important because they uniquely combine cognitive and affective components of learning. They indicate what learning might become if only all elements in education are brought to their highest level.

I mention these, not because the centers are finding it easy to do. It represents an attempt to help students find some aspects of school to be fulfilling, moments of great insight, filled with wonder and awe, and exhilaration. School work is typically regarded by students as just that —work. Much of school learning is seen by students (and some teachers) as drab things to do simply because someone in authority has required it. Students come to view school as little more than meaningless drudgery—at least in contrast to television and the excitement they find outside of the school.

I am sure that students in our schools do have occasional peak learning experiences—but they are rare indeed. Our students tend to seek these memorable experiences outside the classroom in sports, social events, and even in illegal and violent activities. Perhaps we too may learn how learning in the schools can be vivid and one source of fulfillment for most of the students in our schools.

References

J. H. Block, editor. *Schools, Society, and Mastery Learning.* New York: Holt, Rinehart and Winston, 1974.

J. H. Block and L. W. Anderson. *Mastery Learning in Classroom Instruction.* New York: Macmillan Publishing Co., Inc., 1975.

J. Block and R. B. Burns. "Mastery Learning." See: L. S. Shulman, editor. *Review of Research in Education* 4. Itasca, Illinois: F. E. Peacock Publishers, 1976.

B. S. Bloom, editor. *Taxonomy of Educational Objectives: Cognitive Domain.* New York: David McKay Co., 1956.

B. S. Bloom. "Peak Learning Experiences." See: M. Provus, editor. *Innovations For Time to Teach.* Washington, D.C.: National Education Association, 1966.

B. S. Bloom. "Learning for Mastery." Chapter 3 in B. S. Bloom, J. T. Hastings and G.

F. Madaus. *Handbook on Formative and Summative Evaluation of Student Learning.* New York: McGraw-Hill Book Company, 1971.

B. S. Bloom. *Human Characteristics and School Learning.* New York: McGraw-Hill Book Company, 1976.

S. Bloom. *Peer and Cross-Age Tutoring in the Schools.* Washington, D.C.: National Institute of Education, 1976.

J. E. Brophy and T. L. Good. "Teachers' Communication of Differential Expectations for Children's Class Room Performance: Some Behavioral Data." *Journal of Educational Psychology* 61:365–74; 1970.

J. B. Carroll. "A Model of School Learning." *Teachers College Record* 64: 723–33; 1963.

R. H. Dave. "The Identification and Measurement of Environmental Process Variables That Are Related to Educational Achievement." Unpublished doctoral dissertation, University of Chicago, 1963.

L. Dolan. "The Affective Consequences of Home Support, Instructional Quality, and Achievement." Unpublished doctoral dissertation. University of Chicago, 1980.

R. Dreeben. *On What Is Learned in School.* Reading, Massachusetts: Addison-Wesley Publishing Co., 1968.

E. Faure, *et al. Learning To Be.* Paris: UNESCO; London: Harrap, 1972.

J. Henry. *Culture Against Man.* New York: Random House, 1965.

E. Kifer. "The Effects of School Achievement on the Affective Traits of the Learner." Unpublished doctoral dissertation, University of Chicago, 1973.

K. Marjoribanks, editor. *Environments for Learning.* London: National Foundation for Educational Research Publishing Company, Ltd., 1974.

A. H. Maslow. "Cognition of Being in the Peak Experiences." *Journal of Genetic Psychology* 94:43–66; March 1959.

National Center for Education Statistics. *The Condition of Education.* Washington, D.C.: U.S. Government Printing Office, 1976.

N. V. Overly, editor. *The Unstudied Curriculum.* Washington, D.C.: Association for Supervision and Curriculum Development, 1970.

L. A. Stringer and J. C. Glidewell. *Early Detection of Emotional Illnesses in School Children: Final Report.* Missouri: St. Louis County Health Department, 1967.

K. Torshen. "The Relation of Classroom Evaluation to Students' Self-concepts and Mental Health." Unpublished doctoral dissertation, University of Chicago, 1969.

R. Wolf. "The Measurement of Environments." See: A. Anastasi, editor. *Testing Problems in Perspective.* Washington, D.C.: American Council on Education, 1966.

Learning for Mastery

8

Each teacher begins a new term (or course) with the expectation that about a third of his students will adequately learn what he has to teach. He expects about a third of his students to fail or to just "get by." Finally, he expects another third to learn a good deal of what he has to teach, but not enough to be regarded as "good students." This set of expectations, supported by school policies and practices in grading, becomes transmitted to the students through the grading procedures and through the methods and materials of instruction. The system creates a self-fulfilling prophecy such that the final sorting of students through the grading process becomes approximately equivalent to the original expectations.

This set of expectations, which fixes the academic goals of teachers and students, is the most wasteful and destructive aspect of the present educational system. It reduces the aspirations of both teachers and students; it reduces motivation for learning in students; and it systematically destroys the ego and self-concept of a sizable group of students who are legally required to attend school for ten to twelve years under conditions which are frustrating and humiliating year after year. The cost of this system in reducing opportunities for further learning and in alienating youth from both school and society is so great that no society can tolerate it for long.

Most students (perhaps over 90 percent) can master what we have to teach them, and it is the task of instruction to find the means which will enable our students to master the subject under consideration. Our basic task is to determine what we mean by mastery of the subject and to search for the methods and materials which will enable the largest proportion of our students to attain such mastery.

In this paper we will consider one approach to learning for mastery and the underlying theoretical concepts, research findings, and techniques required. Basically, the problem of developing a strategy for mastery learning is one of determining how individual differences in learners can be related to the learning and teaching process.

Background

Some societies can utilize only a small number of highly educated persons in the economy and can provide the economic support for only a small proportion of the students to complete secondary or higher education. Under such conditions much of the effort of the schools and the external examining system is to find ways of rejecting the majority of students at various points in the educational system and to discover the talented few who are to be given advanced educational opportunities. Such societies invest a great deal more in the prediction and selection of talent than in the development of such talent.

The complexities of the skills required by the work force in the United States and in other highly developed nations means that we can no longer operate on the assumption that completion of secondary and advanced education is for the few. The increasing evidence (Schultz, 1963; Bowman, 1966) that investment in the education of humans pays off at a greater rate than does capital investment suggests that we cannot return to an economy of scarcity of educational opportunity.

Whatever might have been the case previously, highly developed nations must seek to find ways to increase the proportion of the age group that can successfully complete both secondary and higher education. The problem is no longer one of finding the few who can succeed. The basic problem is to determine how the largest proportion of the age group can learn effectively those skills and subject matter regarded as essential for their own development in a complex society.

However, given another set of philosophic and psychological presuppositions, we may express our concern for the intellectual and personality consequences of lack of clear success in the learning tasks of the school. Increasingly, learning throughout life (continuing learning) will be necessary for the largest proportion of the work force. If school learning is regarded as frustrating and even impossible by a sizable proportion of students, then little can be done at later levels to kindle a genuine interest in further learning. School learning must be successful and rewarding as one basis for insuring that learning can continue throughout one's life as needed.

Even more important in modern society is the malaise about values. As the secular society becomes more and more central, the values remaining for the individual have to do with hedonism, interpersonal relations, self-development, and ideas. If the schools frustrate the students in the latter two areas, only the first two are available to the individual. Whatever the case may be for each of these values, the schools must strive to assure all students of successful learning experiences in the realm of ideas and self-development.

There is little question that the schools now do provide successful learning experiences for some students—perhaps as high as one-third of the students. If the schools are to provide successful and satisfying learning experiences for at least 90 percent of the students, major changes must take place in the attitudes of students, teachers, and administrators; changes must also take place in teaching strategies and in the role of evaluation.

The Normal Curve

We have for so long used the normal curve in grading students that we have come to believe in it. Our achievement measures are designed to detect differences among our learners, even if the differences are trivial in terms of the subject matter. We then distribute our grades in a normal fashion. In any group of students we expect to have some small percent receive A grades. We are surprised when the percentage differs greatly from about 10 percent. We are also prepared to fail an equal proportion of students. Quite frequently this failure is determined by the rank order of the students in the group rather than by their failure to grasp the essential ideas of the course. Thus, we have become accustomed to classify students into about five categories of level of performance and to assign grades in some relative fashion. It matters not that the failures of one year performed at about the same level as the C students of another year. Nor does it matter that the A students of one school do about as well as the F students of another school.

Having become "conditioned" to the normal distribution, we set grade policies in these terms and are horrified when some teacher attempts to recommend a very different distribution of grades. Administrators are constantly on the alert to control teachers who are "too easy" or "too hard" in their grading. A teacher whose grade distribution is normal will avoid difficulties with administrators. But even more important, we find ways of convincing students that they can only do C work or D work by our grading system and even by our system of quiz and progress testing. Finally, we proceed in our teaching as though only the minority of our students should be able to learn what we have to teach.

There is nothing sacred about the normal curve. It is the distribution most appropriate to chance and random activity. Education is a purposeful activity and we seek to have the students learn what we have to teach. If we are effective in our instruction, the distribution of achievement should be very different from the normal curve. In fact, we may even insist that our educational efforts have been unsuccessful to the extent to which our distribution of achievement approximates the normal distribution.

"Individual differences" in learners is a fact that can be demonstrated in many ways. That our students vary in many ways can never be forgotten. That these variations must be reflected in learning standards and achievement criteria is more a reflection of our policies and practices rather than the necessities of the case. Our basic task in education is to find strategies which will take individual differences into consideration but which will do so in such a way as to promote the fullest development of the individual.

The Variables for Mastery Learning Strategies

A learning strategy for mastery may be derived from the work of Carroll (1963), supported by the ideas of Morrison (1926), Bruner (1966), Skinner (1954), Suppes (1966), Goodlad and Anderson (1959), and Glaser (1968). In presenting these ideas we will refer to some of the research findings which bear on them. However, our main concern here is with the major variables in a model of school learning and the ways in which these variables may be utilized in a strategy for mastery learning.

Put in its most brief form the model proposed by Carroll (1963) makes it clear that if the students are normally distributed with respect to *aptitude* for some subject (mathematics, science, literature, history, etc.) and all the students are provided with exactly the same instruction (same in terms of amount of instruction, quality of instruction, and time available for learning), the end result will be a normal distribution on an appropriate measure of achievement. Furthermore, the relationship between aptitude and achievement will be relatively high (correlations of +.70 or higher are to be expected if the aptitude and achievement measures are valid and reliable). Conversely, if the students are normally distributed with respect to aptitude, but the kind and quality of instruction and the amount of time available for learning are made appropriate to the characteristics and needs of *each* student, the majority of students may be expected to achieve mastery of the subject. And, the relationship between aptitude and achievement should approach zero. It is this basic set of ideas we wish to develop in the following.

1. Aptitude for Particular Kinds of Learning
We have come to recognize that individuals do differ in their aptitudes for particular kinds of learning and over the years we have developed a large number of aptitude tests to measure these differences. In study after study we have found that aptitude tests are relatively good predictors of achievment criteria (achievement tests or teacher judgments).

Thus, a good set of mathematic aptitude tests given at the beginning of the year will correlate as high as $+.70$ with the mathematics achievement tests given at the end of the course in algebra, or some other mathematics subject.

The use of aptitude tests for predictive purposes and the high correlations between such tests and achievement criteria have led many of us to the view that high levels of achievement are possible only for the most able students. From this, it is an easy step to some notion of a causal connection between aptitude and achievement. The simplest notion of causality is that the students with high levels of aptitude can learn the complex ideas of the subject while the students with low levels of aptitude can learn only the simplest ideas of the subject.

Quite in contrast to this is Carroll's (1963) view that *aptitude* is the amount of time required by the learner to *attain* mastery of a *learning task*. Implicit in this formulation is the assumption that, given enough time, all students can conceivably attain mastery of a learning task. If Carroll is right, then learning mastery is theoretically available to all, if we can find the means for helping each student. It is this writer's belief that this formulation of Carroll's has the most fundamental implications for education.

One type of support for this view is to be found in the grade norms for many standardized achievement tests. These norms demonstrate that selected criterion scores achieved by the top students at one grade level are achieved by the majority of students at a later grade level. Further support is available in studies where students can learn at their own rate. These studies show that although most students eventually reach mastery on each learning task, some students achieve mastery much sooner than do other students (Glaser, 1968; Atkinson, 1967).

Can all students learn a subject equally well? That is, can all students master a learning task at a high level of complexity? As we study aptitude distributions in relation to student performance we have become convinced that there are differences between the extreme students and the remainder of the population. At the top of the aptitude distribution (1 percent to 5 percent) there are likely to be some students who have a special talent for the subject. Such students are able to learn and to use the subject with greater fluency than other students. The student with special aptitudes for music or foreign languages can learn these subjects in ways not available to most other students. Whether this is a matter of native endowment or the effect of previous training is not clear, although this must vary from subject to subject. It is likely that some individuals are born with sensory organs better attuned to sounds (music, language, etc.) than are others and that these constitutional characteristics give them special advantages in learning such subjects over others. For other subjects, special training, particular interests, etc. may develop these high level aptitudes.

At the other extreme of the aptitude distribution, we believe there are individuals with special disabilities for particular learning. The tone deaf individual will have great difficulty in learning music; the color blind individual will have special problems in learning art; the individual who thinks in concrete forms will have special problems in learning highly abstract conceptual systems such as philosophy. Again, we believe these may constitute less than 5 percent of the distribution, but this will vary with the subject and the aptitudes.

In between are approximately 90 percent of the individuals where we believe (as does Carroll) that aptitudes are predictive of rate of learning rather than the level (or complexity) of learning that is possible. Thus, we are expressing the view that, given sufficient time (and appropriate types of help), 95 percent of students (the top 5 percent + the next 90 percent) can learn a subject up to a high level of mastery. We are convinced that the grade of A as an index of mastery of a subject can, under appropriate conditions, be achieved by up to 95 percent of the students in a class.

It is assumed that it will take some students more effort, time, and help to achieve this level than it will other students. For some students the effort and help required may make it prohibitive. Thus, to learn high school algebra to a point of mastery may require several years for some students but only a fraction of a year for other students. Whether mastery learning is worth this great effort for the students who may take several years is highly questionable. One basic problems for a master-learning strategy is to find ways of reducing the amount of time required for the slower students to a point where it is no longer a prohibitively long and difficult task for these less able students.

We do not believe that aptitude for particular learning tasks is completely stable. There is evidence (Bloom, 1964; Hunt, 1961) that the aptitude for particular learning tasks may be modified by appropriate environmental conditions or learning experiences in the school and the home. The major task of educational programs concerned with learning to learn and general education should be to produce positive changes in the students' basic aptitudes. It is likely that these aptitudes can be most markedly affected during the early years in the home and during the elementary years of school. Undoubtedly, however, some changes can take place at later points in the individual's career.

However, even if marked changes are not made in the individual's aptitudes, it is highly probable that more effective learning conditions can reduce the amount of time required to learn a subject to mastery for all students and especially for the students with lower aptitudes. It is this problem which must be directly attacked by strategies for mastery learning.

2. Quality of Instruction

Our schools have usually proceeded on the assumption that there is a standard classroom situation for all students. Typically, this has been expressed in the teacher-student ratio of 1:30 with group instruction as the central means of teaching. There is the expectation that each teacher will teach the subject in much the same way as other teachers. This standardization is further emphasized by textbook adoption which specifies the instructional material to be provided each class. Closely related to this is the extensive research over the past 50 years which seeks to find the one instructional method, material, or curriculum program that is best for all students.

Thus, over the years, we have fallen into the "educational trap" of specifying quality of instruction in terms of good and poor teachers, teaching, instructional materials, curriculum—all in terms of group results. We persist in asking such questions as: What is the best teacher for the group? What is the best method of instruction for the group? What is the best instructional material for the group?

One may start with the very different assumption that individual students may need very different types and qualities of instruction to achieve mastery. That is, the same content and objectives of instruction may be learned by different students as the result of very different types of instruction. Carroll (1963) defines the *quality of instruction in terms of the degree to which the presentation, explanation, and ordering of elements of the task to be learned approach the optimum for a given learner.*

Much research is needed to determine how individual differences in learners can be related to variations in the quality of instruction. There is evidence that some students can learn quite well through independent learning efforts while others need highly structured teaching-learning situations (Congreve, 1965). It seems reasonable to expect that some students will need more concrete illustrations and explanations than will others; some students may need more examples to get an idea than do others; some students may need more approval and reinforcement than others; and some students may even need to have several repetitions of the explanation while others may be able to get it the first time.

We believe that if every student had a very good tutor, most of them would be able to learn a particular subject to a high degree. A good tutor attempts to find the qualities of instruction (and motivation) best suited to a given learner. And, there is some evidence (Dave, 1963) that middle-class parents do attempt to tutor their children when they believe that the quality of instruction in school does not enable their children to learn a particular subject. In an unpublished study, the writer found that one-third of the students in an algebra course in a middle-class school were receiving as much tutorial instruction in the home in algebra as they were receiving group instruction in the school. These students received relatively high grades for the algebra course. For these students, the relationship between their mathematics aptitude scores (at the beginning of the year) and their achievement in algebra at the end of the year was almost zero. In contrast, for the students who received no additional instruction other than the regular classroom instruction, the relationship between their mathematics aptitude scores and their algebra achievement scores was very high (+.90). While this type of research needs to be replicated, it is evident in this small study that the home tutoring help was providing the quality of instruction needed by these students to learn the algebra—that is, the instruction was adapted to the needs of the individual learners.

The main point to be stressed is that the quality of the instruction is to be considered in terms of its effects on individual learners rather than on random groups of learners. Hopefully, the research of the future may lead to the definition of qualities and kinds of instruction needed by various *types* of learners. Such research may suggest more effective group instruction since it is unlikely that the schools will be able to provide instruction for each learner separately.

3. Ability to Understand Instruction

In most courses at the high school and college level there is a single teacher and a single set of instructional materials. If the student has facility in understanding the teacher's communications about the learning and the instructional material (usually a textbook), he has little difficulty in learning the subject. If he has difficulty in understanding the teacher's instruction and/or the instructional material, he is likely to have great difficulty in learning the subject. *The ability to understand instruction may be defined as the ability of the learner to understand the nature of the task he is to learn and the procedures he is to follow in the learning of the task.*

Here is a point at which the student's abilities interact with the instructional materials and the instructor's abilities in teaching. For the student in our highly verbal schools it is likely that this ability to understand instruction is primarily determined by verbal ability and reading comprehension. These two measures of language ability are significantly related to achievement in the majority of subjects and they are highly related (+.50 to +.60) to grade-point averages at the high school or college level. What this suggests is that verbal ability (independent of specific aptitudes for each subject) determines some general ability to learn from teachers and instructional materials.

While it is possible to alter an individual's verbal ability by appropriate training, there are limits to the amount of change that can be produced. Most change in verbal ability can be produced at the preschool and elementary school levels with less and less change being likely as the student gets older (Bloom, 1964). Vocabulary and reading ability, however, may be improved to some extent at all age levels, even though there is a diminishing utility of this approach with increasing age. Improvements in verbal abilities should result in improvements in the individual's ability to understand instruction.

The greatest immediate payoff in dealing with the ability to understand instruction is likely to come from modifications in instruction in order to meet the needs of individual students. There is no doubt that some teachers do attempt to modify their instruction to fit a given group of students. Many teachers center their instruction at the middle group of their students, others at the top or bottom group—these are, however, reflections of the teacher's habits and attitudes. They are, by no means, determinants of what it is *possible* for a teacher to do. Given help and various types of aids, individual teachers can find ways of modifying their instruction to fit the differing needs of their students.

Group Study procedures should be available to students as they need it. In our own experience we have found that small groups of students (two or three students) meeting regularly to go over points of difficulty in the learning process were most effective, especially when the students could cooperate and help each other without any danger of giving each other special advantages in a competitive situation. Where learning can be turned into a cooperative process with everyone likely to gain from the process, small-group learning procedures can be very effective. Much depends on the composition of the group and the opportunities it gives each person to expose his difficulties and have them corrected without demeaning one person and elevating another. In the group process, the more able students have opportunities to strengthen their own learning in the process of helping another person grasp the idea through alternative ways of explaining and using the idea.

Tutorial help (one-to-one relations between teacher and learner) represents the most costly type of help and should be used only where alternative procedures are not effective. However, this type of help should be available to students as they need it, especially where individuals have particular difficulties that can't be corrected in other ways. The tutor, ideally, should be someone other than the teacher, since he should bring a fresh way of viewing the idea or the process. The tutor must be skillful in detecting the points of difficulty in the student's learning and should help him in such a way as to free the student from continued dependence on him.

Another approach to variations in the students' ability to understand instruction is to vary the instructional material.

Textbooks may vary in the clarity with which they explain a particular idea or process. The fact that one textbook has been adopted by the school or by the teacher does not necessarily mean that other textbooks cannot be used at particular points in the instruction when they would be helpful to a student who can't grasp the idea from the adopted textbook. The task here is to be able to determine where the individual student has difficulty in understanding the instructions and then provide alternative textbook explanations if they are more effective at that point.

Workbooks and programmed instruction units may be especially helpful for some students who cannot grasp the ideas or procedures in the textbook form. Some students need the drill and the specific tasks which workbooks can provide. Other students need the small steps and frequent reinforcement which programmed units can provide. Such materials may be used in the initial instruction or as students encounter specific difficulties in learning a particular unit or section of the course.

Audio-visual Methods and Academic Games. Some students may learn a particular idea best through concrete illustrations and vivid and clear explanations. It is likely that film strips and short motion pictures which can be used by individual students as needed may be very effective. Other students may need concrete material such as laboratory experiences, simple demonstrations, blocks and other relevant apparatus in order to comprehend an idea or task. Academic games, puzzles, and other interesting but not threatening devices may be useful. Here again, the point is that some ways of communicating and comprehending an idea, problem, or task may be especially effective for some students although others may not use or need such materials and methods. We need not place the highest priority for all on abstract and verbal ways of instruction.

With regard to instructional materials, the suggestion is not that particular materials be used by particular students throughout the course. It is that each type of material may serve as a means of helping individual students at selected points in the learning process—and that a particular student may use whatever variety of materials are found to be useful as he encounters difficulties in the learning.

Throughout the use of alternative methods of instruction and instructional material, the essential point to be borne in mind is that these are attempts to improve the *quality of instruction* in relation to the ability of each student to *understand the instruction.* As feedback methods inform the teachers of particular errors and difficulties the majority of students are having, it is to be expected that the regular group instruction could be modified so as to correct these difficulties. As particular students are helped individually, the goal should be not only to help the student over particular learning difficulties but also to enable him to become more independent in his learning and to help him identify the alternative ways by which he can comprehend new ideas. But, most important, the presence of a great variety of instructional materials and procedures should help both teachers and students to overcome feelings of defeatism and passivity about learning. If the student can't learn in one way, he should be reassured that alternatives are available to him. The teacher should come to recognize that it is the learning which is important and that instructional alternatives exist to enable all (or almost all) of the students to learn the subject to a high level.

4. Perseverance

Carroll defines *perseverance as the time the learner is willing to spend in learning.* If a student needs to spend a certain amount of time to master a particular task, and he spends less than this amount in active learning, he is not likely to learn the task to the level of mastery. Carroll attempts to differentiate between spending time on learning and the amount of time the student is actively engaged in learning.

Perseverance does appear to be related to attitudes toward and interest in learning. In the International Study of Educational Achievement (Husén, 1967), the relationship between the number of hours of homework per week reported by the student (a crude index of perseverance) and the number of years of further education desired by the student is +.25.

We do believe that students vary in the amount of perseverance they bring to a specific learning task. However, students appear to approach different learning tasks with different amounts of perseverance. The student who gives up quickly in his efforts to learn an academic subject may persevere an unusually long time in learning how to repair an automobile or in learning to play a musical instrument. It would appear to us that as a student finds the effort rewarding, he is likely to spend more time on a particular learning task. If, on the other hand, the student is frustrated in his learning, he must (in self-defense) reduce the amount of time he devotes to learning. While the frustration level of students may vary, we believe that all students must sooner or later give up a task if it is too painful for them.

While efforts may be made to increase the amount of perseverance in students, it is likely that manipulation of the instruction and learning materials may be more effective in helping students master a given learning task, in spite of their present level of perseverance. Frequency of reward and evidence of success in learning can increase the student's perseverance in a learning situation. As students attain mastery of a given task, they are likely to increase their perseverance for a related learning task.

In our own research we are finding that the demands for perseverance may be sharply reduced if students are provided with instructional resources most appropriate for them. Frequent feedback accompanied by specific help in instruction and material as needed can reduce the time (and perseverance) required. Improvement in the quality of instruction (or explanations and illustrations) may reduce the amount of perseverance necessary for a given learn task.

There seems to be little reason to make learning so difficult that only a small proportion of the students can persevere to mastery. Endurance and unusual perseverance may be appropriate for long-distance running—they are not great virtues in their own right. The emphasis should be on learning, not on vague ideas of discipline and endurance.

5. Time Allowed for Learning

Throughout the world schools are organized to give group instruction with definite periods of time allocated for particular learning tasks. A course in history at the secondary level may be planned for an academic year of instruction, another course may be planned for a semester, while the amount of instructional time allocated for a subject like arithmetic at the fifth-grade level may be fixed. Whatever the amount of time allowed by the school and the curriculum for particular subjects or learning tasks, it is likely to be too much for some students and not enough for other students.

For Carroll, the time spent on learning is the key to mastery. His basic assumption is that aptitude determines the rate of learning and that most, if not all, students can achieve mastery if they devote the amount of time needed to the learning. This implies that the student must not only devote the amount of time he needs to the learning task but also that he be *allowed* enough time for the learning to take place.

There seems to be little doubt that students with high levels of aptitude are likely to be more efficient in their learning and to require less time for learning than students with lower levels of aptitude. Whether most students can be helped to become highly efficient learners in general is a problem for future research.

The amount of time students need for a particular kind of learning has not been studied directly. One indication of the time needed comes from studies of the amount of time students spend on homework. In our review of the amount of time spent by 13-year-old students on mathematics homework in the International Study of Educational Achievement (Husén, 1967), we find that if we omit the extreme 5 percent of the subjects, the ratio is roughly 6 to 1. That is, some students spend 6 times as much time on mathematics homework as do others. Our studies of use of time suggest that this is roughly the order of magnitude to be expected.

If instruction and student use of time become more effective, we believe that most students will need less time to learn the subject to mastery and that the ratio of time required for the slower and the faster learners may be reduced from about 6 to 1 to perhaps 3 to 1.

In general, we find a zero or a slightly negative relationship between final grades and amount of time spent on homework. In the International Study (Husén, 1967) the average correlation for twelve countries at the 13-year-old level is approximately $-.05$ between achievement test scores in mathematics and number of hours per week of homework in mathematics as reported by students. Thus, the amount of time spent on homework does not seem to be a very good predictor of achievement in the subject.

We are convinced that it is not the sheer amount of time spent in learning (either in school or out of school) that accounts for the level of learning. We believe that each student should be allowed the time he needs to learn a subject. And, the time he needs to learn the subject is likely to be affected by the student's aptitudes, his verbal ability, the quality of instruction he receives in class, and the quality of the help he receives outside of class. The task of a strategy for mastery learning is to find ways of altering the time individual students need for learning as well as to find ways of providing whatever time is needed by each student. Thus, a strategy for mastery learning must find some way of solving the instructional problems as well as the school organizational (including time) problems.

One Strategy for Mastery Learning

There are many alternative strategies for mastery learning. Each strategy must find some way of dealing with individual differences in learners though some means of relating the instruction to the needs and characteristics of the learners. We believe that each strategy must include some way of dealing with the five variables discussed in the foregoing.

Were it not so costly in human resources, we believe that the provision of a good tutor for each student might be one ideal strategy. In any case, the tutor-student relationship is a useful model to consider when one attempts to work out the details of a less costly strategy. Also, the tutor strategy is not as farfetched as it may seem at first glance. In the preschool period most of the child's instruction is tutorial—usually provided by the mother. In many middle-class homes the parents continue to provide tutorial help as needed by the child during much of his school career.

Other strategies include permitting students to go at their own pace, guiding students with respect to courses they should or should not take, and providing different tracks or streams for different groups of learners. The nongraded school (Goodlad and Anderson, 1959) is one attempt to provide an organizational structure that permits and encourages mastery learning.

A group of us at the University of Chicago have been doing research on the variables discussed in the previous pages. In addition, some of us have been attempting to develop a strategy of teaching and learning which will bring all (or almost all) students to a level of mastery in the learning of any subject. Our approach has been to supplement regular group instruction by using diagnostic procedures and alternative instructional methods and materials in such a way as to bring a large proportion of the students to a predetermined standard of achievement. In this approach, we have tried to bring most of the students to mastery levels of achievement within the regular term, semester, or period of calendar time in which the course is usually taught. Undoubtedly, some students will spend more time than others in learning the subject, but if the majority of students reach mastery levels at the end of the time allocated for the subject, mastery will have affective as well as cognitive consequences.

We have had some successes and some dismal failures with this approach. We have been trying to learn from both the successes and the failures. In the near future we hope to have some of these ideas applied to a large number of classrooms in selected school systems. Initially, we have chosen to work with subjects which have few prerequisites (algebra, science, etc.) because we believe it is easier to secure mastery learning in a given time period in such courses. In contrast are subjects which are late in a long sequence of learning (6th grade reading, 8th grade arithmetic, advanced mathematics, etc.). For such subjects, it is unlikely that mastery learning can be attained within a term for a group of students who have had a long history of cumulative learning difficulties in the specific subject field.

In working on this strategy we have attempted to spell out some of the *preconditions* necessary, develop the *operating procedures* required, and evaluate some of the *outcomes* of the strategy.

Preconditions

If we are able to develop mastery learning in students, we must be able to recognize when students have achieved it. We must be able to define what we mean by mastery and we must be able to collect the necessary evidence to establish whether or not a student has achieved it.

The specification of the objectives and content of instruction is one necessary precondition for informing both teachers and students about the expectations. The translation of the specifications into evaluation procedures helps to further define what it is that the student should be able to do when he has completed the course. The evaluation procedures used to appraise the outcomes of instruction (summative evaluation) help the teacher and student know when the instruction has been effective.

Implicit in this way of defining the outcomes and preparing evaluation instruments is a distinction between the teaching-learning process and the evaluation process. At some point in time, the results of teaching and learning can be reflected in the evaluation of the students. But, these are *separate* processes. That is, teaching and learning are intended to prepare the student in an area of learning, while evaluation (summative) is intended to appraise the extent to which the student has developed in the desired ways. Both the teacher and the learner must have some understanding of what the achievement criteria are and both must be able to secure evidence of progress toward these criteria.

If the achievement criteria are primarily competitive, i.e., the student is to be judged in terms of his relative position in the group, then the student is likely to seek evidence on his standing in the group as he progresses through the learning tasks. We recognize that competition may be a spur to those students who view others in competitive terms, but we believe that much of learning and development may be destroyed by primary emphasis on competition.

Much more preferable in terms of intrinsic motivation for learning is the setting of standards of mastery and excellence apart from interstudent competition, followed by appropriate efforts to bring as many students up to this standard as possible. This suggests some notion of absolute standards and the use of grades or marks which will reflect these standards. Thus, it is conceivable that all students may achieve mastery and the grade of A. It is also possible in a particular year in a specific course for few or none of the students to attain mastery or a grade of A.

While we would recommend the use of absolute standards carefully worked out for a subject, we recognize the difficulty of arriving at such standards. In some of our own work, we have made use of standards derived from previous experience with students in a particular course. In one course, students in 1966 were informed that the grades for 1966 would be based on *standards* arrived at in 1965. The grades of A, B, C, D, and F would be based on an examination which was parallel to that used in 1965 and the grades would be set at the same performance levels as those used in 1965. The students were informed that the proportion of students receiving each grade was to be determined by their performance levels rather than by their rank order in the group. Thus, the students were not competing with each other for grades; they were to be judged on the basis of levels of mastery used in 1965.

We do not believe this is the only way of arriving at achievement standards, but the point is that students must feel they are being judged in terms of level of performance rather than a normal curve or some other arbitrary and relative set of standards. We are not recommending national achievement standards. What is being recommended are realistic performance standards developed for each school or group, followed by instructional procedures which will enable the majority of students to attain these standards.

One result of this way of setting achievement standards was to enable the students to work with each other and to help each other without being concerned about giving special advantages (or disadvantages) to other students. Cooperation in learning rather than competition was a clear result from this method of setting achievement criteria.

In the work we have done, we attempted to have the teacher teach the course in much the same way as previously. That is, the particular materials and methods of instruction in the current year should be about the same as in previous years. Also, the time schedule during the course was about the same. The operating procedures discussed in the next section supplemented the regular instruction of the teacher. We have proceeded in this way because we believe a useful strategy for mastery learning should be widely applicable. If extensive training of teachers is necessary for a particular strategy, it is less likely that it will receive widespread use.

Operating Procedures

The operating procedures we have used are intended to provide detailed feedback to teachers and students and to provide specific supplementary instructional resources as needed. These procedures are devised to insure mastery of each learning unit in such a way as to reduce the time required while directly affecting both quality of instruction and the ability of the student to understand the instruction.

Formative Evaluation. One useful operating procedure is to break a course or subject into smaller units of learning. Such a learning unit may correspond to a chapter in a textbook, a well-defined content portion of a course, or a particular time unit of the course. We have tended to think of units as involving a week or two of learning activity.

Using some of the ideas of Gagné (1965) and Bloom (1956) we have attempted to analyze each unit into a number of elements ranging from specific terms or facts, more complex and abstract ideas such as concepts and principles, and relatively complex processes such as application of principles and analysis of complex theoretical statements. We believe, as does Gagné (1965) that these elements form a hierarchy of learning tasks.

We have then attempted to construct brief diagnostic-progress tests which can be used to determine whether or not the student has mastered the unit and what, if anything, the student must still do to master it. We have borrowed the term *Formative Evaluation* from Scriven (1967) to refer to these diagnostic-progress tests.

Frequent formative evaluation tests pace the learning of students and help motivate them to put forth the necessary effort at the appropriate time. The appropriate use of these tests helps to insure that each set of learning tasks is thoroughly mastered before subsequent learning tasks are started.

Each formative test is administered after the completion of the appropriate learning unit. While the frequency of these progress tests may vary throughout the course, it is likely that some portions of the course —especially the early sections of the course—may need more frequent formative tests than later portions. Where some of the learning units are basic and prerequisite for other units of the course, the tests should be frequent enough to insure thorough mastery of such learning material.

For those students who have thoroughly mastered the unit, the formative tests should reinforce the learning and assure the student that his present mode of learning and approach to study is adequate. Since he will have a number of such tests, the student who consistently demonstrates mastery should be able to reduce his anxiety about his course achievement.

For students who lack mastery of a particular unit, the formative tests should reveal the particular points of difficulty—the specific questions they answer incorrectly and the particular ideas, skills, and processes they still need to work on. It is most helpful when the diagnosis shows the elements in a learning hierarchy that the student still needs to learn. We have found that students respond best to the diagnostic results when they are referred to particular instructional materials or processes intended to help them correct their difficulties. The diagnosis should be accompanied by a very specific prescription if the students are to do anything about it.

Although we have limited evidence on this point, we believe that the formative tests should not be assigned grades or quality points. We have marked the tests to show *mastery* and *nonmastery*. The nonmastery is accompanied by detailed diagnosis and prescription of what is yet to be done before mastery is complete. We believe that the use of grades on repeated progress tests prepares students for the acceptance of less than mastery. To be graded C repeatedly, prepares the student to accept a C as his "fate" for the particular course, especially when the grades on progress tests are averaged in as part of the final grade. Under such conditions, there must come a point when it is impossible to do better than a particular grade in the course—and there is little value in striving to improve. Formative evaluation tests should be regarded as part of the learning process and should in no way be confused with the judgment of the capabilities of the student or used as a part of the grading process.

These formative tests may also provide feedback for the teacher since they can be used to identify particular points in the instruction that are in need of modification. The formative evaluation tests also can serve as a means of quality control in future cycles of the course. The performance of the students on each test may be compared with the norms for previous years to insure that students are doing as well or better. Such comparisons can also be used to insure that changes in instruction or materials are not producing more error and difficulty than was true in a previous cycle of the course.

Alternative Learning Resources. It is one thing to diagnose the specific learning difficulties the student has and to suggest the specific steps he should take to overcome these difficulties. It is quite another thing to get him to do anything about it. By itself, the frequent use of progress tests can improve the achievement of students to a small degree. If, in addition, the student can be motivated to expend further effort on correcting his errors on the progress tests, the gains in achievement can be very great.

We have found that students do attempt to work on their difficulties when they are given specific suggestions (usually on the formative evaluation results) as to what they need to do.

The best procedure we have found thus far is to have small groups of students (two or three) meet regularly for as much as an hour per week to review the results of their formative evaluation tests and to help each other overcome the difficulties identified on these tests.

We have offered tutorial help as students desired it, but so far students at the secondary or higher education level do not seek this type of help frequently.

Other types of learning resources we have prescribed for students include: (a) reread particular pages of the original instructional materials; (b) read or study specific pages in alternative textbooks or other instructional materials; (c) use specific pages of workbooks or programmed texts; and (d) use selected audio-visual materials.

We suspect that no specific learning material or process is indispensable. The presence of a great variety of instructional materials and procedures and specific suggestions as to which ones the student might use help the student recognize that if he cannot learn in one way, alternatives are available to him. Perhaps further research will reveal the best match between individuals and alternative learning resources. At present, we do not have firm evidence on the relations between student characteristics and instructional materials and procedures.

Outcomes

What are the results of a strategy for mastery learning? So far we have limited evidence. The results to date, however, are very encouraging.

We are in the process of securing more evidence on a variety of situations at the elementary, secondary, and higher education levels.

Cognitive Outcomes of a Mastery Strategy. In our work to date we have found some evidence of the effectiveness of a strategy for mastery learning. Our best results have been found in a course on test theory where we have been able to use parallel achievement tests for the course in 1965, 1966, and 1967. In 1965, before the strategy was used, approximately 20 percent of the students received the grade of A on the final examination. In 1966, after the strategy was employed, 80 percent of the students reached this same level of mastery on the parallel examination and were given the grade of A. The difference in the mean performance of the two groups represents about two standard deviations on the 1965 achievement test and is highly significant.

In 1967, using the same formative evaluation tests as used in 1966, it was possible to compare the 1966 and the 1967 results after each unit of learning. Thus, the formative evaluation tests became quality control measures. Where there were significant negative differences between the results on a particular test from 1966 to 1967, the instructor reviewed the specific learning difficulties and attempted to explain the ideas in a different way. The final results on the 1967 summative evaluation instrument, which was parallel to the final achievement tests in 1965 and 1966 were that 90 percent of the students achieved mastery and were given grades of A.

Similar studies are underway at different levels of education. We expect to have many failures and a few successes. But, the point to be made is not that a single strategy of mastery learning can be used mechanically to achieve a particular set of results. Rather, the problem is one of determining what procedures will prove effective in helping particular students learn the subject under consideration. It is hoped that each time a strategy is used, it will be studied to find where it is succeeding and where it is not. For which students is it effective and for which students is it not effective? Hopefully, the results in a particular year can take advantage of the experience accumulated over the previous years.

Affective Consequences of Mastery. We have for the past century conceived of mastery of a subject as being possible for only a minority of students. With this assumption we have adjusted our grading system so as to certify that only a small percent of students (no matter how carefully selected) are awarded a grade of A. If a group of students learns a subject in a superior way (as contrasted with a previous group of students) we still persist in awarding the A (or mastery) to only the top 10 or 15 percent of the students. We grudgingly recognize that the majority of students have "gotten by" by awarding them grades of D or C. Mastery and recognition of mastery under the present relative grading system is unattainable for the majority of students—but this is the result of the way in which we have "rigged" the educational system.

Mastery must be both a subjective recognition by the student of his competence and a public recognition by the school or society. The public recognition must be in the form of appropriate certification by the teacher or by the school. No matter how much the student has learned, if public recognition is denied him, he must come to believe that he is inadequate, rather than the system of grading or instruction. Subjectively, the student must gain feelings of control over ideas and skills. He must come to recognize that he "knows" and can do what the subject requires.

If the system of formative evaluation (diagnostic-progress tests) and the summative evaluation (achievement examinations) informs the student of his mastery of the subject, he will come to believe in his own mastery and competence. He may be informed by the grading system as well as by the discovery that he can adequately cope with the variety of tasks and problems in the evaluation instruments.

When the student has mastered a subject and when he receives both objective and subjective evidence of the mastery, there are profound changes in his view of himself and of the outer world.

Perhaps the clearest evidence of affective change is the interest the student develops for the subject he has mastered. He begins to "like" the subject and to desire more of it. To do well in a subject opens up further avenues for exploration of the subject. Conversely to do poorly in a subject closes an area for further study. The student desires some control over his environment, and mastery of a subject gives him some feeling of control over a part of his environment. Interest in a subject is both a cause of mastery of the subject as well as a result of mastery. Motivation for further learning is one of the more important consequences of mastery.

At a deeper level is the student's self-concept. Each person searches for positive recognition of his worth and he comes to view himself as adequate in those areas where he receives assurance of his competence or success. For a student to view himself in a positive way, he must be given many opportunities to be rewarded. Mastery and its public recognition provide the necessary reassurance and reinforcement to help the student view himself as adequate. It is the opinion of this writer that one of the more positive aids to mental health is frequent and objective indications of self-development. Mastery learning can be one of the more powerful sources of mental health. We are convinced that many of the neurotic symptoms displayed by high school and college students are exacerbated by painful and frustrating experiences in school learning. If 90 percent of the students are given positive indications of adequacy in learning, one might expect such students to need less and less in the way of emotional therapy and psychological help. Contrariwise, frequent indications of failure and learning inadequacy must be accompanied by increased self-doubt on the part of the student and the search for reassurance and adequacy outside the school.

Finally, modern society requires continual learning throughout life. If the schools do not promote adequate learning and reassurance of progress, the student must come to reject learning—both in the school and later life. Mastery learning can give zest to school learning and can develop a lifelong interest in learning. It is this continual learning which should be the major goal of the educational system.

References

Atkinson, R. C., Computerized instruction and the learning process. Technical Report No. 122, Stanford, California. Institute for Mathematical Studies in the Social Sciences, 1967.

Bloom, B. S., *Stability and change in human characteristics*. New York: John Wiley & Sons, 1964.

Bloom, B. S. (Ed.), *Taxonomy of educational objectives: Handbook I, cognitive domain*. New York: David McKay Company, 1956.

Bowman, M. J., The new economics of education. *International Journal of Educational Sciences*, 1966, 1:29–46.

Bruner, Jerome, *Toward a theory of instruction*. Cambridge, Massachusetts: Harvard University Press, 1966.

Carroll, John, A model of school learning. *Teachers College Record*, 1963, 64: 723–733.

Congreve, W. J., Independent learning. *North Central Association Quarterly*, 1965, 40: 222–228.

Dave, R. H., The identification and measurement of environmental process variables that are related to educational achievement. Unpublished doctoral dissertation, University of Chicago, 1963.

Gagné, Robert M., *The conditions of learning*. New York: Holt, Rinehart, & Winston, 1965.

Glaser, R., Adapting the elementary school curriculum to individual performance. Proceedings of the 1967 Invitational Conference on Testing Problems. Princeton, New Jersey: Educational Testing Service, 1968.

Goodlad, J. I. and Anderson, R. H., *The nongraded elementary school.* New York: Harcourt, Brace & World, 1959.

Hunt, J. McV., *Intelligence and experience.* New York: Ronald Press Co., 1961.

Husén, T. (Ed.), *International study of educational achievement in mathematics: A comparison of twelve countries,* Volumes I and II. New York: John Wiley & Sons, 1967.

Morrison, H. C., *The practice of teaching in the secondary school.* Chicago: University of Chicago Press, 1926.

Schultz, T. W., *The economic value of education.* New York: Columbia University Press, 1963.

Scriven, Michael, The methodology of evaluation. In Stake, R. (Ed.), *Perspectives of curriculum evaluation.* Chicago: Rand McNally & Co., 1967.

Skinner, B. F., The science of learning and the art of teaching. *Harvard Educational Review,* 1954, 24: 86–97.

Suppes, P., The uses of computers in education. *Scientific American,* 1966, 215: 206–221.

The Role of the Educational Sciences in Curriculum Development

9

INTRODUCTION

Curriculum study and reorganization is at present of great concern to many nations. Until about 15 years ago, curriculum revision was only minor—when it did take place—and was usually of a patchwork character. A new section was added to a syllabus and a little might be taken out.

It would require only a very brief investigation in many countries to reveal that particular courses of study and syllabi in 1965 are in large part the same as the courses of study and syllabi 50 years earlier. Furthermore, the changes which have taken place in many of these courses of study are usually such as to further reduce whatever organic unity the course originally possessed.

In contrast to these minor revisions are the more serious curricular reorganizations which are now taking place in secondary school mathematics and science and to a lesser degree in the social studies and languages. These more intensive efforts are such that few teachers can teach them without participating in further study and training. In each instance, the new courses of study have required the efforts of many specialists to construct them and, even then, they require tryout under different conditions, evaluation, and modification before they are regarded as ready for use in the classroom.

Thus, we have two patterns of curriculum change. One is the partial and piecemeal change in which a few subject specialists are appointed as an *ad hoc* committee to make some modification (every 5 or 10 years) but not so much that present teachers would find the modified course "uncomfortable." The other is the development of a curriculum or course in which a team of specialists bring about a fundamental change —so fundamental that few of the present teachers can teach it without

[1]This paper is in part based on a report submitted in 1963 to the Government of Israel. The writer served as UNESCO Advisor to Israel on the creation of a Center for Curriculum Development and Educational Research.

further training. Study, research, and evaluation are needed in this second type of curriculum change to make a satisfactory course of study. It is this second type of curriculum research and development which is likely to become the pattern in many countries. And, fortunately or unfortunately, it is likely that fundamental changes in the curriculum will be needed much more frequently than once or twice in a hundred years.

While there may be many ways in which these more fundamental changes will be made, it is likely that systematic and careful curriculum change will be made only in those countries which create curriculum development and educational research centers adequate to this very complex task.

But why is this new pattern of curriculum development coming into being? Why can't curriculum modification still follow the simpler and more comfortable pattern that has apparently been used in many countries for so long?

In many subjects, the rapid growth of new knowledge, the changing conception of the subject itself and its relation to other subjects, and the basic changes in the scholarly and research methodologies require more than piecemeal curriculum modification to keep some semblance of relationship between the subject as taught in the schools and the subject as viewed by the specialists in the field. Perhaps the most fundamental change is that the specialist is less concerned with his subject as a "history" of what has been produced in the past and increasingly he regards his subject as a "way of inquiring" and as a way of thinking about and investigating the nature of the world or some area of human experience.

But even more fundamental than the changes in the specialist's approach to his subject are the changes in the larger aims of education and in the uses of education. The rapid changes in the nations, the political and economic changes in the social system, and the new interests and aspirations of the people all make new demands on the educational system. Education must be more than a system for maintaining an elite from one generation to another or for conferring status on individuals who seek it. Education is now called upon to develop individuals to their highest capability, to increase the amount of competence in a nation and to develop intelligence, citizenship qualities, and the basic values of the society. These demands on the educational system require a curriculum which is more than coverage of subject matter. The schools cannot fulfill these educative functions primarily by discarding the largest proportion of the students as unfit and selecting a few who, for a variety of conditions and circumstances, already possess the qualities of memory, verbal ability, and motivation which the schools have for so long prized most highly.

Curriculum change is required not only because of changes in the subject matter and in the society. The students in the present schools are different in many ways from the students before World War II. Child-rearing practices throughout the world are resulting in different personal qualities being developed in children. There is less and less motivation available to do a task without knowing why. Blind obedience to authority is much less common among pupils than it was two or three decades ago. Many other changes have taken place in the students in the schools. In many countries today the largest portion of the students in both elementary and secondary education are the children of parents who are essentially illiterate. Contrast this with the educational situation of 30–50 years ago, where the pupils in the elite schools such as the Gymnasium, Lycée and "Public Schools" studied the same books that their parents had studied and the classics used in the classroom were a part of the library in the home. The students in the schools and, consequently, the curriculum task of the schools are now very different from what they were no more than 15 years ago.

Finally, curriculum changes are resulting from new knowledge about the learning process. The theories of learning and the methods of educational research and measurements give us the means of investigating the effects of particular methods of teaching and particular curricula. Not all that is "learned" is remembered. Much that is learned is not used or usable. Much that is learned cannot be understood or related to other learning. These newer educational theories and methods raise serious questions about existing curricula and they permit us to put new curricula to an empirical tryout and evaluation. No longer do we have to accept the old curriculum on faith. Also, new curricula are not acts of faith—they represent new hypotheses which should be empirically tested before they become an accepted part of the educational program.

In short, a number of major forces operating directly or indirectly on the schools and the educational system require more and more deep-seated curriculum reorganization and development. Such curriculum change will increasingly require the combined efforts of many types of specialists if the reorganizations of curricula are to be adequate to the demands and pressures which give rise to them. A Center for Curriculum Development and Educational Research would appear to be one means for insuring that new curricula will be more adequate than present ones. Such a Center, if properly organized, should insure that the many problems involved in curriculum development are systematically attacked and that the evidence derived from specialists, research investigations, and evaluation studies are properly treated in the different stages of curriculum development. It is likely that only through such a Center can the different institutions, organizations, and committees be fruitfully involved in creating and securing widespread adoption of new curriculum developments.

FUNCTIONS OF A CENTER FOR CURRICULUM DEVELOPMENT AND RESEARCH

The purpose of education and the schools is to change the thoughts, feelings and actions of students. If a course, unit of instruction, or an educational program is effective, it is because the students have grown and changed to some significant extent as a result of the learning experiences in which they were involved.

The curriculum may be thought of as a plan for changing student behavior and as the actual set of learning experiences in which students, teachers, and materials interact to produce the changes in students.

The three questions which curriculum development[1] must answer are also the three questions with which a Center for Curriculum Development and Research must deal.

A. What are the changes in students which should result from the curriculum, that is, what are the objectives of the curriculum?

B. What are the learning experiences which will bring about the changes specified in the objectives? What material, teacher and student interactions are planned?

C. How effective are the learning experiences in bringing about the desired changes in students? What evaluative evidence can be collected to determine the effectiveness or lack of effectiveness of the curriculum?

A. What are the objectives of the curriculum?

Every school and educational unit or program does have objectives. Most frequently these objectives are implicit rather than explicit. All too frequently apparent agreement is reached among curriculum constructors because they do not make the objectives explicit or because they

[1]The view of curriculum which underlies this paper is largely drawn from the work of TYLER, RALPH W. (1950). *Basic Principles of Curriculum and Instruction*. Chicago: University of Chicago Press.

state objectives in such a general and ambiguous way that they serve as slogans rather than as sources of direction.

The objectives are the statements of the ways in which students should change if the curriculum is effective. They state in an operational form the types of knowledge, cognitive abilities, interests, attitudes and other characteristics of the students which should change significantly as a result of the unit of learning, the course of study, or the entire school program.

Objectives are both the statement of the desired outcomes of the curriculum and the specifications for the design of a curriculum. They may be stated in different ways but they should be so stated as to indicate the ways in which the student is to feel, act, or think in relation to some subject content or area of experience. In curriculum planning, it is frequently found useful to prepare a two-dimensional table in which the content or topics of a particular subject matter or course are placed on one dimension of the table, while the objectives or changes to take place in students (in relation to the content) are indicated on the other dimension of the table. The interrelation of the objectives and content help to specify the learning tasks as well as the evaluation and examination problems.

The determination of the objectives of an educational unit or program is in many ways the most difficult task in curriculum construction. There are so many objectives which are possible or to which education could make a contribution, that some selection must be made if the time and means available to the schools are to be utilized most productively.[2] All objectives cannot be attained at the same time and experience suggests that a school will be most effective if it concentrates its efforts on a few major objectives.

The determination of educational objectives must take into consideration the changes in the very forces which raise questions about the present curriculum—the subject matter, the society, the students, the educational philosophy and the value system of the society, and the theory and principles of learning. The curriculum builders must be provided with the means of answering a number of questions about each of these matters before a satisfactory resolution of the objectives and content can be made.

[2]Some of the possible objectives of the schools are indicated in the books:
> B. S. BLOOM, (Editor) *Taxonomy of Educational Objectives, Handbook I: Cognitive Domain.* David McKay and Co., New York (1956).
> D. R. KRATHWOHL, B. S. BLOOM and B. B. MASIA. *Taxonomy of Educational Objectives, Handbook II: Affective Domain.* David McKay and Co., New York (1964).

The answers to these questions will usually require a team of experts from the different educational sciences. In some cases, the research already done in the different disciplines and the wisdom and experience of the experts may be sufficient to answer these questions. In other cases, specific investigations for the purpose will be required.

In the following sections, the writer will comment briefly on the questions and procedures under each of the major headings and will suggest the types of experts and investigations needed.

1. *Subject matter.* Each subject or area of human experience has its own characteristic methods of inquiry, its own field of interest, and its own content. History and mathematics are very different in basic structure, types of thinking required, relevance for organizing human experience, as well as present implications and applications. Specialists in each field—at the highest level—may be asked to serve as experts in curriculum development. For this task, the educational sciences are all the disciplines and subjects represented in the curriculum (mathematics, physical sciences, biological sciences, social sciences, literature, music, languages and linguistics, philosophy, etc.). Such specialists may be asked to help determine:

(a) What contribution the field may make to the education of an individual?

(b) What contribution the study of the subject may make to other more general aims of education?

(c) What are the essential ideas, content and principles of the field which should, as a minimum, be included in a study of the subject?

(d) What are the possible structures and organizing principles of the field which may serve to interrelate and give meaning to the more detailed aspects of the subject? (e.g. Set Theory in mathematics, Atomic Theory in physics, etc.)

(e) What are the special weaknesses in the present curriculum in the light of the major changes which have already taken place in the specialist's conception of the subject field, its methods of inquiry, and its relevance for contemporary problems?

(f) Finally, the specialist may express his views on the kinds of learning experiences which are of greatest value for the student studying his subject field.

It is likely that each country has a number of capable subject specialists in its universities, research institutions, and teacher training institutions. A Curriculum Center must find ways of involving such specialists in its curriculum revisions and in its development of new curricula. The special problem here is to determine the proper role of the specialist. His understanding of his own subject does not mean that he is an expert on the teaching of this subject to 15-year-old-students.The curriculum constructors can learn a great deal from the specialists in the subject field, but it should be remembered that the specialist's contribution is as an expert in his subject—not as an expert in curriculum construction. It is likely that a resolution of the views of different experts will require more time and discussion in some fields than in others. Where a subject is international in scope (e.g. mathematics, science, foreign language, etc.) efforts should be made to determine the thinking or views of expert groups in other countries—especially through the literature of the field. For this purpose it may be useful to have some persons connected with the Curriculum Center become informed on the foreign literature of each subject field.

2. *The society.* Each nation and society has its own special problems, concerns and interests. These special qualities of the nation and its subgroups must find a place in the educational program, otherwise the curriculum of each nation might be identical with that of every other nation.

In this area, investigations by sociologists, psychologists, economists, political scientists, and historians may be needed. Some of the questions to be answered by studies as well as by the use of expert opinion are the following:

(a) What are the critical problems of contemporary life?

(b) What aspects of contemporary life have special relevance for the aims and purposes of education?

(c) What are the aspirations of the people? Do these differ for different groups of the population?

(d) What are the problems, misconceptions, ideas, values, practices, etc., of particular groups?

(e) If a society is undergoing rapid transformation, it becomes crucial to determine the most probable changes which are likely to take place in the next decade or two. Thus, in a society where economic and social planning has a significant place in the national scene, it is most important that the planners be brought into relation to curriculum development.

Curriculum development is a type of social planning since it is concerned with the kinds of learning students will need if they are to play a significant part in the society as it develops in the future. Educational planning and social planning must be interrelated at many points if they are to be mutually reinforcing. All too frequently there is a marked disjunction between the schools and the contemporary problems and changes taking place in a society. A Curriculum Center would be considerably strengthened if it had on its staff a person trained in the social sciences who could bring together the necessary experts to answer questions about the society and who could carry out special investigations as needed in this area.

3. *The students.* Each school system must adapt its educational program to the special characteristics of its students. The educational objectives and the nature of the learning experiences must be in part determined by the kinds of students in the school and by the cultural conditions in which they develop. Also, the educational objectives at a particular educational grade or level of school are, in part, determined by the level of educational development the students have already reached.

The rigidity of the schools in many countries and the availability of education to only a small "elite" has tended to obscure the relations between the characteristics of the students and the educational objectives.

Some of the questions about students which need to be answered for curriculum development purposes are the following:
   (a) What are the special needs of the students generally and what are the needs particular to specific subject matter?
   (b) What can the schools contribute to meeting present and future needs of students?
   (c) What are the present interests of students and what are their (or their parents) aspirations for the future?
   (d) What specific educational problems are raised by the home environments and peer groups in which the students develop?
   (e) How do the attainments of the learners under the present curriculum differ from desirable standards of attainment?
   (f) What are some of the special problems of students now and what are likely to be some of their problems in the future?
   (g) What are the sources of dissatisfaction, frustration, anxiety, etc. of students in relation to the schools?

Questions such as these require many different techniques of investigation and many different kinds of experts. The clinical psychologist and the guidance expert may contribute expert opinion on these questions as well as conduct appropriate studies. The educational measurement specialist should provide objective and relatively precise information on present standards of attainment, the particular strengths and weaknesses of students in relation to specific subjects, and he may also provide information on the aptitudes, interests and aspirations of the students. The educational psychologist and the sociologist can also make contributions to these questions.

The basic problem is one of how to collect and organize the information available from different sources in such a way that it can contribute to curriculum development. In many countries information on these questions is available, but it is difficult to locate because different individuals and organizations each have only a limited portion of the needed information. A Center for Curriculum Development will need at least one person with background in educational psychology and educational measurement to make an inventory of what is already known, to determine future needs in this area, and to make investigations as needed with the support of other specialists.

4. *Values and educational philosophy.* In a highly stable society the basic values the society prizes become an integral part of the educational philosophy, and the organization and activities of the schools reflect such values. In a society in rapid transition there is usually confusion about the values and the ways in which they can be implemented by the schools. Under such conditions the schools tend to become segmented and each subgroup in the society seeks special control over the schools in order to have its values and educational philosophy find expression in the education of its own children.

An explicit educational philosophy can do much to give meaning and direction to the schools. It can help to determine the hierarchy of educational objectives, and it can serve as the organizing principles for the content, learning experiences, and evaluation procedures of the schools.

Some of the philosophic and value questions which need to be answered for curriculum development purposes are the following:

   (a) What are the basic values of the society at present? Are there any basic values which exist for the entire society or are the values very different for each subgroup in the society?
   (b) Which of these basic values are properly a part of the school philosophy?
   (c) Which of the basic values are likely to be endangered by the changes taking place in the society and what is the role of the schools in preserving some of these values?
   (d) What values must the school develop to meet the social changes which are likely to take place?

Additional questions which relate to an educational philosophy are:

(e) Should the society develop different educational systems for different groups in the society?
(f) What should the proper relation be between general education and specialized education?
(g) What is the appropriate relation between the needs of the individual and the needs of the society and how should these be implemented by the schools?

Every specialist and expert who is in any way related to the educational system is likely to regard himself as having a contribution to make to educational philosophy. While there may be some merit in this, it is not likely that consensus will emerge when all feel equally competent in this area. It is likely that philosophers, historians, and sociologists may be able to make the clearest contributions to answering some of the questions posed in this section. Also, "wise men" who may or may not be specialists in other fields are likely to be able to make significant contributions to these questions.

In some ways these are the most difficult questions to answer since consensus is hard to secure and because of the emotional and political overtones raised by these questions. The curriculum constructors at the detailed level are likely to see the disagreement among "experts" as a reason for not developing and using an explicit educational philosophy. However, it should be recognized that when an explicit educational philosophy is not available, each educator is likely to use his own educational philosophy without making it explicit.

One finds considerable difficulty with regard to the establishment of a particular educational philosophy. Evidently, this reflects the basic difficulties in achieving consensus about such values at present in the larger society. In spite of the difficulty, the importance of an explicit educational philosophy cannot be stressed too much. Without it, education is at the mercy of each new gadget, fad, or point of view. The full power of education to affect the behavior of students and the welfare of the nation is dependent on the solution to this problem. A Center for Curriculum Department must use a variety of experts as well as laymen to participate in making a philosophy of education explicit. It may make use of an educational philosopher to find ways of stating the philosophy so that curriculum makers, educational leaders, teachers and parents may understand its meaning and implications.

5. *The principles of learning.* A theory of learning can be one basis for ordering the possible objectives of education and for the determina-

tion of the objectives which should be given highest priority. Such a view of learning can be used to determine the likelihood that a particular objective can be achieved or not by a particular group of students. Finally, a psychology of learning is of value in determining the appropriateness of particular learning experiences as means of attaining particular objectives.

If a psychology of learning is made explicit, it can be used to answer the following questions:

(a) Which objectives of learning are likely to be achieved and which are most unlikely to be achieved through the learning process?

(b) Which objectives are most likely to be achieved at one level of education and which are more likely to be achieved at a later stage of education?

(c) Which objectives can be achieved over a relatively short period of time and which objectives must be emphasized over a number of years before significant growth is likely to take place?

(d) Which objectives are dependent for their attainment on their being emphasized in both the school as well as out of school environment?

(e) Which objectives can be achieved within a particular course or subject, and which objectives require emphasis in different aspects of the school program?

A psychology of learning can also be utilized to determine the particular conditions under which the interaction of teachers, students and material is most likely to bring about significant growth in the ways specified by the objective.

Although countries differ in the particular learning theory and learning principles they utilize in the schools, knowledge about learning and research on this topic is likely to be of universal significance. This means that the major problem of each country is to draw from the accumulated international knowledge about learning and to develop its own statement of this knowledge in a form which will be useful for its educational system.

The psychologist who has specialized in learning and education should be able to formulate an appropriate learning theory and a set of learning principles. He should be able to relate such a formulation to the questions suggested here. Further, as specific studies and research are needed to answer particular questions in the local setting, he should be able to make significant contributions in this area also.

While it may be too much to expect of a single specialist in this educational science, it is clear that psychology and psychologists have much to contribute to a Center for Curriculum Development.

B. *Development of learning experiences*

Educational objectives are not mere expressions of hopes and desires. Properly conceived and defined they are the specifications of what the educational program is to accomplish. However, objectives are the ends of the educational process and they do not specify the means by which they are to be achieved.

Students learn as a result of the learning experiences they have. Such learning experiences refer to the interaction between the learner and the conditions in the environment. Learning takes place through the active involvement of the student: it is what he does that he learns—not what the teacher does.

The teacher can help to provide an educational experience for the learners by setting up an environment and structuring the situation so as to stimulate the desired types of reactions. The teacher must have some understanding of the interests and background of the students if he is to be effective in determining the likelihood that a given situation will bring about the kind of reaction which is essential to the learning desired.

If the sole objective of education is the development of knowledge, the learning experience required is little more than a relatively passive listening or reading on the part of the student. As a greater variety of objectives become of importance, teachers need help in providing appropriate learning experiences.

The creation of the conditions which bring about appropriate learning experiences for the students is largely an artistic endeavour. Some teachers appear to do this superbly while other teachers appear to be less able to do this. Since the learning experiences take place in the classrooms and laboratories, and even in the privacy of the students own study place, they cannot be completely determined by a Center for Curriculum Construction.

What can be done by a Curriculum Center is to suggest and try out procedures for providing learning experiences. The Center may do this by providing learning materials (textbooks, readings, audio-visual methods, workbooks, programmed materials, etc.) which are interesting to students and which are likely to involve him in appropriate activities and tasks when used properly.

A Curriculum Center may also suggest the ways in which the teachers may be especially effective in providing learning experiences for students. Thus, the Center may develop syllabi and teacher's manuals to guide teachers in their teaching procedures. The Center may also create a pool of suggested learning experiences to be used by teachers in the classroom. Such suggested learning experiences may be described and developed by creative teachers who have actually tried them out with their own students.

The educational psychologist may contribute to the creation of learning experiences by utilizing the body of theory and evidence on learning to specify the conditions which are necessary for each type of objective and learning to take place. However, the educational psychologist and the educational worker may be even more useful in the Curriculum Center in securing evidence on the effectiveness of particular learning experiences and in establishing the special conditions which must be met if the learning experiences are to be effective in specific situations.

Undoubtedly, basic changes in the content and objectives of instruction and changes in learning experiences will require a considerable amount of in-service training of the existing teaching personnel as well as appropriate modifications in the training of new teachers. Teachers' receptiveness to new curricula is dependent on their mastery of the new ideas and on the opportunities they have to try out the new instructional procedures under conditions which reduce their own insecurity and anxiety. For each major new curriculum development there must be an adequate training program for the teachers. If teachers are to become adequate to the new tasks, the Curriculum Center must find ways of providing the necessary training through seminars, special courses in teacher training institutions, workshops, and study circles. It is this training which should enable teachers to adapt learning experiences to the specific local conditions and to the needs and abilities of the students assigned to the teacher. Such training should help teachers to become more creative and free in developing appropriate new learning experiences which will help their students attain the objectives specified for the curriculum.

The Curriculum Center for a particular country may, in the development and research on learning experiences, make use of the experiences in this field available in other countries. This will be most easy to do in the fields of Mathematics, Science, and Foreign Languages, but the work in other fields will also be suggestive.

C. Evaluation of the effectiveness of learning experiences
A new curriculum should not be conceived of as an act of faith. A set of specifications are drawn up which make clear the kind of changes that are to take place in students. Learning experiences and instructional

material are designed to meet these specifications. Whether they do meet the specifications or not is a matter for evaluation. Evaluation procedures can be developed to determine whether or not the students do change in the desired ways to the expected degree. Evaluation evidence can also be used to determine wherein the learning experiences and instructional material need be improved or changed in particular ways. Also, the evaluation data can be used to determine whether the new curriculum works well for some students but not others and where modification is required for particular groups of students.

The specifications of educational objectives and content which are used as a basis for the development of learning experiences and instructional material are also used as the basis for the development of appropriate evaluation procedures.

Although it is desirable to have teachers participate in the development of evaluation procedures, the construction of valid, reliable, and efficient evaluation instruments and techniques requires a small group of well trained specialists in educational measurement and evaluation. This is one of the educational sciences which has had greatest development in the past three decades. Properly used this science can do much to insure that the curriculum is sound and that the learning experiences do have the effects intended.

Ideally, the evaluators should participate in the curriculum construction work and they should prepare the evaluation procedures in cooperation with the other members of the curriculum construction team. Such evaluation procedures give further operational definition to the specifications of educational objectives and content, and they become useful in many aspects of the curriculum construction.

After the curriculum is designed and the evaluation procedures developed, the new curriculum should be experimentally tried out with appropriate samples of students and teachers. If the experimental design is carefully developed and if the evaluation data are appropriately analyzed, it should be possible to determine modifications needed in the curriculum and the likelihood established that similar results may be found if the curriculum is used in other schools with other teachers and students.

The efficient sampling and research designs to experimentally try new curricula require the services of an educational research worker with appropriate training in statistical methods and research procedures. Such a person can insure that the data analysis is appropriate to the curricular hypotheses and that the results can be used to determine the limits within which the curriculum is likely to be effective.

In summary, curriculum development may be seen as first involving a series of value decisions based on available evidence, studies, expert opinion, and a body of theory and research on learning. The results of such value decisions may be expressed in terms of the specification of objectives and content for a particular curriculum or educational program.

A second stage in curriculum development is essentially an artistic and creative synthesis in which learning materials and instructional procedures are devised to set the conditions under which powerful learning experiences are made available to students. While a Curriculum Center may do much to help create new materials and instructional methods, the final utilization of these must depend on the teachers in the system. The training and experience the teachers have had will determine in large part the effectiveness of the learning experiences in realizing the goals of the curriculum.

The third stage in curriculum development is essentially the problem of quality control and feedback of evidence to insure that the curriculum plans are being effectively realized.

While curriculum planning may be centralized in a Curriculum Center in which the appropriate team of specialists in the educational sciences are effectively utilized, the task of execution must be decentralized and much depends on the morale and training of teachers. Curriculum development can be centralized but curriculum adaptation to the particular students must be decentralized.

A Center for Curriculum Development can bring together the necessary resources for effective curriculum construction in a modern and rapidly changing society. It can insure that each of the educational sciences plays its appropriate role in curriculum construction. Such a Center may also do a great deal in helping to prepare teachers for the new instructional tasks. The educational sciences can do much to create the materials and conditions for effective learning. However, it must be recognized that the final determinants of the quality of learning that takes place are the individual teacher and the individual student.

Peak Learning Experiences

10

I magine a classroom learning session which is so powerful that many students have almost total memory of it twenty years later. When these students begin to recall this session, it becomes quite vivid, and they actually appear to be reliving it. This one experience forms a landmark in their school recollections. For a few of these students the session becomes a turning point in their educational careers, and they trace major decisions, new interests, and the formation of particular attitudes and values to this single hour.

Before the reader dismisses the possibility of such powerful learning sessions, he should review his own school career. Can he recall a vivid learning experience from his elementary school, high school, or college days? It may be difficult at first, but an hour of effort alone with one's thoughts is likely to yield one or two memorable class sessions. Some of these may be what we have termed "peak learning" experiences.

Such experiences do occur with a very low frequency, but they are not really accidents. The study of peak learning experiences should reveal the conditions which are essential for creating them; and, hopefully, research should enable teachers to increase the frequency and value of such experiences.

The characteristics of peak experiences have been described by Maslow (1959) in a stimulating paper. Such peak experiences are the rare moments in which an individual has a feeling of the highest level of happiness and fulfillment. Maslow's peak experiences include love experiences, parental experiences, mystic or oceanic experiences, aesthetic experiences, creative moments, orgasmic experiences, certain forms of athletic fulfillment, and the therapeutic or intellectual insight.

Maslow's summary of the characteristics of cognition in the generalized peak experience makes it possible to identify such experiences after they have taken place. With these characteristics in mind, I asked a few friends to attempt to recall peak experiences related to learning situations. Some of their anecdotal accounts made it clear that such moments of highest fulfillment can occur and that there should be more systematic study of these phenomena.

Over a one-year period an assistant, John Stamm, and I asked eighty university students to describe their memorable or vivid classroom learning experiences. We stipulated that these should be only classroom sessions, at the university or pre-university level, which they found to be the most vivid.

About a third of our respondents were not able to recall what we regarded as peak learning experiences, and some of these students were not able to recall *any* very memorable learning experiences. Others were able to recall a memorable teacher or book but not the nature of the learning which had occurred in connection with that teacher or book. For example, one student was able to recall, with great vividness, a teacher who had stood on a desk and scolded the class, but the student could not remember the content of this dramatic speech. We did not classify such events as peak learning experiences because of the absence of detailed recall of learning content.

About two thirds of our interviewees appeared to have a vivid, almost total recall of a learning situation. That is, they were able to report in great detail what the teacher and the class had done, what had been said by the teacher and the students, and what they themselves had done during the session as well as immediately following it. We regard such total recall as *one* possible indication of a peak learning experience.

While we could not, of course, always be certain that the recall was perfectly accurate, it was striking to hear an event that had occurred ten or more years previously described by a person with every confidence that he had remembered the most minute details. We also were able to study several situations in which two or more of our respondents had been in the same session. For these situations there was evidence that recall was quite accurate since many of the same details were reported independently by the respondents. Similarly, when we were able to check out the details with the instructor, there was evidence of very accurate recall by students. While we do not wish to affirm that the students' feeling of total recall was necessarily accurate, we were impressed with the accuracy of recall where we had means of checking it.

When a student could recall a learning situation with great vividness, his description indicated that he was almost totally involved in the situation at the time it occurred. This parallels Maslow's characteristic of a peak experience as being attended to fully and exclusively. In peak learning experiences the student's description of himself in relation to the situation suggests that he was so involved or attentive at the time that everything else receded in importance. As Maslow describes it, the learning situation became the figure while the ground (physical surroundings; educational paraphernalia, such as marks, assignments, tests; time of day; or other classes) disappeared or was trivial in relation to the figure. Closely related to this was a student's frequent comment that he was surprised when the session was over. The time had passed "so quickly" or the student had not noticed the passage of time. One got the impression that so much had occurred during the peak learning experience that the student could not quite understand how a single class period could be so eventful.

The peak learning experiences were described in such a manner that they appeared to be "moments of truth" for the student. Whatever set of ideas or way of thinking the student glimpsed in the peak learning experience was seen as a fundamental truth. The student regarded the experience as valuable in its own right rather than as a means to some learning task or as useful for other purposes. Repeatedly, the students described peak learning experiences as a unit which was temporarily all-encompassing with a fundamental unity of its own.

Frequently, descriptions suggested that the peak learning experience was essentially an aesthetic experience which was seen as true, beautiful, and valuable—whether or not it had some effect on the learning of a subject or had value for other learning. While many students did recall the way in which the peak learning experience had influenced them in subsequent years, the point here is that they had not been classifying, organizing, or judging aspects of the experience while it was happening. They had experienced it fully at the time, while organizing, analytic, and application types of thinking were temporarily suspended. The peak learning experience was good in its own right at the time—only later was it seen as useful and valuable for other learning purposes.

The students' descriptions of their own involvement in peak learning experiences suggest an extreme type of emotional reaction. The students evidently had a momentary loss of fears and anxiety, and their defenses and controls were suspended. Describing the experience as "awe-inspiring" and "wonderful," many students added that it had produced a high level of tension and something of an "emotional jag." Afterwards, some students said they had found it necessary to seek solitude to think over the experience and to come back gradually to a more comfortable emotional state. Others described what appeared to be a way of "talking it out" with others as a way of reducing tension. In general, it seemed that an hour or two had been required before the students could return to a state of emotional equilibrium. Some appeared to have dwelt on the experience for a few days, especially when in the company of others who had been a part of this session.

As a result of the peak learning experience many students were stimulated to explore the ideas or subject matter which had been highlighted. The session had been a disquieting one which could, in part, be put in proper perspective by further learning or by some attempts to consolidate and secure mastery over the ideas, materials, or process which had been its main feature. Many students read further on the subject or attempted to apply the ideas or process to other situations and material. In this deliberate effort to explore, to use, and to generalize the learning outcomes, the students appeared to be trying to hold on to the experience as well as to make it a more definite part of their own thinking and behavior.

The first part of our 80-student sample was interviewed at random from varied sources—dormitories, our own classes, or fields of specialization (e.g., law, liberal arts, education). We wanted a varied group of volunteers and, by chance, found a few instances in which the same instructor or course was mentioned by more than one student. Later, we deliberately inverviewed six students who had been classmates in a course taught by a particularly outstanding teacher. We were surprised and delighted to find that three independently (the students did not know the basis on which we had selected them) described, with much the same detail, the same session as a memorable learning experience. Using this same procedure we later found about four different class sessions which were described as peak learning experiences by two or more students. In describing their own reactions as well as the reactions of others, these students made it clear that some class sessions can be so powerful that a number of the participants have simultaneous peak learning experiences.

Thus, we begin to glimpse two types of peak learning experiences. One is unique to an individual who just happens to be in a situation which triggers off a powerful response in himself. It seems that it is largely the student, rather than the situation, which makes for this type of peak learning experience. That is, the student appears to be at a point in his development where something in the learning situation sets off an emotional response which is different from the response of others in the class. A number of students described such a unique personal type of peak learning experience, but we believe this type to be only a small fraction of all our reports. Such unique and individualized peak learning experiences are difficult to study and are likely to be even more difficult to predict, explain, or control. That they are important to the individual, we do not doubt. However, their value for investigations of the educational process seems to be somewhat less than that of our second type of peak learning experience.

The second type of peak learning experience is one in which a group of students simultaneously have much the same reactions and involvement. Something in the situation causes a number of them to experience a very powerful learning episode—so powerful that they can describe it with great detail and vividness many years later.

It is this second type which we believe has so much promise for educational investigations, for curriculum investigations and planning, and for new insight into the learning process—especially in the affective domain (Krathwohl, Bloom, and Masia, 1964). We have tried to see if we could determine some of the controlling factors of this type of peak learning experience—in hopes that we may eventually find ways of producing such experiences as part of a plan.

We used our analysis of student reports as a basis for selecting educational films which were likely to approximate peak learning experiences. We studied these films and student reactions to them in order to understand the process in greater detail. On the basis of these studies as well as on the analysis of the recalled experiences of our interviewees, we have identified four sets of elements which seem to produce group peak learning experiences. Further research will be necessary to determine whether or not these hypotheses can be carefully tested and whether or not they can, in fact, be used to create such experiences.

The Teacher. While a charismatic instructor does much to create an atmosphere for peak learning experiences, it is necessary that the students regard the teacher as one who is communicating some fundamental truth or some way of viewing phenomena which is both unique and of great moment. A major personality in the arts was featured in one of our educational films. For those who felt, in advance, that this man was something of a charlatan, the viewing of the film was regarded as a waste of time; and they expressed irritation with it. For those viewers who had a high regard for the speaker, the experience of viewing the film was a remarkably powerful one (although not necessarily a peak learning experience).

Contrast. Most peak learning experiences included an element of surprise. The student, expecting one set of events or procedures, had found the learning situation to be very different from that anticipated, sharply contrasting with that previously encountered with the same or with other instructors. Sometimes the teacher's manner or approach to the subject differed greatly from that to which the student had become accustomed. Being caught "off guard" seems very necessary for making this experience stand out from other learning experiences. This may explain why it is recalled with such vividness in after years.

Content. For the student a peak learning experience must include some fundamental truth, some new insight, or some different way of viewing an aspect of the world or the self. Many of the peak learning experiences may have been powerful because something previously accepted by the student was shown to be untrue, misleading, or trivial; and this new approach was demonstrated as being more appropriate, true, or fundamental. It is as though the world which the student had come to accept was shown to be false—while a new world opened to him. at the very moment the old one was being destroyed. When this dramatic shift is made in a single class session, it is little wonder that the student becomes temporarily distraught by the experience.

Lack of Closure. The peak learning experience forms a unit which opens vistas for further learning but is far from complete or final. The new truth, insight, or way of viewing phenomena is partially grasped by the student, but much further learning is necessary before it can be completely understood or mastered. If it is too difficult for the student to understand, it is likely to be forgotten or rejected quickly. The student must feel that he partially understands the revelation, that he can completely understand it if he does the necessary work, and that to master these new ideas is eminently worthwhile.

Our attempts to characterize and explain peak learning experiences are far from complete. While we have tried to sketch their general nature, much more research will be necessary to understand them adequately. Peak experiences cannot be satisfactorily explained by present theories of learning nor are they at present given a significant place in instructional or curricular investigations and plans.

Peak experiences are important because they uniquely combine cognitive and affective components of learning. That they really appear as "peaks" in contrast to what seems to be a very drab "flatland" of school learning is also important. It may be these rare peaks that keep some of our best students searching for just one more of these exhilarating experiences. These peak learning experiences indicate what learning might become if only all elements in education were brought to their highest level.

Because of the rareness of such experiences, there was a note of despair and frustration in the reports of our interviewees. The 80 respondents, reporting 60 peak learning experiences, had had a collective total of 1,200 years of school attendance (over 1 million hours of class sessions). Only 60 class hours of peak learning experiences seem to us, as well as to the students, a pitiably inadequate return for so many years of seeking and yearning for the "might have been." As the process of creating peak learning experiences is better understood, we may find ways of helping students to have more than just one or two peak learning experiences in their entire educational career.

Many teachers can deliberately plan to create several peak learning experiences in a particular term. Such planning should include the four sets of elements described in this paper. The peak learning experience may be a good way of starting a new unit, or it may be a culminating experience at the end of a study. The careful teacher will note which one of these efforts produces the intended effect and repeat it with another group. Several such efforts to shape a particular peak learning experience should finally result in a planned experience which will have similar effects with each new group of students.

Television and films may help to create peak learning experiences, especially if appropriate preparations have been made. Thus the study of a Shakespearean drama when related to a production of the drama by live actors, on film, or by the students themselves may produce a peak learning experience.

Field trips, contemporary events, or laboratory experiences, if properly set, may form peak learning experiences. The skillful teacher finds necessary ingredients for peak learning experiences everywhere around him. This quest can do much to make teaching satisfying and exciting. For the student such experiences become major sources of new enthusiasm and energy for learning.

We begin to see how powerful the educational process can be through peak learning experiences. While such experiences are emotionally disturbing, they appear to lead to tremendous gains in learning. More fundamentally, they help the student reorganize his approach to learning and, indeed, to the world. By appropriate curricular planning, such powerful learning experiences may be created time and time again. If this is done repeatedly, education will have a powerful new force which can influence student learning at all levels.

References

Krathwohl, D. R.; Bloom, Benjamin S.; and Masia, B. B. *Taxonomy of Educational Objectives, Handbook II: Affective Domain.* New York: David McKay Co., 1964.

Maslow, A. H. "Cognition of Being in the Peak Experiences." *Journal of Genetic Psychology* 94: 43–66; March 1959.

EVALUATION

Introduction to Evaluation

GEORGE F. MADAUS
School of Education
Boston College

In these three essays, which span the years 1950 to the present, Benjamin Bloom demonstrates how evaluation can be the handmaiden of instruction and learning. Throughout his career a central message in his teaching and writing has been that evaluation is an essential for the improvement of the curriculum, of teaching and, most importantly, of student learning. He has exhorted educators to produce evaluation procedures that have a positive effect on student learning and on instruction, and that leave both teachers and students with a positive view of themselves, of the subject, and of the learning process. Bloom has done more than exhort, however; he has described in these three essays and elsewhere exactly what steps are to be followed in developing evaluation procedures that lead to the improvement of teaching and learning.

To begin with, the intended objectives of the course must be clearly stated. The content to be mastered and the competencies and skills to be acquired need to be made explicit. But there is more to it than clear specification. The objectives should not be the whims of a particular teacher, curriculum maker, or evaluator. It is essential that these objectives—the content domain and behavioral domain—themselves be evaluated. Teachers, curriculum developers, and program evaluators need to make value judgments about the objectives. They need to answer the important question, "Are these domains of content and skills the correct ones?" Are they "correct" in terms of the operative philosophy of education of the school and teacher? Do they address the needs and capabilities of the learners and teachers? Of the society? When stated objectives survive this evaluation of what is both desirable and possible, they clarify communication between the various publics concerned with instruction—teachers, administrators, evaluators, pupils, and parents. The objectives make explicit what it is a course or program hopes to accomplish, and further, they help educators to know what to look for to determine if the objectives have been realized.

The objectives become the blueprint for developing instructional strategies and for designing and validating the evaluation procedures. This latter function of objectives is the key to recognizing how evaluation procedures can help improve instruction and learning. Bloom goes to the heart of the matter when he reminds us of something we too often forget: students attempt to learn the skills, abilities, and content that are emphasized in the evaluation procedures. The evaluation process de facto defines for the students what to study and how to study by furnishing *models* of what learning is expected.

He further reminds us that if the evaluation procedures are designed and administered by an agency external to the school, rather than by the teacher, then the procedures furnish the teacher with models of what they are expected to teach and what their pupils are expected to learn. This power of the tradition of past exams that he illuminates has apparently been overlooked in the present rush by state legislatures to mandate minimal competency testing for high school graduation. These people would do well to peruse these three essays.

Given the power of evaluation procedures to focus teaching and learning, Bloom warns educators to be acutely aware of the duality of this power; that they must weigh the risks (narrowing teaching and learning) with the benefits (improving the quality of teaching and learning). Policymakers pay heed!

This power of evaluation to influence learning is largely based on a perceptual phenomenon on the part of both teachers and pupils. When the evaluation process is seen to be influential in decisions about a pupil (grading, promotion, certification, etc.), or about teacher or program effectiveness, then it becomes the basis for deciding what is important in the learning process and what is not.

If the objectives call for mastery of higher-order cognitive skills and abilities, the evaluation procedures must permit the pupil to demonstrate these skills. If they do not—if instead they call on the students to demonstrate only recall or recognition—then these will become the skills learned. The evaluation procedures must reflect the objectives in the most direct way possible if they are to influence and reinforce the instructional process designed to achieve these objectives. The key to the validity and fairness of the evaluation procedures is the extent to which they reflect the objectives of instruction. Unfortunately too many educators and evaluators are oblivious to this fundamental principle articulated by Bloom. They equate evaluation with machine scorable multiple-choice tests. This myopia ignores the fact—pointed out cogently in these essays—that many skills and competencies are better judged by more direct techniques: having the students write an essay, observing the student's performance in a science lab, listening to the student's pronunciation of a French passage, etc.

Related to this point is Bloom's insistence on not limiting one's evaluation to recall and recognition of facts. He continually argues the need for assessing all types of skills, abilities, attitudes, and feelings. He points out that only by designing evaluation procedures that permit students to exhibit these multiple skills will there be any assurance that students attempt to acquire them.

However, it is not enough to show that the evaluation procedures reflect the objectives; it is also necessary to establish that teaching was geared to the achievement of the stated objectives. That is, for the evaluation procedures to be fair and valid they have to be geared to the actual educational experience of the students.

When we evaluate a program rather than an individual, Bloom reminds us that the evaluator must establish that the educational experiences designed to realize the objectives are implemented, and further, that the evaluation procedures are direct measures of the objectives and experiences. Too often evaluators have ignored this advice and have incorrectly labeled programs as ineffective when either the proper instructional strategies had not been implemented or the evaluation procedures employed were not direct measures of the objectives of the program.

Another central point in these essays is that evaluation procedures can contribute to the improvement of teaching and learning at several points in the instructional process. Evaluation procedures can assure that the pupil is properly placed, in the first instance. Pretests, interviews, and behavioral checklists can help a teacher decide whether or not the pupil is ready for a particular instructional sequence. Does the pupil have the necessary general prerequisite reading skills for a history course? Does the pupil have the specific prerequisite skills for an algebra II course? Does the pupil have a negative attitude toward science? Frustration and failure can be avoided by identifying pupils who lack these general and specific prerequisites, and then providing them with the necessary remediation. Evaluation prior to the beginning of a course can also identify students who have already mastered many of the objectives and who therefore can profit from different educational experiences, thereby avoiding boredom and its concomitant problems.

Once the pupil is properly placed, evaluation procedures can continue to contribute to the improvement of teaching and of learning, by providing timely and useful information to both the teacher and the student. Throughout Bloom's earlier work in the University of Chicago Examiners' Office, the benefits to the teacher and the learner of frequent, nonjudgmental evaluations was a guiding principle. Later, in his development of mastery learning, this belief was translated into formative evaluation. Evaluation should not be solely for grading and marking, he argues, but also used as a feedback mechanism which helps teachers and learners identify and correct weaknesses while there is still an opportunity to redirect their efforts.

For the teacher, evaluation procedures that provide ongoing, frequent diagnostic information about a pupil or group of pupils permits the readjustment of teaching strategies and the individualization of learning experiences as needed. For students, to learn from their mistakes without the fear of being penalized by a low mark allows them to gauge their progress and to identify, and hopefully correct, misunderstandings, misconceptions, or poor performance. Such corrective, rather than judgmental, feedback helps the student develop a positive self-image about his or her ability to learn. This growing feeling of competence in turn can break the vicious circle of failure, frustration, and low grades. Formative evaluation, for Bloom, is an operating procedure in instruction that reinforces the learning of those who have mastered the material or skill in question and reveals particular points of difficulty for those who lack mastery. Formative evaluation procedures can take many forms in the instructional process; daily quizzes, class recitations, short tests, homework. What is necessary is that the evaluation be free of overtones of grading and that the information describe what the student can and cannot do relative to the domain of content and skill of interest. For Bloom, if evaluation is to improve learning it must not only be timely, but must also provide the teacher and learner with useful descriptive information about strengths and weaknesses.

Long before the current distinction between norm- and criterion-referenced testing became fashionable, Bloom's work in the University Examiner's Office was geared to providing information about what a student had achieved, not about his or her relative standing in a group. Evaluation in Bloom's sense of the term has always involved the development of procedures that are referenced to specific performance criteria: to what an individual can do or cannot do. Only with this information can teachers and students intelligently redirect their efforts toward the realization of course objectives.

A theme central to these essays, then, is that if evaluation is used to properly place pupils, and then frequently while instruction is still is progress to redirect instruction and learning, most pupils should master the course objectives by the time the teacher has to assign a grade for the course. Despite this emphasis on using evaluation procedures for placement, diagnosis, and prescription, these three essays show that Bloom has never lost sight of the fact that, like it or not, teachers must eventually grade or certify students. This phase of the evaluation/instructional dyad eventually came to be called—in the second of these three essays —summative evaluation. For summative evaluation procedures to improve learning they must be perceived by pupils as being fair and valid; that is, as being clearly related to what was taught and how it was taught. Bloom points out that this positive perception of summative evaluation procedures does not develop spontaneously; an evaluator must plan carefully and work hard to achieve it. The evaluation procedures must be keyed to the important objectives of the course; they must appraise these objectives as directly as possible; they must give a reliable indication of what the student has learned; and finally, they must be referenced to absolute performance rather than to a pupil's relative rank among his peers.

Carefully designed summative evaluation procedures should also leave the pupil with a feeling that his or her preparatory effort has been worthwhile; that the preparation for the summative evaluation helped the pupil to integrate what has been learned rather than regurgitate it.

If evaluation is used properly to place a student, and for corrective nonjudgmental decisions during instruction, and if summative evaluation is seen as fair, just, valid, and reliable, then evaluation has become an integral part of both teaching and learning. When this happens the student is the beneficiary.

There is one final theme to which Bloom speaks in these three essays. Evaluation procedures, if used properly, can improve curriculum and program design and implementation. Properly designed evaluation procedures can improve decision making on the part of those who design curricula, who administer programs, and who formulate educational policy.

One caveat runs throughout these three essays. Bloom, while emphasizing the potential of evaluation for good, also warns of its potential for harm. Since poorly designed evaluation procedures can seriously narrow and inhibit teaching and learning, an essential question for the practitioner is "How can I minimize possible negative effects?" These essays answer that essential question.

These three essays should be read and reread. There is much in them. Unfortunately too many of the points he makes in these essays have been forgotten. Forgotten by those who denigrate the need for grading and certifying; forgotten by those who equate evaluation with multiple-choice tests; forgotten by those who only measure recall of facts; forgotten by those who refuse to make explicit their objectives so that they can be reasonably examined; forgotten by those who often use inappropriate evaluation techniques and conclude that a program is ineffective when in fact it has not been properly implemented; forgotten by those who see minimal competency testing linked to a high school diploma as a quick technological fix for failing standards. These essays illuminate the folly of these manifestations of evaluation amnesia.

Reread these essays from time to time. If you are like me, you'll see different things each time and better appreciate the depth and soundness of Bloom's vision about what evaluation should and can be. Finally, reflect on the power of the theme central to all Bloom's work—evaluation is an integral component in the improvement of education.

Changes in Evaluation Methods

11

Although educational measurement has existed in some form or other for several thousand years, much of its development into a complex art and technology has taken place during the twentieth century. During much of this century, the field has been dominated by the ideas of psychologists, psychometricians, and statisticians. It is only within the past few decades that educational evaluation has sought to free itself from these ancillary fields in order to find clearer roots in the educational process and educational concerns and problems.

Psychological and educational measurement was primarily concerned with the development and utilization of instruments that could be used for prediction, selection, and certification in relation to students and student achievement. Such functions could be served by specialists far removed from education and educational processes in the schools. And, in fact, most of the educational measurement specialists were trained in psychology and statistics with little grounding in the field of education or even educational psychology.

The more recent field of educational evaluation, which was created by Ralph Tyler in the 1930s, has attempted to make use of the precision, objectivity, and mathematical rigor of the psychological measurement field but, in addition, has sought to find ways in which instrumentation and data utilization could more directly be related to educational institutions, educational processes, and educational purposes. In this chapter, I will attempt to sketch some of the major dimensions of this work as they appear at this time. I am confident that this field will develop in many new ways and that we can only dimly perceive a few of the major lines this work will take in the future.

EDUCATIONAL PURPOSE AND EDUCATIONAL EVALUATION

Educational purposes, goals, and objectives have been with us since the beginning of formal education. Expressed in verbal form, these statements of intentions were useful in giving a general direction to the educational institution, but only rarely were they operational statements which guided either the teacher or the learner.

In sharp contrast, the instruments for educational measurement (external examinations, teachers' tests and final examinations, standardized tests, etc.) have always had a controlling force on what was taught and, even more, on what was learned by students. Since the major rewards and penalties of an educational system are tied to its certification and grading procedures, which in turn are dependent on its examination procedures, the teaching-learning activities of teachers and students are to a large extent guided by what they expect will be tested on these examinations. And in countries throughout the world, the examination procedures have been largely limited to a single objective—the testing of recall of specific information about each school subject.

Perhaps the major innovation of educational evaluation was the development of ways in which the evaluation process could be integrally related to the educational purposes of the classroom, the school, and the educational system. Much progress in this work has been documented in the many books on educational evaluation, taxonomies of educational objectives, and curriculum evaluation. While there are many differing views about how the objectives should be defined, who has responsibility for determining the objectives, and the precise procedures for evaluating each objective, there is much consensus throughout the world on the importance of relating educational evaluation to educational purposes.

Starting with the pioneering work of Ralph Tyler in the 1930s, the development of evaluation procedures for specific types of educational objectives has moved with careful research and experimentation until it has reached the stage of what might be termed a technology. While there are still many opportunities for creativity and artistry in the construction and use of evaluation procedures, the models and techniques for developing evaluation procedures for major classes of cognitive and affective objectives have been specified in relatively clear detail. Having been involved in this work for over three decades, I have been surprised and delighted to find that most of my students can develop the necessary skills for this work in 3 to 6 months in contrast to the several years necessary to develop similar skills in the 1940s. I attribute much of this to the fact that the procedures are now more clearly developed and illustrated in the many books and manuals on educational evaluation.

It is now common practice for all the major educational testing organizations to start the construction of a new educational test with a detailed set of specifications of the content and objectives to be tested and then to check the validity of the test items against the detailed specifications. Similarly, every new curriculum, research project, or evaluation program starts with the specifications to be met in terms of content and objectives and then develops instruments, sampling procedures, a research design, and data analysis in terms of these specifications. The point is that the linkages between educational purposes and educational research or practice start with this almost as the first step in the work. Also, the detailed procedures for making the linkages are so well developed that evaluation workers can be trained to do it well in much less time than was true several decades earlier.

Educational Evaluation as Models
for Teaching and Learning

One of the consequences of the linkage between educational purpose and educational evaluation is that the evaluation procedures become operational definitions of educational purposes. It is now possible to classify the items, problems, and procedures being used in examinations, tests, questionnaires, observational forms, and other evaluation material and techniques to determine what purposes are being represented by the evaluation techniques. Thus, in the work of the International Studies of Educational Achievement (IEA) (Carroll, 1976; Comber & Keeves, 1973; Foshay, 1962; Husén, 1967; Lewis & Massad, 1975; Purves, 1973; Thorndike, 1973; Torney, Oppenheim, & Farnen, 1976), a collection of the evaluation procedures being used within a nation, when properly analyzed, gives more operational information about the educational objectives of a school subject or curriculum than do the verbal statements about the course or curriculum (Bloom, 1974a).

Furthermore, the actual materials of instruction and the observations of teaching-learning situations can be analyzed to determine the appropriate evaluation procedures and, in turn, the relation between the stated objectives and the learning experiences available to students. The evaluation procedures then can be determined in great detail. From these analyses, one can get a better picture of the kinds of learning being developed in a classroom, school, or entire educational system than is likely to be true from observations that might take several years to carry out. These analyses of "the opportunity to learn" have been very effective in predicting (and accounting for) the kinds of learning eventually found on major national or international survey instruments such as those reported in the IEA studies.

There are, however, even more important consequences of the linkage between educational purpose and educational evaluation. One can determine where the linkages are distorted between educational purposes, instruction, and evaluation. Is it that the purposes are beyond the present capabilities of the evaluators to develop appropriate evaluation procedures? If so, then the task of training educational evaluators to construct more valid and appropriate evaluation procedures becomes clear. Is it that the teachers have not yet learned how to provide instruction for particular educational purposes? If so, then the need for preservice and in-service education of teachers becomes clear. If the task of providing such training appears insurmountable for economic reasons or because of the present capabilities and training of the teaching staff, then can the situation be remedied by improvements in the instructional materials; by the use of radio, TV, or educational films; or by the use of peer tutoring and other special instructional procedures?

It is evident that students attempt to learn the skills, abilities, and subject content that they believe will be emphasized in the evaluation procedures they will be judged on. If they believe this is largely rote information, they will study and prepare accordingly. If they believe they will be judged on their ability to use the ideas and processes in new situations, they will learn and prepare to demonstrate such abilities. There has been a great deal of observational studies, as well as more direct experimental research, on how students learn and prepare in relation to different kinds of examinations. The evidence is unmistakable: Students will attempt to learn what they anticipate will be emphasized in the evaluation instruments on which they expect to be judged, graded, and certified. There is little doubt that a series of major changes in the evaluation procedures over a number of years can bring about great changes in the learning of the students—probably more change than could be produced by any other single change in the educational situation. This is, of course, a two-edged sword in that negative changes (reduction in the quality of learning) as well as positive changes (improvements in the quality of learning) can be produced by related changes in the evaluation procedures. But the point of this relation between student learning and evaluation is that the evaluation procedures furnish *models* of what learning is expected and the models are clearer than the more ambiguous statements of educational purposes or the complex range of instructional materials and procedures to which the students have been exposed. The clearest guide that students have as to what learning (largely cognitive) is expected of them is the evaluation instruments on which they will be judged and graded.

Similarly, teachers are also guided by the evaluation procedures as to what they are to teach and what will be expected of their students. Even when the evaluation procedures are made by the teachers themselves, they define the end learning products of their own teaching and they strive to prepare their students to do well on these evaluation instruments. If the evaluation procedures largely deal with rote types of learning, teachers will prepare their students for such types of evaluation. If the evaluation procedures largely deal with application of ideas to new problems, then teachers will attempt to develop these kinds of learning in their students. It has been found that one of the most effective ways of preparing teachers to teach higher mental processes is to develop skills for testing such processes in the teachers and to help them include problems of the appropriate type in their own evaluation procedures.

Evaluation As an Integral Part of Instruction and Learning

Evaluation instruments do serve as models for teaching and learning and, as such, help to guide both instruction and student learning. Evaluation used this way is largely a perceptual phenomenon in that teachers and students have expectations as to the evaluation procedures to be used (sometimes incorrect), and their efforts are guided by these expectations. Thus, the evaluation procedures serve to indicate the goals to be reached at the end of some period of instruction and learning.

Many of us have searched for ways in which evaluation might become a more integral part of the process of teaching and learning during the actual process. We had become aware of the effects of the frequency of testing on the learning of students (typically the more frequent the testing the higher the achievement); the ways in which some teachers analyze the results of their progress tests and quizzes to determine wherein they should stress certain points, review others, and even provide special help for students who have difficulties; and the effects of the kind of testing and the frequency of testing on the preparation that students make as well as the pacing of their learning activities. In addition, we became aware of the effects of group instruction on the differential learning of students within a class.

Much of the research on classroom instruction has demonstrated that students differ in their learning even though theoretically all had equal opportunity to learn in the same classroom. We conceived of this differential learning as errors in both instruction and learning and we took the position that if errors in student learning are systematically corrected at each stage in the learning process, there should be little variation in the final outcomes as measured by a summative evaluation measure. Furthermore, students who are corrected at each stage of learning should achieve at a much higher level than other students who have not been helped when they needed it, even though both groups of students are in the same classroom or are taught similarly by the same teacher.

This systematic corrective learning has been termed mastery learning and there are a number of teaching strategies to achieve such mastery. Central to most mastery learning strategies is the use of *feedback* and *corrective* procedures at various stages or parts of the learning process. While a variety of feedback processes are possible (including quizzes, homework, workbooks, etc.), it has been found that the development and use of brief diagnostic tests have proven to be most effective. Such diagnostic or formative tests are intended to determine what *each* learner has learned in a particular unit, chapter, or part of the course and what he or she still needs to learn. In general, these formative tests are not used to grade or judge the student and their main value is in providing feedback to both teachers and students on the particular aspects or elements of the learning unit that still need to be mastered. The effectiveness of mastery learning work is clearly related to the degree of efficiency of formative tests in pinpointing the learning needs of each student.

The key to the success of mastery learning strategies, however, largely lies in the extent to which students can be motivated and helped to correct their learning difficulties at the appropriate points in the learning process. Many teachers have been very effective in motivating students to do the necessary additional work and in finding ways of providing the correctives they need. The research done so far in the United States, Canada, South Korea, and a number of other countries suggests that the development of a student partner system or providing opportunities for groups of two or three students to work together are very effective methods of motivating each student to do the corrective work, and, in addition, this provides the additional time and help a student may need. Teacher aides, programmed instruction, audio tapes or cassettes, and other instructional material appear to work well in particular situations. In most schools, the corrective work following the formative test feedback is done outside of the regular classroom time.

In the many studies reported by Block (1971, 1974) and by Peterson (1972), there is considerable evidence that mastery learning procedures do work well in enabling about 80 percent of the students to reach a level of achievement which less than 20 percent of the students attain under nonmastery or conventional teaching methods. The time costs for the mastery learning is typically of the order of 10 to 20 percent additional time over the classroom scheduled time for those students who need it.

In a number of studies, it has been found that the extra time and help needed steadily decreases and toward the end of the course, little or no corrective work is needed to attain the criterion of mastery on the formative tests (Bloom 1974b).

While there are many different approaches to the improvement of both instruction and learning through mastery, the effectiveness of most of these approaches is dependent on the use of feedback and corrective procedures. Evaluation plays a central role in providing the feedback on the effects of instruction as well as on the effectiveness of the correction procedures. Properly used, the evaluation is looked upon by both teachers and learners as an indispensable tool for instruction and learning, especially when the formative evaluation is not used to grade or judge either the teacher or the student.

Many countries have been experimenting with different mastery learning strategies. Typically, they are finding that after the formative tests and corrective procedures are developed by evaluation and curriculum specialists, the costs of mastery learning are negligible. Furthermore, they are finding that the outcomes in terms of final achievement, student attitudes toward learning, and improvement in student general ability to learn under school conditions are so great as to represent positive human development in its own right as well as economic benefits that are far greater than might be expected from the time or other costs incurred.

However, for the purposes of this paper, the main point to be stressed is that the use of evaluation as an integral part of instruction and learning has enormous consequences. We must continue to search for additional effective ways in which evaluation can contribute to the teaching-learning process as an integral part of that process.

Evaluation To Determine the Effectiveness of Instruction and Learning

Much of the use of evaluation has been to determine the learning outcomes of particular types of curriculum and instruction. Typically, the attempt is made to construct evaluation procedures that are appropriate to a particular educational program, curriculum, or instructional approach. Then, an appropriate research design and a sampling procedure are chosen to determine whether in fact the educational program, course, etc., did have specific traceable effects on student learning.

Rarely does an educational system restrict itself to a single educational program, curriculum, or instructional approach for all students of a particular age or grade. Evaluation is useful in determining the relative effectiveness of the different approaches to instruction and learning. Evaluation used this way has characteristically been used to determine whether alternative A is, in terms of student learning, more effective than alternatives B, C, D, etc. (alternatives may be programs, courses, curricula, teaching methods, class size, instructional strategies, etc.). In most of the research using this evaluation approach, it has characteristically been found that the "opportunity to learn" particular content and objectives in a particular alternative is highly related to the evaluation results for that alternative. That is, if students are taught x, y, and z they tend to learn x, y, and z, while if they are taught only x and z they learn accordingly. This seems so obvious that one wonders why evaluation is necessary.

However, there are great discrepancies between what an educational program is *intended* to accomplish, what students are *actually given an opportunity to learn,* and what *students actually learn.* The discrepancies have to do with what happens in particular classrooms (opportunity to learn) in relation to what was intended and the evaluation results. Thus, the basic problem of the effects of an educational alternative is dependent on the linkages between the intended effects of a program, what happens in the school or classroom, and the evaluation results. If an educational program is designed to produce a particular set of results, we must insure that the appropriate use of the program actually takes place in the classroom before we can be certain that we are really evaluating the effectiveness of the program. In response to this problem, educational evaluators and researchers now seek to establish what actually takes place in the classrooms they evaluate before claiming they are evaluating the effectiveness of the specific program. Increasingly, evaluators are selecting classrooms and teachers where they are certain that the program is actually being implemented in the intended ways before applying their evaluation procedures.

Once they can satisfy themselves that the classrooms or teachers are fully implementing the intended curriculum, program, or method, the evaluations can determine its effectiveness as well as its difficulties. Then, the research moves to the problems of how the program can be fully implemented in other classrooms—training of teachers, orientation of students, appropriate materials, or the supporting conditions of morale, educational leadership, supervisors, consultants, etc., that are necessary for its full implementation with other teachers and classrooms.

Perhaps the main lesson to be learned from the attempts to evaluate new early childhood educational programs (Head Start), new programs for the disadvantaged students (compensatory education), programmed instruction, new curricula (new mathematics, new biology, etc.), and new teaching strategies is that there are great gaps between the intended new program and its full realization in the classrooms. In fact, one has to search very carefully before finding the few classrooms where the new program is fully realized. Policymakers who sponsor and give economic support to the new educational alternatives must be aware that good intentions (especially new ones) are not enough in education. The problems of how the good intentions can be fully implemented in the classroom must be solved before the new program can be evaluated.

Closely related to the foregoing points is the increasing use of evaluation to determine how an alternative can be modified and improved. New approaches to education are rarely perfect and seldom are they universal panaceas. At one time, evaluation was used primarily to determine whether alternative A was better than B, or C. It mattered little that the statistical significance of the difference between the alternatives was rarely matched by the educational or social significance of the differences. Now, however, evaluation increasingly is being used not only to determine which alternatives are superior, but also how they can be further improved. A new curriculum or program may be excellent in terms of certain characteristics but should be modified in terms of other characteristics. When the evaluation and other data are properly analyzed, they reveal what is excellent about an educational alternative, what is good but could be improved, and what is poor and needs much further work.

For the educational policymaker or administrator, the basic point is that major changes in programs should be instituted only when there is clear evidence that a particular existing program is poor in all respects. Improvements and modifications in existing programs may be more effective than the creation of entirely new programs. Smaller changes cause less dislocation in the schools and may, under appropriate conditions, be more effective in promoting improved instruction and student learning than will completely new programs. It is likely that the enormous expenditure of resources (economics as well as human) of introducing great changes in teachers, materials, and educational points of view will be cost-effective only when all aspects of the new program are working effectively in the classrooms and school.

A final point to be made on evaluation and effectiveness of instruction and learning is that times and conditions change. An educational program that is very effective at one time may in a number of years become less effective. A new curriculum which works superbly in year x may in year x + 5 work very poorly. The deterioration of particular new programs, curricula, and teaching methods has been well documented, especially in relation to some of the major educational changes introduced during the past decade in the U.S. as well as other countries.

Increasingly, educational evaluation is seen as a quality control measure. That is, carefully selected samples of students, classrooms, and schools are surveyed at particular times to determine whether a new program that worked well at one time still continues to work well or to determine whether particular aspects of the program need to be modified at particular points in time if the program is to continue to work well in the classrooms. Sometimes, it is found that the program continues to be effective with some students and some teachers or schools but works less well in certain respects with other students or teachers. Again, the point is that the educational policymakers or administrator must not expect that education can be a fixed and static thing. Times and conditions change and evaluation can reveal when and where the changes require modification and improvements in the educational programs.

Educational Evaluation and Education

Education in Western societies is frequently equated with schooling. We support schools to give our children and youth an education. We empower schools to give formal recognition to the amount and type of education an individual has completed by the use of credits, certificates, and academic degrees. Most of our writing and research on education deal only with schools and schooling.

This equation of education and schooling has been attacked by scholars of education as well as by more radical reformers who insist that much learning can and does take place outside the school. But equally important, research on education and research on various aspects of the society have questioned some of the relations between the school system and other subsystems in the society.

Research into the relationship between the schools and the home environment has been one of the more fruitful areas of study stimulated by these questions. Home is a powerful educational environment, especially during the preschool and primary school years. Studies of home environments in the United States as well as in several other countries reveal the effect of the home on language development, ability to learn from adults, attitudes toward school learning, and aspirations for further education and the occupational careers and life styles associated with education. It is clear that when the home and the school have congruent learning emphases, the child has little difficulty in his later schooling. But when the home and the school have very divergent approaches to life and to learning, the child is likely to be penalized severely by the school, especially when school attendance is required for 10 or more years.

During the past decade, we have begun to recognize some of the problems raised by disparities between home and school. One approach has been to preempt some of the years preceding regular school by placing children in preschool programs. Other attempts have been made to alter some aspects of the primary school. Still other efforts have been made to alter the home environment. There is no doubt that these attempts to alter the relations between home and school have raised many problems. The resolution of these problems and the appropriate relations between home and school will concern us for many years to come.

Schools and peer groups are increasingly in conflict, and the individual appears to learn very different things in these two subsystems of society. Especially during adolescence do we find these two subsystems diverging. The conflicts between the values emphasized by schools and colleges and the values emphasized by various peer groups raise serious questions about the ways in which these two sets of values can be more effectively related. What we desperately need are research and scholarship that will point the way to the resolution of some of the more disturbing conflicts between the schools and adolescent peer groups.

Recent research by economists attempts to understand the relationships between the economic system of a nation and its educational system. It is evident that the relations between education and economics may be very different for societies at different stages of industrialization as well as for societies that have very different political systems. The view that education can be conceived of as investment in human capital has stimulated educators as well as economists to study the economic effects of different approaches to education. The view of education as both a consumer or cultural good and an investment in human capital alters many of our traditional views about education and its effects. This area of research raises long-term problems about the consequences of this view for support of the schools and support of students in the schools.

There are other subsystems in a nation—religion, mass media, the political system, the status system—that have very complex relations with education. Perhaps the main point is that education is not confined to the school system and that very complex educational and other relations are found between the schools as a subsystem and the other subsystems within a society. While we have tended to think of a system of schooling as relatively insulated from other parts of the society, it is likely that the schools will be under pressure to relate more clearly to the other parts of the social system. Undoubtedly, we will come to regard education during the school-attending period (as well as before and after this period) as most appropriately the concern of many aspects of the society. Increasingly we will try to determine what can best be learned in the schools, what can best be learned elsewhere, and what can be learned only through an effective interrelation of different parts of the social system.

Evaluation methods are gradually being developed to appraise the learning of a population both in the school as well as outside of the school. The new ideas on national assessment that are being developed in a number of countries are efforts to determine what has been learned in the schools, what has been learned elsewhere, and what has been learned in the interaction between the schools and other subsystems in a nation. This work is of recent development and it will be some time before evaluators are effective in determining both the extent of the learning as well as the source.

Once again, the point is that education and educational policymakers must learn to use evaluation and evaluation data to secure a broader picture of the educational resources of a nation than may be secured from viewing the schools as the single educational resource. This is probably the most complex problem that educational evaluators and policymakers must face. The challenges posed by these broader issues suggest that international seminars and conferences may be necessary if the problems and progress of various national attempts in this field are to be studied and utilized where relevant by other national groups.

Educational evaluation may contribute to the improvement of education in many countries of the world. The enormous resources being expended in each country for education makes it mandatory that some forms of educational evaluation be used for appraising the effectiveness of particular aspects of a national educational program, for determining where it is in need of modification or major changes, and for determining how to maintain and even improve the effectiveness of the schools as well as the related educational resources of the nation.

The appropriate training of highly competent educational evaluation specialists is a minimum requirement if effective use is to be made of this rapidly developing technology. The support of and the appropriate relations between such specialists, educational policymakers, and the educational institutions of a nation are necessary to maintain educational evaluation at a high level and to ensure that the evaluation methods and results play their appropriate role in the continued maintenance and improvement of complex educational systems.

References

Block, J. H. (Ed.). *Mastery learning: Theory and practice.* New York: Holt, Rinehart & Winston, 1971.

Block, J. H. (Ed.). *Schools, society, and mastery learning.* New York: Holt, Rinehart & Winston, 1974.

Bloom, B. S. Implications of the IEA studies for curriculum and instruction. *School Review,* 1974, *82,* 413–435. (a)

Bloom, B. S. Time and learning. *American Psychologist,* 1974, *29,* 682 -688. (b)

Carroll, J. B. *French as a foreign language in eight countries: International studies in evaluation V.* New York: Wiley, 1976.

Comber, L. C., & Keeves, J. P. *Science education in nineteen countries: International studies in evaluation I.* New York: Wiley, 1973.

Foshay, A. W. (Ed.), *Educational achievements of 13-year-olds in twelve countries.* Hamburg: UNESCO Institute for Education, 1962.

Husén, T. (Ed.), *International study of achievement in mathematics: A comparison of twelve countries* (2 vols.). New York: Wiley, 1967.

Lewis, E. G., & Massad, C. E. *English as a foreign language in ten countries: International studies in evaluation IV.* New York: Wiley, 1975.

Peterson, P. *A review of the research on mastery learning strategies.* Unpublished manuscript, International Association for the Evaluation of Educational Achievement, 1972. (Also available from Stanford Center for Research and Development in Teaching, Stanford, California.)

Purves, A. C. *Literature education in ten countries: International studies in evaluation II.* New York: Wiley, 1973.

Thorndike, R. L. *Reading comprehension education in fifteen countries: International studies in evaluation III.* New York: Wiley, 1973.

Torney, J. V., Oppenheim, A. N., & Farnen, R. F. *Civic education in ten countries: International studies in evaluation VI.* New York: Wiley, 1976.

Some Theoretical Issues Relating to Educational Evaluation

12

Nature and Use of Specifications

There has been some controversy recently about the need for specifications as to the desired outcomes of a course of instruction.[1] Much of this controversy has been engendered by investigators who have observed teachers in the process of teaching a group of young children. Teachers appear to respond to individual students during the instructional period, and they appear to alter procedures and interactions rapidly as they focus on the needs of individuals or subgroups in the class. When probed, the teachers have difficulty in stating their objectives or in relating what they do in class to a set of long-term objectives for the subject matter.

Other fuel has been added to the controversy by curriculum makers who have great difficulty in getting subject-matter experts to state their objectives in other than the most general and vague terms. In contrast, curriculum makers find the subject matter experts more explicit in defining the subject-matter content that should be learned and quite skilful in suggesting instructional procedures to make explicit the ways in which they would like the interactions among teacher, student, and learning material to take place.

Quite in contrast to this reluctance to state or use specifications is the great need for and rather avid use of specifications by persons working with instructional technology or evaluation. Workers on instructional materials find it difficult to determine what to include in programmed instructional material, computer-aided instruction, educational films, or other learning materials unless they know precisely what is to be learned by the students. If specifications are not available from other sources, these workers find it difficult to start their work until they have constructed an appropriate set.

[1] E. W. Eisner et al., "Educational Objectives: Help or Hindrance?" *School Review*, LXXV (Winter, 1967), 258–82; Philip W. Jackson and Elizabeth Belford, "Educational Objectives and the Joys of Teaching," *School Review*, LXXIII (Autumn, 1965), 267–91; W. J. Popham, J. M. Atkin, and J. Raths, "The instructional Objectives Controversy" (Symposium, Annual Meeting of the American Educational Research Association, Chicago, February, 1968).

Persons constructing evaluation instruments to be used by more than a single teacher or a single school also find it difficult to begin their work until a set of specifications is provided. Here again, if specifications are not available, these workers find it necessary to construct them or to create a committee or other type of consensus mechanism to develop a set of specifications against which they can construct and validate an evaluation instrument.

If one takes these statements about teachers, curriculum constructors, educational technologists, and evaluators at their face value, one finds real conflict between the first two and the latter two. Yet, if one probes to a deeper level, it is quite likely that all four groups have a set of specifications in mind which differ only in explicitness, detail, and form.

No teacher can work with a group of students for a term or more without some model or framework to guide him with respect to the learning desired or expected of his students. At the very minimum he must have a set of expectancies which guide his teaching in order that his students will be ready for the next grade or course in a sequence. Thus, the second-grade teacher is in part guided by what the third-grade teacher expects to do in reading, arithmetic, and the like. The sequence of expectations in our graded schools makes it impossible for any teacher to ignore what is required by the educational system and to do exactly as he pleases with his students. Minimal requirements for students with respect to various learning and developmental tasks are made very clear to all teachers, although the teachers may be more or less free with respect to the way in which they teach and to the timing of their instruction on particular topics or material during the term or year. Beyond these minimal requirements, teachers are quite free as to what they may expect or desire of their students. In some instances the teacher may wish to do unique things with individual students while in other instances the teacher may attempt to get all students to develop in similar ways.

It is possible that most experienced teachers have their minimal requirements so clearly in mind that they take them for granted and see little reason to state them as objectives or content to be learned.

The curriculum makers who are reluctant to state their objectives are not reluctant to state the content or ideas they wish to have developed through the curriculum. Perhaps their resistance is to the formulation of educational objectives, a formulation which they believe represents meaningless "pedagese." In instances in which the curriculum makers are scholars and experts in their own subject field, it is likely that they will place primary emphasis on the instructional treatment of the ideas and subject matter rather than on the learning processes that might and should take place in individual students. Some curriculum makers regard curriculum making as an artistic process which should not be specified in advance. Such curriculum makers may be less opposed to an analysis of the objectives included, after the curriculum has been constructed.

For the educational technologists and evaluators, the clearer the specifications are in terms of both content and behaviors, the better. Such specifications define the problems they must solve in the construction of instructional materials or evaluation instruments, and such specifications provide the criteria against which the materials and instruments are validated.

It would seem to this writer that it is virtually impossible to engage in an educational enterprise of any duration without having some set of specifications to guide one—whether one is a student, teacher, administrator, curriculum maker, educational technologist, evaluator, or guidance worker. What may be different from worker to worker is the explicitness of the specifications, the forms in which they are cast, the sources from which they are derived, and the extent to which they are used for various decisions.

Explicitness of Specifications

It is quite possible for the specifications that guide a teacher or curriculum worker to be implicit in his actions, processes used, or products developed rather than stated in precise and explicit form. One may work for many years as a teacher without making his purposes explicit in verbal form. Unfortunately, specifications which are implicit are difficult to communicate to others, they are rarely analyzed and clearly revised, and they do not serve as clear guides to particular decisions or actions. Implicit specifications may shift without the educational worker's being clearly aware of any change, and, because of poor communication, the attainment of the specifications may defy any attempt at systematic appraisal.

If education and educational materials are to be systematic in their effects and open to inquiry, the specifications for them must be put forth in some explicit form. One cannot determine whether two or more educative actions, experiences, or products are consistent or inconsistent with each other, whether they are additive or nullify each other, or whether they have positive or negative effects on the students unless they can be exposed to analysis and inquiry. If education is to be open, public, and examinable, the specifications for it must be explicit, and either the process of education or the outcomes of the process must be examinable in relation to such specifications. Trust in professionals is a highly desirable goal for any field, including education, but each profession must either police itself, if it is to merit the confidence of the public that supports or uses it, or expose itself to external scrutiny when the confidence of the public is impaired.

If the purposes and specifications for education are not explicit, then it is possible for them to be altered by social pressures, by new fads and fashions, and by new schemes and devices which may come and go with momentary shifts on the educational scene. Implicit purposes are difficult to defend, and the seeming vacuum in purpose invites attack and substitution of explicit purposes by a constant stream of pressures and pressure groups.

That *all* the purposes and specifications for education cannot be made explicit does not mean that *no* purposes or specifications should be made explicit.

Purposes and specifications which are explicit tend to be those which are relevant for groups of students. Such purposes and specifications may attempt to describe the ways in which students are to be altered by the educational activities. Although in actual fact the students may vary in the extent to which they are altered by the educational activities, all are expected to be modified to some degree in the ways specified.

It is possible to develop specifications for the changes to take place in an individual student, but this has rarely been done by teachers. Such specifications are more likely to be developed by tutors, guidance workers, or other professionals who work primarily with individuals on a one-to-one basis. Perhaps the current emphasis on individualization of learning may result in the development of such specifications.

In addition to change in relation to the purposes and specifications which were made explicit, it is possible for groups of students to change positively (or negatively) in ways not included in the specifications. Some of these changes are not intended by the teachers or curriculum makers and may either be accidental, in that no one could have foreseen them, or occur as foreseeable effects of the educational activities if the teachers and curriculum makers are fully cognizant of human behavior and the forces which produce change.

Finally, there may be other changes which take place in individual students as the result of specific activities of the teachers which are designed to affect these individuals. These may be implicit in the teacher's activities but, for a variety of reasons, are not made explicit. Such implicit purposes may not be made explicit because they are fulfilled only as the teacher senses a particular need of the student in the actual process of interacting with the student—that is, they cannot be or are not planned in advance. Other implicit purposes may be achieved unconsciously by the teacher's interactions with individual students or groups of students.

The point to be made is that not all purposes of education can or should be made explicit. However, it is the thesis of this chapter that, insofar as possible, the purposes of education and the specifications for educational changes should be made explicit if they are to be open to inquiry, if teaching and learning are to be modified as improvement or change is needed, and if each new group of students is to be subjected to a particular set of educative processes.

The Form of Specifications

Education may be regarded as consisting of some content or subject matter to be learned (topics in science, areas of living, material to be studied, ideas, etc.) as well as processes to take place in individuals (retention of information, problem solving, attitude formation, and the like). Thus, the explicit specifications may take the form of descriptions of the ways in which each group of students is to be altered by interaction with the material of instruction and the process of instruction. Most teachers and curriculum makers have little difficulty in defining the content or subject to be included. They may have greater difficulty in defining the processes which they desire or expect to take place in individuals.

Various workers have differed as to the appropriate degree of specificity in defining these processes. Some would insist on great detail with each behavior defined and stated with considerable precision.[2]

To be able to solve linear equations

To be able to repair a television set

Given a list of thirty chemical elements, the learner must be able to recall and write the valences of at least twenty-five

To be able to write three examples of the logical fallacy of the undistributed middle

[2]R. F. Mager, *Preparing Instructional Objectives* (Palo Alto, Calif.: Fearon Publishers, 1962); Popham, Atkin, and Raths, *op. cit.*; R. M. Gagné, "The Analysis of Instructional Objectives for the Design of Instruction," in *Teaching Machines and Programmed Instruction*, ed. Robert Glaser (Washington; Department of Audiovisual Instruction, National Education Association, 1965), pp. 21–65.

Others[3] make use of more generalized statements of objectives such as the following:

Familiarity with dependable sources of information in the biological sciences

Ability to analyze arguments and propaganda

Ability to recognize unstated assumptions

Ability to apply social science generalizations and conclusions to actual social problems

Ability to make mathematical discoveries and generalizations

Responds emotionally to a work of art or musical composition

Enjoys reading books on a variety of themes

The degree of specificity sought (as represented in these two examples) is determined in part by the extent to which the curriculum makers or teachers wish to anticipate and program the work and activities of students and teachers. If the changes in students are to take place primarily because of the interaction of a student with specific learning material, the specifications must be most detailed. If the changes are to take place through the interaction of student, teacher, and material, the specifications are usually less detailed in order that the teacher may have greater freedom to use those procedures and instructional processes which he may believe to be most appropriate in a given set of circumstances and at a given moment in time.

Another reason for the difference in specificity has to do with the view of learning and education accepted by the curriculum maker, instructional-material producer, or teacher. If the worker believes that each element to be learned must be included in the instruction, he will be most detailed in his specifications. Thus Thorndike,[4] in the teaching of arithmetic, specified several hundred detailed objectives to be attained. Some would insist that this is training rather than education. In contrast is the view that students can learn to generalize from a small number of appropriate learning experiences. For example, if there are about thirty major principles in physics and literally several million possible applications of these principles, this view of learning would attempt to determine how a small number of illustrations and applications could gen-

---

[3]R. W. Tyler, *Basic Principles of Curriculum and Instruction* (Chicago: University of Chicago Press, 1951); B. S. Bloom (ed.), *Taxonomy of Educational Objectives, Handbook I: The Cognitive Domain* (New York: David McKay Co., 1956); D. R. Krathwohl *et al.*, *Taxonomy of Educational Objectives, Handbook II: The Affective Domain* (New York: David McKay Co., 1964).

[4]E. L. Thorndike, *The Psychology of Arithmetic* (New York: Macmillan Co., 1926).

eralize into "the ability to apply principles of physics to new problems." The main point to be made is not that the more precise and detailed the specifications, the better. One level of detail may be better from one point of view, while a more general set of specifications may be better from another point of view.

Other specifications may be in the form of a series of tasks or problems to be solved. Such tasks or problems may be analyzed to determine the content and processes which are included in them, or they may be used as illustrations of the content and purposes already made explicit in a table of specifications. The value of such a set of tasks or problems is that they do make explicit what the student is to do, although they may not be very effective in defining the intent behind the materials to be used. As such, they are more effective in determining what is to be done by the student than as specifications for alternative sets of materials or as criteria for a range of evaluation procedures. The development of test-item banks is one way in which test items may be used to illistrate the specifications and to give operational definitions to them.

Finally, the specifications may be in the form of learning activities in which the student is to engage. Here again, the astute analyst may infer the content and behaviors which are implicit in the learning activities, but he is hard-pressed to determine what learning activities may be substituted for the stated ones or precisely what evaluation procedures are relevant for appraising the effectiveness of the learning activities.

The basic problem in developing a set of specifications is to make the desired outcomes of learning sufficiently explicit that they can be used to communicate what is desired to other teachers, curriculum workers, educational technologists, and evaluators. If the specifications can be made explicit enough to communicate clearly to others, they can be used to furnish the criteria for many alternative learning tasks, a variety of evaluation procedures, and a variety of interactions among students, teachers, and materials. Furthermore, the specifications can be judged for their appropriateness for a given group of learners, for their relevance to students with particular characteristics, and for their relations to prior as well as to later educational specifications.

The Source of Specifications
A set of specifications may, in part, be drawn from an analysis of the important ideas or subject matter available in a subject field. This requires some decisions about what in the subject field is most significant, what will contribute most to the student's development, and what aspects of the subject are likely to be most relevant and important for

other learning the student is likely to do in this or in related subjects. Different conceptions of the subject field are likely to result in different priorities with regard to content and behavior. For example, if a subject is viewed as closed and likely to change very little in the future, the specifications may stress knowledge and comprehension of a systematic account of what has been learned by scholars in the field. However, if the subject is viewed as open and highly changeable in the future, the specifications may stress inquiry objectives, higher mental processes, and the processes used in developing the subject rather than the products of previous research and scholarship. Under this view, the content may be selected both because of some view about its importance and because of beliefs about its value in developing these more complex behaviors.

Different views about the relation of the subject to other learning (and to other subjects) may also result in different priorities with regard to content and behaviors. If a subject is seen as being clearly related to other subjects, the specifications must take this into consideration, and the learning of one subject will not be viewed as an end in itself. If learning is seen as developmental and sequential, the specifications should show how one set of learnings is to be related to previous and subsequent learning. If a subject is seen as related to ongoing processes in contemporary life as well as arising from historical processes, the specifications should take these views into consideration.

The subject matter of a field furnishes the content and processes to be considered in a curriculum. However, the subject matter to be included in a set of specifications, while guided by what a particular group of subject experts may suggest, must transcend the limitations of the subject specialists. However competent he is in his own subject, a subject expert may not be fully aware of what a group of students in the freshman year of high school can learn and what is important to such students. A young person is to be educated and the specifications as to what he is to learn are dependent on his previous educational development, his abilities and skills, and his aspirations and motivations. A curriculum and a set of specifications for it should be the product of the best thinking of wise and expert men about what will best promote the fullest development of the individual as a man, as a citizen, and as a contributing member of a society. It is likely that no one set of specifications will suffice for all students, teachers, and schools.

The behavioral part of the specifications is likely to emerge from some views about the subject, but this also may arise in part from research as well as from views about the nature of the students, the nature of the society, a philosophy of education, and a conception about the nature of learning. Students differ in many ways, and the specifications must in part be based on selected characteristics of the students who are to be changed by the educative process. The educational objectives and the nature of the learning experiences must be partly determined by the kinds of students in the school and by the cultural conditions in which they develop.

Each nation and society has its own special problems, concerns, and interests. These special qualities of the nation and its subgroups must be reflected in the educational program. Implications for the specifications of a curriculum must be drawn from studies of contemporary society as well as from studies of trends for the future. Social scientists who are experts on the society, both as it is and as it is coming to be, should play a vital role in furnishing the raw data for curriculum planning. Curriculum development is a type of social planning, since it is concerned with the kinds of learning students will need if they are to play a significant part in the society as it develops in the future. Educational planning and social planning must be interrelated at many points if they are to be mutually reinforcing. All too frequently there is a marked disjunction between the schools and the contemporary problems and changes taking place in society.

In a highly stable society, the basic values which the society prizes become an integral part of the educational philosophy, and the organization and activities of the schools reflect these values. In a society in rapid transition, there is usually confusion about values and the ways in which they can be implemented by the schools. An explicit educational philosophy can do much to give meaning and direction to the schools. It can help to determine the hierarchy of educational objectives, and it can serve to provide the organizing principles for the content and learning experiences. The specifications for a course as well as those for an entire curriculum should reflect the educational philosophy of the school and, if possible, the educational philosophy of the society.

A theory of learning can be one basis for ordering the possible objectives of education and for the determination of the objectives which should be given highest priority. Such a view of learning and evidence in support of it can be used to determine the likelihood that a particular objective can be achieved (or not) by a particular group of students. Finally, a psychology of learning is of value in determining the appropriateness of particular learning experiences as means for attaining particular objectives.

The point of all this is that specifications should not be the whims of particular teachers, subject experts, or curriculum makers. The specifications properly result from a very complex analysis of the conditions and context in which the learning is to take place. The specifications for one place and time may not be appropriate for another place and time. It is unlikely that any single person has a comprehensive grasp of the entire situation. Only as a variety of resources are brought to bear can the specifications fully take into consideration the multitude of information and conceptions that are necessary.

Use of Specification for Making Decisions

One objection to the making of specifications and, especially, to the stating of objectives is that it has no effect on the curriculum, the instruction, the evaluation, or even the learning of students. Some people view the stating of objectives as a meaningless charade advocated by educationists which, once done, can easily be forgotten. If educational objectives are regarded only as the introductory statements for a course, a set of instructional materials, or a dean's speech to a new group of students, then they are best forgotten, and to state them is a pointless exercise.

But educational specifications can and should have far-reaching consequences for all that follows in an educational enterprise. We can state a few of the educational decisions which require an explicit set of specifications with regard to content and objectives.

What is to be included or excluded in a particular subject, curriculum, or educational program? There is so much to be learned, so much to be understood, so many specifics in any field of learning that some set of considerations must guide the curriculum maker or teacher. If the specifications are clear and understandable, they provide criteria for determining what in the subject matter is useful and what is not, what should be emphasized and what need not be emphasized, and which details can be omitted and which are absolutely essential.

Furthermore, the specifications can be utilized to determine how the materials should be treated. Is a particular item of information to be learned in its own right, or is it to be learned in order that some larger theory or concept can be understood? Is a principle to be learned in order to be remembered, is it to be learned in order to develop the ability to apply principles, or is it to be learned because it is part of a process of inquiry in the subject? Thus, decisions about how the subject matter is to be learned can follow from decisions about the specifications.

Decisions about the teaching-learning process in the classroom also are dependent upon a set of specifications. When to use a lecture or discussion; when to use secondary sources, primary sources, or firsthand experience; when to use independent learning, group processes, or discovery-learning strategies; when to use programmed instruction, computer-assisted instruction, or workbooks, and drill procedures, etc.—these are decisions which, in part, are dependent on the use of a set of specifications. It may be true that a teacher depends on feelings, hunches, and a quick grasp of a particular learning situation to determine what to do and how to do it. Without a set of specifications, however, these decisions are likely to be repetitions of what he has always done or expressions of what the teacher likes, believes he is good at, and gives him fewest problems. If the decisions are to promote the learning of students rather than to make the interests and attitudes of the teacher central, the teacher and teaching must be guided by some set of specifications which have been carefully developed and which are workable for the subject matter and the students involved.

Decisions about the evaluation process are also dependent on a set of specifications. What types of evaluation procedures are to be used: open book or closed book, essay or recognition-form questions, products or processes, observation of the student or observation made by the student, cognitive tasks or affective responses of the students, frequent testing or comprehensive examinations, formative or summative evaluation—these are all possibilities for evaluation which may be used in various combinations depending on the specifications. Decisions about the particular objectives and content to be appraised, the weight and importance to be given to particular aspects of the evaluation, and even the standards to be used are largely dependent upon the specifications. Again, evaluation can be determined by the particular predilections of the evaluator, his skills, his habits, etc., or it can be determined by an explicit set of specifications which furnishes a blueprint for what should be evaluated and how it should be evaluated. The "state of the art" of evaluation is far more complex than the skills and habits of a particular examiner or evaluator. A set of specifications can, with proper technical facilities, provide for evaluation that transcends what can be evaluated by a particular teacher or evaluator.

Evaluation of Non-specified Outcomes of Instruction

One argument against the use of specifications is that there are differences between the outcomes of learning and instruction and the learnings which were specified in advance. This argument may be developed in two ways. First, not all of the outcomes that have been specified are achieved. This, of course, is one of the main reasons for evaluation. That is, if one attempts to evaluate for all the specified outcomes of instruction, it is possible to determine which ones have been achieved to a satisfactory degree and which have not. Thereafter, the problem becomes reduced to research and inquiries to determine why certain outcomes have not been attained and to the development of alternative procedures to attain them. It is quite possible, even after considerable time and effort has been expended, that certain outcomes are really impossible to attain with a given group of students and teachers under a given set of conditions. If this conclusion is finally reached, the specifications may have to be altered accordingly. One does hope that means can be developed to attain those outcomes which a group of teachers and curriculum makers firmly believe to be desirable and important, but it is recognized that not all that one reaches for is attainable.

The second argument is that individuals vary, teachers vary, and the learning process is so complex that students learn far more than can be specified in advance. That this may be so should not be seen as an argument against specifying and evaluating the outcomes that are desired. It should be regarded as an argument for inquiry and research into the nature of the non-specified outcomes.

Some of the non-specified outcomes may be regarded as desirable from the viewpoint of curriculum makers and teachers, and, if possible, they should be studied and evaluated. If the curriculum and the instruction stimulate some students to read and study far beyond the requirements of the course, this may be regarded as desirable. The extent to which this occurs may be appraised by relatively informal evaluation procedures. If the curriculum inspires some students to seek additional courses or other learning experiences in the subject, this may also be regarded as desirable, and it may be studied by appropriate methods. If the instruction results in some student's seeking interrelationships between what he has studied in one course and what he has studied in other courses, between the course and contemporary problems of the society, or between the course and his own personal problems, this may also be appraised. All of these "desirable" outcomes should be studied in an effort to understand the effects of instruction and perhaps to seek ways in which such effects may become more widespread. It is possible, on reflection, that some of these effects may become so predictable and widespread that they may be included in the specifications. The other desirable effects may be regarded as plusses which occur in an unpredictable way, and, one should be content when and if they occur.

However, there may be side effects of the instruction and curriculum which are clearly undesirable. These may be difficult to detect, but they need to be identified and corrected, if possible. If some students develop considerable cognitive competence in a subject but learn to dislike the subject with great intensity, this is clearly an undesirable consequence, and it should be appraised in order to determine why it occurs and how it can be altered. If the curriculum, the evaluation methods, and the standards that are used lead many students to regard themselves in a negative way or to develop a negative attitude toward school and learning, this is most unfortunate and should be investigated and, hopefully, corrected. If teacher attitudes are positive toward some students and negative toward others, the effects of this should be ascertained and corrected.

Increasingly there is evidence that middle-class children are encouraged while lower-class children may be discouraged by teachers and by particular aspects of the curriculum. Especially in a rapidly changing society, we must search to determine the intended as well as the unintended effects on children of particular practices, methods, curriculums, teachers, and organizational characteristics of education. Public education cannot be permitted to develop some children at the expense of others or to develop some desirable characteristics in children at the price of developing even more far-reaching negative characteristics in them.

It is quite likely that many of the unintended positive as well as negative outcomes of instruction can be detected by competent observers who approach the problem in a clinical way. An understanding of learning and of human development should enable competent observers of the process of learning and instruction in actual classrooms to predict many of these side effects. Once they have been detected and identified, it is possible to devise evaluation procedures to determine their frequency and their qualitative characteristics.

The point of all this is that there are undoubtedly many outcomes of instruction and curriculum that cannot be specified in advance. Such outcomes should be investigated by clinical and other techniques in the hope that the desirable outcomes can be strengthened and the undesirable outcomes corrected or eliminated. One need not limit evaluation to only the desired and specified outcomes of instruction if there is some reason to believe that certain additional outcomes are likely to take place. While the medical analogy is not entirely appropriate, it does suggest the importance of searching for the side effects of a particular treatment. All too frequently, the side effects of medical treatment are as important as the desired main effects.

Effects of Evaluation

It is possible to measure the length of a bar of metal in such a way that the measurement process does not appreciably alter the shape or size of the bar. Precautions must be taken to insure that the body heat of the measurer does not affect the expansion of the metal and that the weight of the measuring instrument does not alter the shape of the metal.

More complex processes of studying, testing, or measuring in the physical and biological sciences can have greater consequences on the phenomena being investigated, and more elaborate controls and precautions must be taken to insure that it is the phenomena which are being investigated rather than the "phenomena as influenced by the research procedures."

Whatever the case may be in the natural sciences, the effects of study, testing, or measurement in the social sciences are such that frequently the phenomena being investigated may be markedly altered, distorted, or affected in other ways by the process of investigation. Samoa being studied by Margaret Mead is altered in the very process by the presence of Dr. Mead and her methods of study. Human beings may rarely be studied without being affected by the study procedures. Especially in education, the process of studying or testing may have so much effect on students, teachers, and others that what we are investigating cannot be completely separated from the investigation process itself.[5] To measure a child's intelligence is to appreciably change the child and his parents, as well as to affect the way in which teachers and others come to view the child.

If, as is asserted here, the process of evaluation has an effect on the learner and the teacher, as well as on others involved in education, it is necessary to understand the possible effects and to deal with them intelligently. If these effects are understood and utilized properly, they can do much to enhance the student's learning as well as his regard for himself. If the effects are not used well, they can do great damage to the student as well as to the educational system. The point to be made is that the effects of evaluation can be maximized or minimized, but they cannot be entirely controlled. Also, the effects can be positive or negative, and only rarely can they be entirely neutralized.

Some of the effects of evaluation take place in advance of the actual use of the evaluation instrument. In England, children begin to prepare for the "11 +" examination a year or two in advance of the actual time of

[5]D. A. Goslin, *The Search for Ability* (New York: Russell Sage Foundation, 1963).

the examination. In the United States, college entrance examinations have a similar influence. Teachers also anticipate an examination, especially an external examination, and they direct some of their teaching effort (both group and tutorial instruction) to preparing their pupils for the anticipated examination. Parents also do whatever they can to increase their children's chances of successfully completing an anticipated examination, including placing their children in schools which they believe will give them the best preparation, coaching their children, or using whatever other tactics they believe will be efficacious.

The effects on the students at the time of the examination may be relatively small, except for anxiety aroused by the examination and frustration, self-doubt, or a sense of accomplishment engendered by the student's interaction with the examination. There is no doubt that many students are exhausted at the end of an important examination, but most of these effects disappear relatively quickly.

The postexamination effects may be very profound, depending on the uses made of the examination results. The result of some examinations, such as an intelligence test or a major external examination, may be to mark an individual for the rest of his life. An I.Q. index, the results of a school or college entrance examination, or the results of the matriculation examinations in many countries may determine the individual's educational and vocational career, his own view of himself, and the ways in which others regard him. These major examinations create self-fulfilling prophecies in which later success or failure or the educational and vocational openings available are largely determined by the results. It is no secret that teachers may rationalize their difficulties in instruction by pointing to the I.Q. or standardized test scores of their students. Parents also come to judge their children, positively as well as negatively, in terms of their I.Q.'s or other examination results. And the child himself will come to view himself partly in terms of his performance on certain crucial examinations.

Maximal and Minimal Effects of Evaluation
Not all examinations have the same effect on students, teachers, parents, or instruction. Not all examinations have powerful effects on the way in which the student views himself or the way in which others (including employers) view the individual.

Examinations which are regarded as measuring important and relatively stable characteristics of the individual have the greatest effect. Thus, the I.Q. score is regarded as so important because it is widely believed that it is highly stable, that it determines the individual's capacity to learn, and that little can be done to alter it. While each of these assumptions can, in part, be questioned, it is the beliefs of school people and laymen (including the student himself) which make the intelligence test so important and which have such marked influences on the use of the results of such tests. Other tests which may be regarded in the same way are aptitude tests, personality measures, vocational interests tests, and, sometimes, tests of reading ability.

Examinations which are used to make important decisions at major disjunctions in the educational system also have great effects. The examinations which are used for certification of the completion of an educational program, for the selection of students for particular programs or streams of education, and for the determination of which students are to be admitted to advance programs of education are so critical in the lives and careers of students that they not only have effects on the student and the educational system but they also influence the entire society. Such examinations have a profound effect on the curriculum and instruction: They determine who will have certain opportunities and who will not, and they determine the type of person who will be admitted to (or denied entrance into) particular occupations and professions. In the larger sense these examinations help to shape the society's view of itself and of the variations among the members of the society.

Examinations for which the results become part of the student's permanent record or which are made public also have great effects. If the results of a particular examination are referred to repeatedly in making critical decisions about the student (or adult), the examination will have a marked influence on the student and on the adults who are interested in or concerned with him. Here is the whole issue of invasion of privacy. Insofar as examination results are made a part of the permanent record of the student and such a record may be made available to other teachers, school authorities, and employers, they must be regarded as important by the student, and to do well or poorly on them is a matter of vital concern to the student and others. It is quite possible that administrative convenience has led to an overemphasis on some examinations. Undoubtedly, administrative convenience has led to the creation of a few landmarks in the student's records rather than to the development of a truly cumulative record which highlights the pattern of development of the individual over his entire educational career.

Examinations which are used to judge the effectiveness of teachers, schools, or systems of education have great effect on the institutions involved. While such examinations may have little direct influence on the students tested, they may have marked influence on the curriculum, on the patrons of the institution, and on the staff and administration of the institution. Undoubtedly, the responsiveness of the institution and the staff to the examination results is determined by the extent to which the results are made public and the extent to which the results can be related to specific practices and persons in the institution.

It is possible for examinations to have minimal effects on students, staff, and patrons. *Perhaps the least effect is likely when the examination results are not related to individuals, practices, or institutions.* If the examinations are related to anonymous individuals and institutions with a minimum of comparison among individuals or institutions and with a minimum of publicity, the results are unlikely to have much effect on either individuals or institutions. *Examinations are likely to have little effect if they are considered to be measuring trivial things which are not regarded as important by the students, teachers, patrons, and others.* Thus, a test of handwriting elegance is unlikely to have much influence on students or schools at present, while sixty years ago it might have been regarded as of the utmost importance. *Finally, examinations which are not used for making significant decisions by or about individuals or institutions, and where this is known in advance by the examinees, are likely to have minimal effects on the individuals and institutions.*

Perhaps the main point to be made about the effect of examinations is that it is largely a perceptual phenomenon. That is, if students, teachers, or administrators believe that the results of an examination are important, it matters very little whether this is really true or false—the effect is produced by what individuals perceive to be the case.

Positive Versus Destructive Effects of Evaluation

Evaluation is a two-edged sword which can enhance student learning and personality development or be destructive of student learning and personality development. It can have positive or negative effects on teachers, curriculum, and school systems. While it is unlikely that examinations and other methods of appraising the learning progress of students can be eliminated, it is possible to use evaluation procedures wisely, so that they may have a beneficial effect on learning and teaching. This is a matter of designing and using evaluation with a clear awareness of its possible effects and with a sensitivity to the ways in which the evaluation will be perceived by students, teachers, school authorities, and school patrons or the public.

If the primary use of evaluation is to render judgments of pass or fail, good or poor, the person being evaluated is likely to respond as one who is being tried by a judge. He is concerned about the fairness of the decision. Where students or teachers believe the evaluations to be unfair, they either overtly express their sense of mistreatment or brood about it and feel resentment against the evaluation process as well as the educational system which has used the process. Where students have no way of determining the fairness or soundness of the evaluation and where it is used repeatedly to indicate failure, poor performance, or other negative judgments about students, they are likely to develop a sense of frustration and their motivation for learning must suffer. Thus, some colleges may use achievement examinations at the end of the freshman year to arbitrarily eliminate as high as 40 percent of the entrants. Under such conditions, the students are penalized by their rank order on the examinations rather than by the inadequacy of their performance. When the examination system is "rigged" in this way, the students are placed in a competitive system in which "beating the system" and survival are more important than the learning which is presumably being tested. To "win" under such conditions is to lose in terms of one's view of himself and of his relations with others, and to suffer some deterioration in personal values. This is especially true where passing the examination by cramming, studying the tricks of examiners, memorizing material just for the examination, and other examination-taking strategies are separable from learning the subject.

Quite in contrast is the use of evaluation procedures which are regarded as valid by teachers and students, where the system of grading or marking is regarded as fair and just, and where there is a clear relation between what is taught and what is examined. Under such conditions, the students and teachers can enter into the learning process with a clear sense of purpose, and the appraisal of what has been learned may be regarded with concern and anxiety but, at the same time, is relevant and fair. Motivation for learning can be very high under such conditions, and students can give their efforts to those aspects of the learning which they regard as important. To pass or to do well on such examinations is likely to be regarded by the students as worthwhile, and this success is likely to lead to a strengthening of the student's sense of adequacy and of his commitment to the learning. Even to fail such an examination leaves the student with the sense of having entered into a worthwhile learning process and no great feeling of disgrace if one has done his best.

The basic questions to ask about examinations and other evaluation procedures are whether they have a positive effect on student learning and instruction and whether they leave both teachers and students with a positive view of themselves and of the subject and learning process. A primary task of teachers and examiners is to design the examinations and the evaluation process so that they will have these positive effects. We are able to state a few of the necessary conditions for this to take place. First, the examinations must be valid in the sense that they must examine for those aspects of the learning which are regarded by teachers and students as important and desirable learning outcomes. The examinations must also be valid in that they examine for these learning outcomes by the most direct methods. The evaluation techniques— whether they be observations of processes, products (such as term papers), reports of observations or experiments; recall or recognition questions; open-book or closed-book examinations; viva voce; etc.— must be seen by students and teachers as directly related to the learning or performance desired. Second, the examinations must be regarded as reliable and objective in the sense that chance and error must play a minimal part in determining the adequacy of each examinee's performance. That is, the sampling of the learning outcomes must be adequate enough to minimize the likelihood that chance failures or successes determine the final outcomes, and the scoring procedures must minimize subjectivity on the part of the readers or scorers. Finally, the standards for grades or pass-fail must be defined in terms of adequacy of learning rather than in terms of rank order of students and competition. That is, the student must be left with the sense that he has been judged in terms of what he has been able to do rather than in terms of who else took the examination at the same time as he did.

In addition to these elements, a well-designed examination with adequate previous indications to the student of what is to be expected of him can leave the student with a feeling that his preparation for it was eminently worthwhile. Such an examination can make the preparation for the examination an important learning experience if it requires him to bring the parts of the subject together in new ways—that is, if the examination causes him to interrelate and integrate the elements of the subject so that he finally perceives them in ways different from the ways he experienced them as he learned the parts or elements separately. This of course requires that the examining art be brought to its highest level and that the expectations for the learning be adequately communicated to the students in advance of their special preparation for the examination.

Formative Versus Summative Evaluation

Much of what we have been discussing in the section on the effects of examinations has been concerned with what may be termed "summative evaluation." This is the evaluation which is used at the end of the course, term, or educational program. Although the procedures for such evaluation may have a profound effect on the learning and instruction, much of this effect may be in anticipation of the examination or as a short- or long-term consequence of the examination after it has been given.

Quite in contrast is the use of "formative evaluation" to provide feedback and correctives at each stage in the teaching-learning process. By formative evaluation we mean evaluation by brief tests used by teachers and students as aids in the learning process. While such tests may be graded and used as part of the judging and classificatory function of evaluation, we see much more effective use of formative evaluation if it is separated from the grading process and used primarily as an aid to learning.

Frequent use of formative evaluation during a course may be very effective in pacing student learning. Each student is faced with many competing demands on his time and energies. Unless he is unusually well organized and purposive, he is likely to give his major efforts to those demands which are more compelling and less attention and care to those demands which he believes can be postponed to some later time. In highly sequential learning, especially, it is of the utmost importance that the student learn one task before another if he is to master the entire sequence. The use of formative evaluations after each separable unit or task in the learning process can do much to motivate the student to the necessary effort at the appropriate time.

Another use of formative evaluation is to provide feedback to the instructor after the completion of each unit in the sequence of instruction. Where a significant proportion of the students have made particular errors or have had difficulty with an important element of the learning tasks, this should be taken as a symptom of weakness in the instruction or instructional material. If these errors are regarded as critical, especially for later learning tasks, it is most desirable that the instructor review the ideas, preferably through alternative ways of explaining or describing the element in question. Ideally, the instructor should probe to determine why the idea was not understood or should seek other ways of clarifying what has gone wrong. The use of formative evaluation for this purpose requires that the instructor analyze the accuracy of item responses rather than be content with a description of the distribution of scores on the total test. Formative evaluation used in this way is a healthy corrective to the teaching process, since it finds difficulties early enough to do something about them as the sequence of learning-teaching develops.

Probably the most effective use of formative evaluation is to provide feedback to students on their learning of particular portions of the learning sequence. If a student has mastered all or a high proportion of the test items in the formative test (perhaps 85 percent or more of the items), this can assure him that his learning is going well and that he should continue his present learning procedures. Such mastery information can serve to reinforce the learning (and the learning process) and can do much to decrease the student's anxiety about his learning. Since it is likely that high performance on a number of formative evaluation tests will be predictive of high performances on the summative evaluation instruments, the student who does well on the formative tests can be confident of his learning even in advance of the summative evaluation.

For students who have not mastered a particular unit of learning, the formative evaluation can provide feedback as to precisely where he is having difficulty. Here the formative test must be analyzed to indicate the particular elements still to be learned as well as the relation of these elements to other elements in the unit of learning. Such feedback to the student is most useful when it not only identifies what the student must still learn but also suggests very specific instructional materials and procedures that he should use to learn these ideas. If the students can be motivated to correct their difficulties and if the appropriate resources are made available to them (including tutors, special materials, etc.), it is quite likely that the majority of them can achieve mastery over each unit in the sequence of instruction.

We have found that such formative evaluation procedures are most effective when they are separated from the grading process and are presented primarily as aids in the teaching-learning process. Thus, when each formative test is graded, it is likely that those students who repeatedly receive C grades or less will match their efforts in the course to the final grade they expect. In contrast, when students are assured that they can learn the material if they will correct their difficulties during the progress of the course, they can be motivated to put forth the necessary extra effort at the appropriate time in the course. Further motivation for this extra effort can be produced if there is any assurance that their efforts will eventually be rewarded by high grades on the summative evaluation instruments as well as by the thorough mastery of the subject being studied.

The use of formative evaluation suggests that evaluation in relation to the process of learning and teaching can have strong positive effects on the actual learning of students as well as on their motivation for the learning and their self-concept in relation to school learning. Much can be written on the process of testing and test construction in formative evaluation, but the main point being made here is that evaluation which is directly related to the teaching-learning process as it unfolds can have highly beneficial effects on the learning of students, the instructional processes of teachers, and the use of instructional materials by teachers and learners. This is one method by which individualization in the learning process can be related to the attainment of a common set of objectives by a large proportion of the students.

Changing Conceptions of Examining at the University of Chicago

13

THE IMPROVEMENT OF EXAMINATIONS

The Board of Examinations was founded at the University of Chicago in 1931. In planning the new curriculum in general education, the faculty wished to separate the examining and judging functions from the pedagogical functions. They wished to have the instructor serve primarily to help students learn, and they believed that an ideal student-teacher relationship was impossible when the teacher also had the responsibility for judging and grading the student. The planning group was concerned about the ways in which some instructors overemphasized their functions as graders and judges, but they were even more concerned about the students who deliberately cultivated the instructor in order to secure a higher grade as well as the students who hesitated to express serious interest in a subject or problem because it might be taken as evidence of "apple-polishing." They believed an independent examination system could do much to correct this.

The faculty was also interested in having students assume increasing responsibility for their own education. By stating the requirements for graduation in terms of examinations to be successfully completed, they believed the student could be helped to see that he had responsibility for decisions about the rate at which he would complete the College program, as well as decisions about his own class attendance and the amount and method of study.

The faculty was also concerned about improvement in the quality of examinations and wished to have a staff of competent testers do what they could to improve the quality of examining in the College. Under the leadership of the chief examiner, a staff was assembled whose competence lay primarily in their understanding of psychometrics. These examiners, who were largely recruited from the Department of Psychology, had a thorough grasp of the statistical problems in connection with examining. They were also unusually skillful in the development of objective test forms as well as in the improvement of objectivity in the more subjective essays. This staff organized the entire examining program, and in their writings and in their methods of working set the fundamental principles on which the work to the present day is based.

Perhaps some idea of the problems they encountered may be seen in a brief characterization of the testing then current in this and other programs of higher education. Examining was largely done by the individual instructor who expended a minimum of effort on the task. College instructors have generally thought of their major functions as research and teaching and have regarded examining as a necessary evil which had to be done for the sake of the registrar and the records. Typically, the final examination for a course was constructed by the instructor a short time before it was needed, and many an instructor stayed up late the night before the examination to prepare it. As a result, the final examination was likely to be something of a hit-and-miss affair in which favorite questions were repeated and in which the sampling of the learning tasks was relatively inadequate. Usually the examination consisted of a number of vague essay questions for which the grading was highly subjective and influenced largely by the quality of the handwriting, the presence of phrases and references the instructor recognized as familiar (usually his own), and by the extent of fatigue and boredom of the instructor at the time he graded a particular paper. The many studies on subjectivity in grading need not be mentioned here. Suffice it to say that the grade the student finally received was determined by a tremendous number of accidental and personal circumstances. While such a state of affairs has characterized examining in other colleges as well as in this one, it was clear that the improvement of examining could only be achieved as the result of the investment of considerable time and effort on the task of examining as well as the recruitment of individuals who had special competence or talent in the art and practice of examining.

Thus, the major problem faced by the Board of Examinations in 1931 was the improvement of the examination as a measuring instrument. Since the faculty desired to place upon the student major responsibility for securing an education, it eliminated requirements with regard to class attendance and set the degree requirements in terms of comprehensive examinations. The comprehensive examination, as the sole basis on which the student's progress toward the degree was determined, had to be as good a measure of academic achievement as it was possible to devise. Each examination had to contain a representative sample of the types of questions and problems the student should be able to solve as a result of the study of the ideas and materials included in an entire year of study in a particular field. In order to measure over the total range of problems of a course, each examination had to be a very efficient measuring device. For this reason the first comprehensive examinations tended to be largely made up of objective or recognition types of questions which could be answered in a minimum of time.

In order to help students determine whether they were progressing satisfactorily during the year, evidence had to be gathered at a number of points during the year. For this purpose the examiners developed quarterly as well as midquarterly examinations which included the types of problems the students would encounter later on the comprehensives. These examinations served a purely advisory function in that they were intended solely to help the student gauge his progress, and the results did not become a part of his permanent record or transcript. A third type of examination prepared by the examiners involved aptitude tests which could be used both to advise a student on the order in which he should take particular courses and to help him in making decisions about the size of the academic load he should carry if he engaged in extra-curricular activities or part-time work. Still a fourth kind of examination constructed by this group consisted of scholarship tests which were largely measures of the student's achievement in various subject matter in the high school.

In the preparation of these different types of examinations the examiners spent much time and energy and they were aided by the members of the instructional staff. Perhaps a major contribution of this work was the increasing recognition on the part of the faculty that the construction of a good examination required a great deal of time and effort. The examination construction task became one spread out over the entire academic year rather than one to be done just prior to the use of the test. Considerable improvement was also to be noted in the format and printing of examinations. The original Board of Examinations made extensive use of the photo-offset process of printing because it gave them flexibility in the organization of examination material and because it enabled them to include a great variety of illustrative materials, such as tables, graphs, and pictures.

In their attempt to improve the validity of examinations, the examiners constantly sought to determine: What are fair questions to be asked in the light of the educational experiences to which the students have been exposed? The educational experiences were defined by the lectures and discussions, the textbooks, and the outline of the course specified by the syllabus. The examiners attended classes and had many meetings with the faculty to be sure that questions which had been formulated were fair and appropriate for students who had made good use of the educational experiences offered. The faculty went over each question to be sure it was an answerable one in the light of the content of the course and to be sure there were no errors of fact in the items.

In order to insure that it was a reliable examination and that the student's grade was not dependent on accidental circumstances, the examiners included a large number of questions in each of the comprehensive examinations. Typically, 400 to 600 questions were included in each six-hour comprehensive, and the reliability figures were phenomenally high for these examinations—usually being about +.95 or higher. In part, these high reliability figures were the result of the large number of questions and the amount of time allotted for the particular examination. High reliability was also the result of very systematic coverage of the entire course by the variety of questions. The original group of examiners set a standard of reliability for comprehensive examinations which we have consistently tried to emulate. In general, it may be said that the comprehensive examinations used in the College rarely have reliability figures below +.90, with the usual one being +.95 or higher.

Perhaps the major effort of the examiners was expended in the improvement of objectivity. This they did by using extremely ingenious recognition forms of questions which could be graded by clerks on the basis of a scoring key agreed to in advance by the examiners and the instructional group. They also devised techniques for analyzing the responses to essay questions in order to secure a high degree of consistency between two or more judges. To further insure objectivity, the examiners devised a procedure of removing identifying information from the papers and substituting a number. From the time the paper came to the Examiner's Office until the final grade had been assigned, the grading was done without knowledge of the identity of the student involved. This has meant that the student's grade was determined solely by the quality of the work exhibited on the examination rather than by his relations with either instructors or examiners throughout the year. While these precautions to insure objectivity have not always been highly prized by instructors, it is safe to say that, as far as measurement is concerned, it insures the fairest estimate of the quality of the work without consideration of individual personal circumstances.

Another area which was given attention by this group was the specification of the conditions under which tests should be administered. The early group of examiners experimented with various techniques for administering examinations and attempted to devise what they considered to be as nearly the ideal conditions for test administration as possible. The seating arrangements, the duties and functions of proctors, and the instructions to be given to students were all given a considerable amount of attention. In general, the procedures for test administration set up by this group have been adhered to for some twenty years. The adequacies of these procedures have been testified to by the very infrequent complaint of cheating or of violation of examining rules over these many years. This is remarkable when one considers that the student's final grade is determined solely on the basis of the comprehensive examination and that he is under considerable pressure to show as high a test performance as possible.

The examiners also studied the conditions under which scoring of an examination would be most accurate. They devised a system of scoring procedures by means of readers, clerical workers, and machines which has been both efficient and accurate. Each paper is checked in several ways to insure that the individual student is not penalized by careless or inaccurate appraisal of his performance. As a further check on the accuracy of grading, the student was given the right to request a review of his paper if he was of the opinion that the grade assigned was not a fair index of his performance. The examiners also set up a system of derived scores which placed all of the examination results in a standard form such that the results for different examinations could be easily compared. By this system all examination results are translated into scores with a mean of 20 and a standard deviation of 4. This derived score system has been continued throughout the history of the Board. While new members of the faculty have to be instructed on the use of this system, this can be done relatively easily, and it makes the task of interpreting test results and advising students far simpler than would otherwise be the case. Since examination results must finally be translated into a letter grade, the examiners specified the procedures for judging the final distribution in order to set grades. In general, they made use of the normal distribution in arriving at grades and supplemented this by a number of statistical checks in order to set grades. The staff of instructors and the examiners cooperate in making the final judgments about the grade distribution.

The emphasis of this original group of examiners may be seen in the types of work and research they reported in the literature. A number of publications had to do with the methods of constructing particular test forms[1] as well as the extent to which these types of questions were valid, reliable, and objective.[2,3] Quite a large number of studies were reported involving predictions. These reported the correlation between comprehensive examination achievement and such other variables as high school grades, specific aptitude tests, scholarship tests, interest tests, and tests of intelligence or scholastic aptitude.[4] Finally, there were a number of studies reporting on statistical developments, such as new statistical formulas, new applications for particular formulas, as well as more efficient methods of computing.[5] In general, these research reports indicated the magnitude of the examining task and the attention given by this group to the development of improved examination instruments.

Since this was a pioneer college examining group, they found it necessary to spend some time in training others to make use of their examination procedures. Although the Board of Examinations was an independent group in its relation to the faculty, the task of examination construction was always conceived of as a cooperative activity between faculty and examiners. Most of the members of the College faculty were given some directions and training in examining in order to help them carry on particular parts of the examining function. Since the examination construction task was a fairly sizeable one, the examiners trained their own assistant and associate examiners. The Board of Examinations was also conceived of as a laboratory for developing and trying out measuring and statistical theories and as such furnished opportunities for graduate students in psychology and education to secure training and to do research on psychometric methods. In some instances, also, individuals from other colleges were provided with apprenticeship experiences in examining. Some of these apprentices later became major examiners in other institutions.

EXAMINING AS A PART OF THE EDUCATIONAL PROCESS

The period 1931 to 1939 was the first period in the work of the Examiner's Office during which the primary emphasis was on the development of sound examining methods and techniques and of improved examination instruments. The test questions developed in this first period were largely centered on information or what might be considered to be understanding of subject matter. It was possible for a capable examiner to construct this type of knowledge question on the basis of a careful reading of the textbooks or syllabi and by noting the content of lectures and other classes. Toward the close of this period the faculty of the College began to reach out for methods of developing a greater variety of competencies in students. The faculty was not satisfied with knowledge as the primary outcome of instruction. They wished to have students learn methods of reasoning and attacking a great variety of problems, since they regarded the fundamental task of general education as that of enabling the individual to understand the world in which he lived and to attack the significant problems he encountered both as a man and as a citizen. As they began to explore this greater range of educational competence, they experimented with new methods of teaching, new types of instructional materials, and new methods of organizing courses. These were major changes in the philosophy of general education and in the curriculum and methods, and these in turn required corresponding changes in examining procedures.

As the faculty became more and more aware of what it was they sought to accomplish by means of general education and as they introduced innovations in their teaching methods and curricular materials, they wanted evidence which would help them determine whether these new methods were effective in bringing about the changes in students that they were intended to produce. Examining had to be seen as part of the total educational process and as having consequences beyond the accurate certification of achievement or beyond the production of good examinations.[6]

The staff regarded the task of an educational program as one of changing the behaviors of students. Such behavioral changes included the thinking, actions, and feelings of the individual learners. The faculty were not always crystal-clear in defining the behavioral changes they were seeking to accomplish, and the translation of their objectives into examination tasks frequently required tremendous leaps of the imagination. It became evident that this new type of examination construction task required individuals who were thoroughly trained in the subject matter of a particular course, who were familiar with and sensitive to the instructional materials and methods used in the course and who, in addition, had acquired the techniques of examining. The original group of examiners trained a number of people who could perform this dual function of being sensitive to the instructional task as well as being skillful in the techniques of examining. Most of the examiners since 1939 were selected because they were outstanding teachers in the particular courses involved and then given training in the techniques of examining.

Since this was a period of rapid growth and change in curriculum, it was necessary then that the examining process be an integral part of the total educational process. Thus, although emphasis was given to production of good examinations, the examining staff had to be extremely sensitive to the effect of the examining on the total educational process. Given this conception, the examining staff began to look upon the comprehensive examinations in a somewhat different way than had been true previously. In the first instance they began to see the production of examinations as a way of helping a staff clarify its educational purposes. The original statements of the educational objectives tended to be general and vague. These statements began to acquire meaning and precision as the examiners, working closely with the staff, explored ways in which evidence could be gathered to reveal whether or not the student had acquired the particular competence stated in the objective. One clear consequence of this sharpening of the statement of objectives was that the staff began to recognize that certain instructional methods, such as the lecture and demonstration, which they had been using, were not very appropriate as means for helping students develop certain of the intellectual skills and abilities desired. As a result, the instructional staff began to experiment with methods of teaching by discussion in order to implement certain of these problem-solving objectives. Likewise, as they became clearer about their objectives, the materials they used for instruction shifted from textbooks and secondary sources to original writings and to primary experiences with art, music, science and other materials or phenomena. Clarification of objectives also enabled the different instructors teaching in a particular course to become somewhat more consistent in their methods of teaching and in their use of the instructional materials.

Since the examinations were oriented to the objectives of instruction, they served to help a staff determine the extent to which it had achieved the objectives desired. Reports, which were prepared by the examiners for the instructional staff at the end of each year, helped the staff determine the strengths and weaknesses of the course and were used as the basis for continual improvement of the course. This close relation between examination development and the educational process meant that with every major change in the view of the educational process, there had to be a corresponding change in the comprehensive examination. In order to keep abreast of the curricular developments, it was found necessary to prepare new forms of the examination each year. In other words, the examination had to be much more sensitive to the educational process than had originally been true, and the possibilities of preparing parallel forms of the examination year after year were no longer true with a rapidly changing and developing curriculum.

Through questionnaire studies and informal talks with faculty and students, the Board of Examinations became very much aware of the ways in which the kinds of examinations used influenced the kind of preparation students made. Released copies of old examinations, the syllabi, and the "grapevine" helped students orient to the objectives and purposes of the course. As students learned about the kinds of tasks they had to perform on examinations, they organized their study and preparations with these tasks in mind. Unless the examinations were closely interrelated with the objectives, instructional methods and materials of curriculum, examining and instruction worked in opposition to each other. Thus, when the examination consisted of knowledge questions while the instruction emphasized problem-solving skills, students tended to memorize and cram information (and ignore much of the instruction) in order to pass the examination. On the other hand, when the examinations were of the open-book type and students were allowed to bring their notes and materials to the examination, their study in preparation for the examination involved attempts to apply the methods and principles of the course to new situations and problems. The examinations tended to motivate the students not only as to the kind but also as to the amount of preparation. Preparation for the examination was also important in getting students to seek for interrelations among the various topics, methods, and problems included in the course.

As we became more and more aware of the relation between examining and the total educational process, it became clear that the students needed and desired evidence of the extent to which they were progressing toward the achievement of the objectives of the College program. The quarterly examinations and other examinations offered during the year had to be as closely oriented to the objectives of the course as the comprehensive. It was also found useful to the student to give him a relatively complete report on the extent to which he had achieved the objectives of the course. For this purpose a rather elaborate set of scoring procedures and reports on performance were made available to students after they had completed each of the comprehensive examinations. These reports helped the student discover his weaknesses and strengths and revealed the relationships among the tasks and objectives in the different parts of the entire program. The diagnostic report booklets also helped students become aware of some of the elements which make the entire curriculum a highly integrated one. Students used these reports as the basis for further study of a particular area as well as to find ways in which the subject matter and objectives of one course were related to other courses in the College program.

As the staff and examiners worked with different objectives, they had to experiment with new ways of securing evidence on achievement of certain of the objectives. Test forms were developed, including essay questions, laboratory examinations, as well as long-term projects, which could be included as part of the comprehensive examination evidence. The examinations shifted from the more straightforward use of recognition and objective test forms to a great variety of test forms needed to secure evidence on the different objectives. Since many of the objectives emphasized problem-solving skills and abilities and methods of dealing with new problems and materials, the examiners developed original problems. Frequently they found it necessary to base questions on new materials which were given the student to read either at the time of the examination or just prior to it. The open-book type of examination came into frequent use because it provided relatively realistic and valid examination situations. For this type of examination, the student was permitted to bring his notes and his study materials to the examination and refer to them as he needed.

The examiners also became concerned about the effect of aptitude and scholarship tests on the types of preparation students made prior to coming to the College. It was found that the aptitude tests which stressed subject-matter competence were objects of considerable attention and study by prospective students as well as their secondary school teachers. In a number of schools students were coached on the particular materials and questions included in the aptitude and scholarship examinations. Clearly, this put some students at an advantage as compared with other students. This was additional evidence that examining could not be considered apart from the total educational process. In order to minimize the effect of coaching as well as to decrease the influence of the College tests on the secondary school curriculum, the examiners attempted to develop aptitude tests which would not emphasize particular school subjects. The examiners found that a psychological examination, a test of reading comprehension and a test of writing competence were better predictors of achievement in the College than the tests which emphasized particular school subjects.

The freshman week testing program shifted from the problems of predicting the student's performance on comprehensive examinations to one of placement. It was found possible to develop tests which could be used to determine the extent to which the entering student had already attained major objectives of the curriculum although he may have attained this competence through quite different educational experiences than the College offered. Since the College emphasized demonstrated competence rather than records of the amount of time spent in courses, the student's requirements for the degree could be determined by the use of these placement tests. This placement as well as the help which the advisers and instructors have been able to give the students on the basis of the placement tests has markedly reduced the failure rate and has done much to individualize the student's program of work in the College. Thus, it may be seen that the freshman week has become much more closely linked with the educational process and with major decisions about the student's academic career than had been true previously.

This increased emphasis on examining as part of the total educational process meant that the development of and study of the examination as an instrument or technique became to a lesser extent the primary tasks, while the intimate relation between the examination and other parts of the educational process became focal. Problems of objectivity and reliability had been given major consideration and were the subject of much study in the first years of the Board. While such problems are always important in examining, it was found possible to achieve satisfactory reliability and objectivity without making them so central in the work of the later group of examiners. In part, this was because the second group of examiners could draw upon the experience of the original group and could achieve a high level of objectivity and reliability by following the sampling procedures, the techniques for examination construction, and the scoring procedures which had been developed previously. In part, also, it had been found that the use of six-hour comprehensive examinations almost guaranteed that a reliable sample of problems and questions would be developed. Finally, reliable examinations were further insured by the procedures of test administration, item analysis, and examination revisions which had become the routine of the Board of Examinations. Objectivity was also attained as the result of the general procedures for constructing tests and appraising tests evidence used systematically by the Board. In particular, the utilization of recognition form questions, the use of two or more readers to grade essays, and the careful specification of essay problems to both the students and the readers were significant aspects of our general procedures for insuring objectivity. There is no doubt that increases in objectivity and reliability are always possible, but the question really is whether much of the energy and thought of the examiners needs to be devoted to this aspect after a relatively high minimum has once been attained. Thus if a reliability figure is in the neighborhood of .92, is it worth the investment of considerable effort and thought to raise this to .95? In general we have thought it more profitable to devote our efforts to other problems of examining and the relation of examining to other aspects of the educational process.

Perhaps the greatest amount of effort was devoted to improving the validity of the comprehensives and other examinations. The faculty of the College severely taxed the Board of Examinations by asking them to secure evidence on the extent to which students were attaining the primary objectives of instruction. Since these objectives were changing and since they were objectives for which little testing experience had been accumulated in the past, it was necessary to devote a considerable amount of attention to determining whether, in fact, performance on a particular type of question or problem was a valid index of the extent to which the student had attained a specified objective of instruction. The statements of the faculty with regard to purposes and objectives became the primary source for validation of the tests. A number of studies were made in which the rating of the faculty as to the attainments of individuals was correlated with the results of tests given to those same students. Although these frequently yielded high relationships, there was always considerable question as to whether the faculty was judging accurately with regard to the individual students and whether they had very much evidence in the discussion classes as to the student's attainment of certain of the objectives. It was found necessary to devise other procedures for the validation of these examinations.

The most direct means of validation was to secure judgments of competent faculty persons and examiners to determine whether specific tests required the student to evidence the particular behaviors specified in the statements of the educational objectives. This became the most important technique for validation of tests, and it, of course, worked especially well when the test devised was a relatively direct test of the objective. Thus, to use a simple illustration, if the objective specified that the student be skillful in the interpretation of economics data, a very direct test could be devised in which the student was presented with a variety of economics data and asked to write out interpretations of them. However, it was possible to devise somewhat less direct tests of the same types of competence. Thus, the student could be presented with data, offered a series of possible interpretations, and asked to judge the accuracy and relevance of each interpretation. While this latter type of test might be more economical of the student's time as well as more efficient to score, there is a much more difficult task of establishing its validity. Two methods for determining the validity of such indirect tests were used. One method was to determine the relationship between the results of the indirect test and the results from a more direct test. A more difficult but very useful method was to interview students and to determine whether the reactions and behaviors which they were able to report while attacking the problems were the kinds of behaviors specified in the statement of objectives. A

number of studies were made of this sort of validation and although it is
a type of *a posteriori* validation, it has been extremely useful as a basis
for determining principles of examining appropriate to specified kinds
of objectives as well as in revealing gross errors of validity.[7] In general, it can be seen that considerable effort is required to develop valid
testing instruments when the source of validation is the definition of
the objectives desired and when these are continually changing.

The changing emphasis in examining may be seen in the types of
studies which were carried on and reported by members of the Board
of Examinations. Since 1939, there have been relatively few studies of
the examinations directly and an increasingly large number of studies on
the relation between examinations and other parts of the educational
process. Thus, there have been a number of studies to determine the
effectiveness with which the admission tests are selecting students who
can achieve the objectives of instruction at the level of quality desired
and at the pace set in the instructional program.[8] While these studies
have usually attempted to relate performance on the admissions tests
to performance on the comprehensive examinations, some studies
have been done to determine the relation between the admission tests
and such variables as: the student's participation in the discussion
classes; frequency of attendance at class; and the extent to which
assignments are done regularly. Detailed studies involving the admissions tests have been made to determine why particular students fail,
the conditions under which failure is likely to take place, as well as
reasons for dropping out of college.[9] Other studies were attempts to
validate placement tests and to determine the consequences of the
placement testing program.[10,11] Here attempts were made to determine
the relation between placement-test performance and the student's
previous training and experiences as well as between the student's
placement in the College and his later achievement in sequential
courses or in other parts of the College curriculum.

A more fundamental kind of study typical of this period has been the
attempt to determine the ways in which students change as a result of
instruction.[12] Students have been tested over a sample of problems
before and after instruction and the results reported to the faculty.
These studies have usually stimulated the faculty to reconsider their
objectives as well as curricular methods. There were a number of
instances in which little or no gain was evidenced as a result of instruction. In one case a particular kind of reading skill showed no change as a
result of almost a year of instruction which had definitely emphasized
this particular skill. Reporting this study to the faculty influenced them

to think more clearly about their instructional methods and to revise procedures which in succeeding years have been more successful. There were also instances in which very remarkable gains were found. For one skill in the analysis of art material it was found that students showed great gains as the result of a period of instruction. It was further found that these students continued to increase in this skill *after* the period of instruction relevant to this objective was at an end. This we believe is an illustration of a type of "threshold" phenomenon in which, once a level of competence is reached, the student is likely to make use of new experiences in such a way as to continue to increase in his skill or ability in the area. We are of the opinion that this is a very general case and believe there are many illustrations of it in such areas as foreign language skills, motor skills (e.g., automobile driving), computational skills, music, etc.

Another type of study was the attempt to determine the extent to which instruction has enabled students to integrate and synthesize their achievement. Here we found it possible to make use of factorial analysis techniques to determine the extent to which performance on a variety of achievement tasks and objectives was more consistent after instruction than before.[13,14] Recently we have been much aided in these studies of interrelationships among types of learning by the Taxonomy of Educational Objectives[15] which makes it possible to classify types of objectives in a number of different subject fields as a preliminary to determining the magnitude of the interrelationships among these objectives. In general, we have found several types of objectives which are highly related across a number of different subject fields. Such studies, of course, only become the starting point for a further inquiry into improved ways of relating and synthesizing the outcomes of instruction.

The extent to which the work of the examiners bears on the total educational process may also be seen in the questionnaire and interview studies of student opinion on different aspects of the educational program.[16] Such studies enable the instructional staff to make use of student reactions as one symptom of the value of particular materials and methods and their understanding of the purposes of the course. Closely related to this type of study have been our attempts to determine the effectiveness of different methods of instruction. Since both instructional methods and the comprehensive examinations arise in relation to the objectives of the course as formulated by the faculty, it was possible to investigate the relation between the achievement of these objectives and the methods of instruction used. As the faculty experimented with lectures and discussion, demonstrations and laboratory work, we attempted to relate the examination results to these methods. Prompted by these early investigations, we have attempted to study teaching methods somewhat more directly. We first began studying discussion and lecture methods by observation of the actual conduct of the class as well as by a rather careful study of recordings of these lectures and discussions.[17] This provided quite fruitful evidence, but there were indications that much more was going on in a lecture or discussion than could be observed from these overt activities. This prompted us to attempt investigations of the kinds of thinking students do during a lecture or discussion.[18] These have revealed some major differences between lectures and discussions as well as between different ways of conducting a lecture or discussion. These have also led us to further study of the relation between a student's thinking and his personal characteristics.[19] Finally, both the data on the student's thinking and his personality have been related to his achievement on the comprehensive examination. These types of studies have enabled us to determine more clearly the conditions under which the discussion or lecture is likely to bring about the kinds of changes specified in the educational objectives as well as the conditions under which particular students are enabled to achieve these objectives.

Examining in Relation to Social Processes

In the past few years we have been invited by several of the graduate and professional departments of the University to study some of the problems involved in selection of students as well as to study some of the factors involved in successful work at these advanced levels. These were departments with small numbers of students carefully selected on the basis of previous academic achievement and aptitude tests. The departments were concerned primarily with the development of creative and outstanding professional workers. Since the numbers of students involved were small, they were especially interested not only in making predictions but also in understanding the kinds of learning situations which would best promote the development of the individual student. This type of study evidently required a more varied set of techniques than our usual entrance or placement tests.

    Our studies of learning situations in the College also highlighted the problems of individual students and the relation between learning and personality. We decided it would be profitable to further extend our research into personality and temperament as it affected the student's College career. We hoped to develop techniques for securing personality evidence which could be used to further our understanding of the effect of the College environment on the student as well as to determine situations which could promote the individual's development most effectively.

In this research and examination development we have been much influenced by the work of clinical psychologists and psychoanalysts, cultural anthropologists, and social psychologists. More specifically, the work of Henry Murray[20] and the OSS Assessment Staff[21] have suggested working concepts, techniques, and the cooperative relations required in research teams needed to implement this work.

The early work of the Board was conducted as though we had assumed that the individual was to be measured and compared with a standard group of some kind. It was also carried on as though we had assumed that the act of measuring was to be focused on the individual student with no reference to the environment from which he had come, with little reference to the educational environment in which he was presently learning and with almost no reference to the social environment in which he moved at present or to which he would go after leaving school. In effect, we were concerned only with the production of examining instruments and with the application of these to the individual student. In our second phase we have been concerned about the interaction of a student with an educational environment. Our examining here has been directed both to the modifiability of the educational practices as well as to the changes being produced in the student. However, we have operated as though the student were the bearer of the effects of his previous environment experiences and would be in the future the bearer of the effects of the educational experiences he was receiving in the College. Again, the individual was being abstracted from the environment from which he had come or to which he was going. In our more recent work we are attempting to consider the interactions of the individual and his environment with somewhat fuller consideration than had been true previously. Although we are giving greatest emphasis to the present environment, we are also attempting to consider his past as well as prospective future environment.

Whereas most of our previous work focused on cognitive characteristics of the individual, that is, his intelligence, intellectual skills and abilities, and his knowledge and understanding of specific subject matter, our more recent work has begun to emphasize character and personality as well as relations between the individual and his work and between the individual and others. While much of our evidence-collecting had been confined to work samples which were clearly related to academic subject matter, our more recent methods of testing make use of a great variety of evidence of behaviors which are analyzed by noting the temperament and character processes which are consistently present.

At present much of this work is exploratory and experimental, and almost none of it has as yet affected our more regular practices as examiners or the practices of teachers and students in our educational programs. The workers involved in this research and development are, for the most part, trained in clinical and social psychology. They have conceived of their task as one of testing certain hypotheses by intensive and individual testing on small numbers of subjects and then, on the basis of these more costly and clinically oriented feelings, attempting to discover more economical methods of gathering evidence which can be applied to large groups of subjects. Thus, in some of our early efforts we studied groups of 20 or 30 cases at a cost of as high as $200 per case, while our more recent work has involved expenditures of no more than a few dollars per case.

In the pilot studies we made use of a battery of individually-administered projective tests, lengthy interviews, art production as well as a very complete battery of scholastic aptitude, perceptual, cognitive, interest, and attitude tests. As our methods and hypotheses become more precise, we find it possible to rely on short group-administered attitude and interest tests as well as biographical data. In our early work it was necessary to make use of teams of workers to interpret and coordinate the different types of evidence. In some cases as many as 50 man-hours were necessary to secure and interpret the evidence on a single case. In our more recent efforts clerical and machine-scoring methods have been used extensively, while a single worker can do all the interpreting and summarizing of the evidence.

One is forcibly reminded of parallels in industry in which initial costs for developing a product are quite high in time and money as compared with decreasing costs for producing the product with increased understanding of it and as many economies are introduced by perfecting the technical methods. However, without the necessity of straying into other fields for illustrations, one finds that the initial methods were characterized by very low levels of reliability and objectivity, while the more recent methods of testing have levels of reliability and objectivity which are as high as we attain on our best examinations.

Most of this research has centered on the attempt to define patterns or types of personality and character and then to secure evidence as to the prevalence of these types in a group of subjects. It is in both the methods of defining the type and in the testing procedures that this work differs sharply from the earlier types of testing we have employed at the Board of Examinations.

In each case we have started with some attempt to secure a personality or character description of the ideal or well-functioning member of a group. We have proceeded in three ways to secure these descriptions. One is to secure a description from the literature of clinical psychology or social anthropology as to the existence of a type of person or syndrome of personality symptoms. In this way we have secured a description of the *stereotyped person,* the *concrete vs. abstract thinker,* and the *creative scientific worker.*[22] Another method has been to interview both faculty and students to secure a description of the well-functioning student in a particular school or department. In this way we have secured descriptions of the well-functioning graduate student in elementary education, in physics, and in one of the theology schools. Still a third method has been to select successful and unsuccessful students in a particular department and attempt to discern consistent differences in the personality and character structures of the two groups. In this way we have attempted to describe students in a general education program.

In all of these attempts to build models of the type sought, we have attempted to discriminate between explicit statements about the ideal or well-functioning individuals and inferences which could be drawn from statements describing specific individuals and the school setting or situation. We have then attempted to test one series of descriptions against another in order to discern a consistent set of symptoms, behaviors, and characteristics of the individual and role.

After the descriptions had been secured in whatever terms were possible, we attempted to organize them into the needs-press categorizations of H. A. Murray. This enabled us to distinguish between the overt behaviors of individuals and the inferences we could draw about the covert behaviors or processes which were implicit in the descriptions or which could be hypothesized as being required. The use of a single system such as this also permitted and facilitated communication among our team of workers. Furthermore, this system enabled us to relate our descriptions to projective testing techniques as well as a number of other tests which were available.

A third step in our procedures was to select and administer a battery of tests, interviews, questionnaires, and other evidence-gathering procedures to a selected group of subjects and then try to organize the evidence in relation to the model which had been previously determined. In interpreting and relating the evidence, we have continually referred to psychoanalytic theory and the theory about personality included in the Murray work. Such theories were used to draw inferences about underlying processes and motivations which are of explanatory value in explaining the data. These differ from inferences about test data which are based on the face validity of the test or on the empirical relations between the test and some criterion. Again, a major criterion for testing an inference of this type is the consistency with which it could be used to explain or interpret data from a number of different sources.

Finally, the evidence is summarized in qualitative and quantitative descriptions of the individual which can then be related to the criteria of success established by the faculty or group involved. These have yielded relationships which are exceedingly high and although many of the studies have been based on small samples, the results are such as to warrant considerable optimism about the methodology and techniques used.

These studies are reported in some detail in a forthcoming book.[23] The results yield great promise at several different levels. At the highest and most abstract level they reveal the promise of a theory and method of testing which differs considerably from the others which we have employed. This method can be used in conjunction with our other methods to improve on the selection process for colleges and universities. The method also holds out great hope for the development of diagnostic techniques which may help teachers at all levels of the schools to be more effective in aiding students develop desirable ways. In addition, the method should be useful in determining whether individual students are educable by given means and in the different ways specified by educational objectives. At the moment, certain educational objectives appear to be less likely of attainment with some types of students than with others, although both groups are equal with respect to scholastic aptitude. These findings should give rise to reconsideration of both educational objectives and educational procedures.

The method has proved to be useful in attacking the problem of the non-intellectual aspects of achievement prediction. Not only have we been able to increase our correlations between tests given at time of entrance and later achievement criteria, but we also derive from this form of testing an increased insight into the characteristics of the student as well as into the nature of the educational situation and its effects on the student.[24] Thus, we are able to understand somewhat more clearly the nature and effects of the curriculum, the instructional methods, the materials used, and the objectives and evaluation procedures.

At another level, the results of this testing give some definition of the *role* required of the successful student in education, physics, and theology. These studies need to be replicated with other groups and situations before our results can be generalized, but at least we are able to determine what beyond previous achievement and scholastic aptitude is necessary for success in a particular field. We are now conducting studies on professional models in some of these fields to discern the relation between the student model and the professional model. Furthermore, this type of research appears to be extremely successful in helping us understand the differences between the highly creative worker in a scientific field and the successful but less productive or creative worker in the same field. One would hope that further work of this kind will help to increase the creative productions in a field and to gain some measure of scientific control over this large and socially important problem. Perhaps some of the degrees of chance and randomness which characterize creative productivity can be reduced.

A third result of this type of testing research is the development of techniques of testing which can be effectively applied to some of these problems. We have found that non-projective instruments can be used to secure some of the types of evidence which are usually gathered by means of projective techniques. Attitude and interest tests can be used as major techniques for describing character and personality and, when used properly, can become powerful tools for the production of academic achievement. We have also made use of biographical data and personal-history questionnaires to secure evidence which has hitherto been gathered by means of lengthy test batteries. Such biographical data can be objectively scored and can yield as reliable evidence as some of our better standardized tests. Finally, we have begun to develop techniques for bringing together a great variety of data in such a way as to yield a highly consistent description of the individual. We are also learning how to substitute one type of test for another in such a way that either one will yield similar pictures of the individual.

It is our hope that in the near future we will be able to determine more clearly the ways in which one type of testing compliments another and the types of problems for which each type of testing is peculiarly appropriate. As we increase our range of testing methods and our variety of testing techniques and procedures, we should be able to find ways of attacking an increasingly greater range of problems of human behavior. These should be especially valuable as we try to utilize testing as a means for developing educational procedures which will maximally contribute to the welfare of the individual and the benefit of society.

References

1. Thurstone, L. L., and others. *Manual of Examination Methods.* University of Chicago, Board of Examinations, 1933.

2. Stalnaker, J. M. "The Construction and Results of a Twelve-Hour Test in English Composition." *School and Society,* XXXIX February 1934, pp. 193–198.

3. Haden, E., and Stalnaker, J. M. "A New Type of Comprehension Foreign Language Test." *The Modern Language Journal,* XIX November 1934, pp. 81–92.

4. *Annual Report of the Board of Examiners.* University of Chicago, 1934–1939. (unpublished).

5. Richardson, M. W., and Kuder, C. F. "The Calculation of Test Reliability Coefficients Based on the Method of Rational Equivalence." *Journal of Educational Psychology,* December 1939, pp. 681–687.

6. Tyler, R. W. "Achievement Testing and Curriculum Construction" from *Trends in Student and Personnel Work,* edited by E. G. Williams, University of Minnesota Press, 1949.

7. Bloom, B. S., and Broder, Lois. *Problem-Solving Processes of College Students.* A Supplementary Educational Monograph, University of Chicago Press, Summer 1950.

8. Diederich, P. B. "The Abolition of Subject Requirements for Admission to College." School Review, LVII September 1959, pp. 364–370.

9. Horler, Frances L. *Factors Related to Withdrawal from the Four-Year College of the University of Chicago.* Ph.D. dissertation, Department of Education, University of Chicago, 1950.

10. Bloom, B. S., and Allison, Jane M. "Developing a College Placement Test Program," *Journal of General Education,* III, No. 3, April 1949, pp. 210–15.

11. Bloom, B. S., and Allison, Jane M. "The Operation and Evaluation of a College Placement Program." *Journal of General Education,* IV, No. 3, April 1950, pp. 221–33.

12. Bloom, B. S. "Testing in the Study of Educational Progress." *American Council on Educational Studies,* "Exploring Individual Differences: A Report of the 1947 Invitational Conference on Testing Problems."

13. Furst, E. J. "Effect of the Organization of Learning Experiences upon the Organization of Learning Outcomes: I. Study of the Problems by Means of Correlation Analysis." *Journal of Experimental Education,* XVII March 1950, pp. 215–228.

14. Furst, E. J. "Effect of the Organization of Learning Experiences upon the Organization of Learning Outcomes: II. Study of the Problem by Means of Factor Analysis." *Journal of Experimental Education,* XVIII June 1950, pp. 343–352.

15. Bloom, B. S., ed. *Taxonomy of Educational Objectives: Cognitive Domain.* New York: David McKay Co., 1956.

16. Goebel, Edith, J. *Construction of a Student-Opinion Questionnaire for the Evaluation of a Curriculum.* Master's thesis, University of Chicago, Department of Education, 1947.

17. Axelrod, J., *et al. Teaching by Discussion in the College Program.* Chicago: University of Chicago Press, January 1949 (Out of print).

*

18. Bloom, B. S. "Thought Processes in Lectures and Discussions." *Journal of General Education,* VII, No. 3, April 1953, 160–169..

19. Gaier, E. L., "Selected Personality Variables and the Learning Process." *Psychological Monographs,* Vol. 66, No. 19, Whole No. 349, 1952.

20. Murray, Henry A., *et al. Explorations in Personality.* New York: Oxford University Press, 1938.

21. OSS Assessment Staff. *Assessment of Men.* New York: Rinehart, 1948.

22. Clifford, Paul I. *A study of the Personality Organizations of a Selected Group of Highly Creative Chemists and Mathematicians.* Ph.D. dissertation, Department of Education, University of Chicago, 1953.

23. Stern, G. G., *et al. Methods in Assessment.* Glencoe, Illinois: Free Press, 1956.

24. Harris, David. *An Investigation into the Relationship Between Certain Personality Factors and College Academic Achievement.* Ph.D. dissertation, Department of Education, University of Chicago, 1953.

Index

About the Author

BENJAMIN S. BLOOM is Distinguished Service Professor of Education at the University of Chicago. He is the author or coauthor of a number of major books, including *Taxonomy of Educational Objectives; Stability and Change in Human Characteristics;* and *Human Characteristics and School Learning.*

Dr. Bloom is one of the founding members of the International Association for the Evaluation of Educational Achievement (IEA) and has been a consultant on evaluation and curriculum to nations throughout the world. He is a past president of the American Educational Research Association.